Religion and Daily Life in the Mountains of Iran

Religion and Daily Life in the Mountains of Iran

Theology, Saints, People

Erika Friedl

I.B.TAURIS
LONDON • NEW YORK • OXFORD • NEW DELHI • SYDNEY

I.B. TAURIS
Bloomsbury Publishing Plc
50 Bedford Square, London, WC1B 3DP, UK
1385 Broadway, New York, NY 10018, USA
29 Earlsfort Terrace, Dublin 2, Ireland

BLOOMSBURY, I.B. TAURIS and the I.B. Tauris logo are trademarks of
Bloomsbury Publishing Plc

First published in Great Britain 2021
This paperback edition published in 2022

Copyright © Erika Friedl, 2021

Erika Friedl has asserted her right under the Copyright, Designs and
Patents Act, 1988, to be identified as Author of this work.

For legal purposes the Acknowledgements on p. vii constitute an extension
of this copyright page.

Cover design: Adriana Brioso

All rights reserved. No part of this publication may be reproduced or transmitted
in any form or by any means, electronic or mechanical, including photocopying,
recording, or any information storage or retrieval system, without prior
permission in writing from the publishers.

Bloomsbury Publishing Plc does not have any control over, or responsibility for, any
third-party websites referred to or in this book. All internet addresses given in this
book were correct at the time of going to press. The author and publisher regret
any inconvenience caused if addresses have changed or sites have ceased to
exist, but can accept no responsibility for any such changes.

A catalogue record for this book is available from the British Library.

A catalog record for this book is available from the Library of Congress.

ISBN: HB: 978-0-7556-1673-2
PB: 978-0-7556-3657-0
ePDF: 978-0-7556-1675-6
eBook: 978-0-7556-1674-9

Typeset by Deanta Global Publishing Services, Chennai, India

To find out more about our authors and books visit www.bloomsbury.com and
sign up for our newsletters.

Contents

List of illustrations	vi
Acknowledgements	vii
Note on transliteration	viii
Map of Kohgiluye and Boir Ahmad	ix
The setting	x
Introduction	1
1 Religion and gnostic realism	13
2 God	29
3 Theology, extended	47
4 Saints and clients	63
5 The end of life	79
6 Beyond the grave	95
7 Well-being	109
Notes	127
References	156
Index	170

Illustrations

Map of Kohgiluye and Boir Ahmad

Minnesota Population Center. Integrated Public Use Microdata Series, International: Version 7.2 (dataset). Minneapolis, MN: IPUMS, 2019 — ix

Figures

All images by Reinhold Loeffler

1	Sisakht, 1995, view towards north	xix
2	Sisakht, 2006	28
3	Sisakht, 1997	46
4	Sisakht, 10. Moharram, 1970, in the courtyard of the old mosque	62
5	Khungah, North Boir Ahmad, April 2006	76
6	Imamzadeh Mahmad, Central Boir Ahmad, May 2006	77
7	Sisakht, October 1994	93
8	Sisakht, August 1997	94
9	Sisakht, November 2004	107
10	Dashtak, Sisakht, May 2006	108
11	Sisakht, 1994	124
12	Chin, Central Boir Ahmad, 2006	125

Acknowledgements

Our ethnographic study of a tribal area in Iran over several decades was possible only by incurring a large amount of debt of gratitude for the assistance a great many people provided in Iran, Europe and the United States. Caution prevents me to name the people my husband and I owe most for their selfless assistance in matters of research permits and dealings with authorities. In the town where we mainly lived, I single out two retired teachers, Ms Nushaferin Boir Ahmedi and Ms Golrokh Pakbaz, whose extraordinary perspicacity, knowledge, patience and understanding of my work were and continue to be invaluable. They have to stand in for everybody to whom I am profoundly grateful to. Despite all the help and care, though, mistakes will appear, and they are my own.

At home, special thanks go, as always, to my husband Reinhold Loeffler and to our daughters for their helpful memories, and to friends and colleagues: Professor Elaine Anderson Jayne for her comments on chapters and her editing, and Professors Mary Elaine Hegland, Mohammad Shahbazi and Evelyn Early for their suggestions. Professor Beatrice Beech patiently hatched the term 'gnostic realism' with me, and Professor Kent Baldner helped me to come to terms with what I call 'vernacular logic' so as to avoid judgemental descriptions of what in scientific logic are fallacious arguments. The late Dr Alfred Janata of the Völkerkunde Museum in Vienna taught me to pay attention to ethnographic detail; Professor Hana Azizi of Columbia University and Ms Ela Mehr answered language questions, as did Dr Afsaneh Gaechter at the Austrian Academy of Sciences in Vienna. Dr Ingrid K. Loeffler generously helped with computer issues and the photographs. Throughout the years, Diplom Ingenieur Helmut Friedl and Sylvia Friedl in Austria assisted me and my family way beyond reasonable kin-motivated generosity and tolerance, and Mr Albert and Diplom Ingenieur Dorle Götzelmann's hospitality and inspirations in Germany were invaluable to us.

Financial assistance from Western Michigan University, the Wenner-Gren Foundation for Anthropological Research, the Social Science Research Council, the National Endowment of the Humanities, and the University of Chicago supported various aspects of my research through the years. I thank them all.

Note on transliteration

Luri, spoken in the Province of Kohgiluye/Boir Ahmad and elsewhere in Iran, is an unwritten language close to Middle Persian. To make Luri words easily readable, Luri and Farsi speakers in Iran, including scholars, prefer the Latin alphabet. I follow this trend with a simplified transliteration code based on English, a language and script familiar to many people in Iran, including Lurs. As pronounced, most letters are close to their English sounds, with these exceptions: ā is the vowel in 'law', i as in 'be', ou as in 'low', u as in 'good'; gh is a soft guttural sound between 'g' and 'r'; j as in 'June', z as in 'zero', č as in 'child'; kh is similar to 'ch' in Scottish 'loch' or Hebrew 'Chaim'. Transliterating from the spoken word, I omit customary Persian diacritical marks.

Map of Kohgiluye and Boir Ahmad

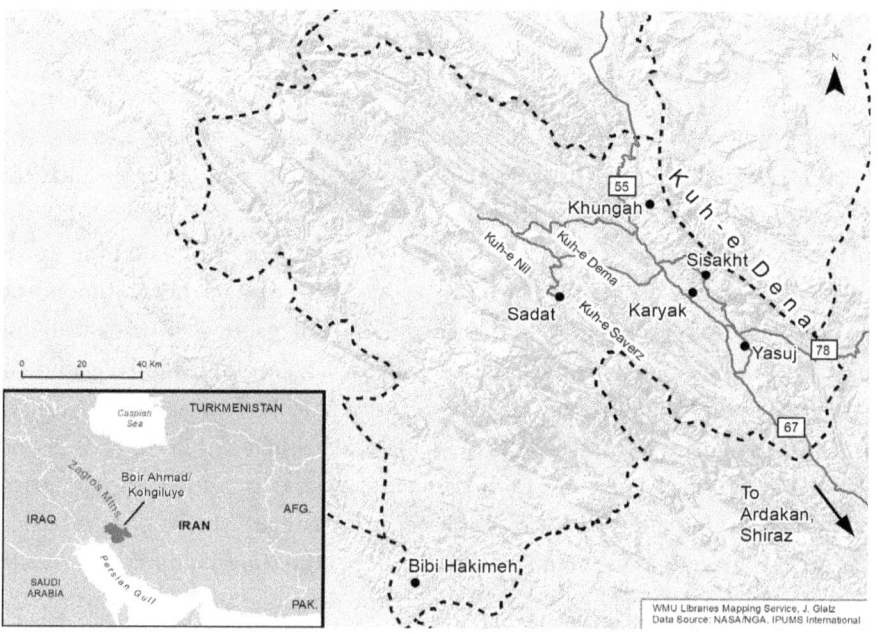

The setting

Place

The southern part of the Zagros range runs roughly northwest to southeast in western Iran. It is a majestic formation of steep, rocky mountains and wooded hills intersected by long rivers carrying snowmelt and rain water towards the Gulf. Few passes cross this barrier between the Gulf and thriving cities on the plateau of central Iran. They were used since antiquity by people on the move, by nomads, traders, soldiers, pilgrims. Despite harsh winters, hot summers and a difficult terrain, the native oak forests, abundant game and verdant alpine pastures have sustained people there for millennia: Palaeolithic hunter-gatherers (18,000 BC) and Neolithic village farmers (around 7,000 BC); settlements along trade routes in the Elamite (2700–539 BC), Achaemenid (553–320 BC) and Sasanian empires (AD 224–651), villages along rivers throughout the centuries, whenever strong central controls allowed safe passage. Nearly everywhere in the area archaeological remains point to earlier, settled, agricultural inhabitants. The most recent tribal, pastoral/transhumant dominance in this part of the Zagros started in the eighteenth century, replacing earlier transhumant and village populations little is known about. Luri-speaking groups inhabit several provinces along the Zagros range.[1] One of them is Kohgiluye-and-Boir Ahmad,[2] (30°54'N and 51°07'E), 6,000 square miles (15,600 square kilometres) of peaks, hills and valleys in the southern part of the Zagros Mountains, with some 720,000 inhabitants in 2016, according to the Population and Housing Census of the Statistical Centre of Iran (2016). Lurs see themselves as original, 'authentic' Iranians and the dialects of their language as true Persian, 'unspoiled' by Arabic. Farsi speakers call Luri a backwoods dialect of Farsi that is hard to understand, and linguists count it as a Middle Persian language (Skjarvo 2010). With rising literacy, television and internet widely available and Farsi as the lingua franca and school language, nearly all Lurs in Boir Ahmad are bilingual now.[3]

Sisakht, the tribal village-turned-town in northern Boir Ahmad where we spent most of our time, was founded in the late nineteenth century. It grew by immigration from adjacent areas such as from Bakhtiari to the west, where the last Boir Ahmad khan's lineage is said to have come from.

Tribal life

Until the late 1960s the local pre-ceramic, pre-wheel material culture reflected a strong hunting and gathering tradition and a pastoral/nomadic lifestyle.[4] For example, the interiors of the one-room rectangular dwellings (of stone-and-mud or mudbrick) were organized like the earlier tents: at one short end the stack of household goods, bedding and food provisions (in tents piled as a centre-divide), and felt-mats or rugs spread on the dirt floor to sit and sleep on. People used stones as tools with dexterity. For some dishes women milled grain by hand on flat stone slabs with a stone rolling pin, and routinely hulled expensive, rare rice in wooden mortars with pestles.[5] Women spun wool and goat hair on drop spindles described for Neolithic Anatolia (Maner 2018) and wove storage bags and floor covers on horizontal wooden looms that could be rolled up and loaded on donkeys for migrations. Bags for storing water and cooking-fat and for churning butter were made of animal hides. Cooking pots were of iron, food-trays of copper, imported from bazars or made by migrant blacksmiths; bowls were of wood, tinned copper and steel. To this inventory people added new tools and ceramic and plastic utensils after the mid-1960s, bought from itinerant traders or in the bazar.

The diet was based on wheat, barley and legumes, grown by men on dry and irrigated fields.[6] Women made several kinds of unleavened flatbread from wheat, barley and fermented acorn-meal, roasted over an open fire in an iron bowl, on hot stones, in ashes as they 'always' had done, they said,[7] before the paper-thin wheat flatbread (*nun tiri*) became the norm. This staple food was augmented by native wild greens such as artichokes, spinach and several kinds of onion plants as well as berries and fruits from native and cultivated fruit trees.[8] The 'best' food was declared to be meat from game and sheep, roasted over an open fire.

A strong Lur identity was audible in local music and visible in dance, rug-patterns and the women's attire, pointing to a Central Asian heritage, and in men's traditional costume with characteristic felt-hats. With the local populations' increasing economic, professional and cultural ties to the dominant Persian/modern culture, these garments became more ornate, expensive and reserved for high cultural status occasions like weddings. Rich folkloric wisdom and a great variety of ideas and rituals in the area have roots in antiquity.[9]

Patrilineally organized kin groups used the ecological niches for agro-pastoral enterprises. Power, authority and responsibilities for economic and political welfare rested in adult men. This encouraged authoritarian, often violent relationships within the household, with young women and children at the lowest rung of the social ladder and men demanding their obedience. Men's violence and bravery in war and as robbers were valourized and supported a markedly androcentric, authoritarian ideology. Labour was gender indexed with near-total interdependence, and with older men and women using younger ones, especially girls, as servants. Vulnerable sheep and goats provided meat mostly for status occasions, as did hunting; fields provided wheat and barley, and gathering provided acorn-meal and greens. Food was always scarce, though, and people remembered hunger times and seasons when they ate acorn-meal and locusts or rustled sheep from other tribal groups to stay alive. Raids on villages outside the tribal area provided occasional additional food.

The self-regulated, transhumant small groups moved seasonally, some over longer distances from southern winter quarters to northern valleys. Others, such as the people of Sisakht, mostly used black goat hair tents and branch huts seasonally in pastures surrounding their settlement. Land was controlled and utilized by tribal units, often fought over under the leadership of the groups' khans and section chiefs (*kadkhodā*). Various British military reports from the early twentieth century describe local people as 'dangerous, wild, strong, formidable, lawless, well-armed, plucky', with fighters able to move '80 miles' in a day (Christian 1919: 66/7). Surrounding villages feared raids of the 'wild tribes', but there was little security within the territory either, as local people remember to this day. Khans and sub-tribal chiefs built forts and shifting alliances. Aided by their riflemen, they often feuded with each other over tributes and labour from the people they controlled.[10] Mullahs and other Islamic dignitaries politically cooperated with the tribal leaders to each other's mutual benefit. Garrod (1946: 37) reported a fairly large, well-tolerated population of Seyeds with 'more than due needs of sanctity' in the early twentieth century in villages throughout the area. In several villages with shrines, Seyeds constituted the majority of the inhabitants. Their influence among the tribal Lurs can be felt to this day, especially in local Islamic tenets and rituals they encouraged and in the area's many shrines of purported saintly descendants of the Prophet Muhammad.

As population pressure on local resources and the chiefs' lifestyle expenses increased, the tribal elite's often-voiced claim of being 'first among equals' and of providing management and assistance for their tribal people changed into a more self-serving ideology. It justified the turning of a professed communal ethic into entitlement behaviour that motivated the chiefs to behave like landlords ruling their peasants. In the 1930s, Qobad Nikeqbal, the chief of Sisakht at the time, was well known and appreciated for his leadership successes, while the last, final local chief's exhortative habits cost him the allegiance of his people: Ali (Agha) Nikeqbal died a poor, lonely man in 2004.

Serious efforts to integrate this 'lawless area' (and others in Iran) into the state were made in the early twentieth century under Reza Shah, mostly to the detriment of the tribal economy and culture (Cronin 2006). But only after the demise of the tribal elite's powers that followed the last paramount khan's assassination by the government, in 1963, did government authorities assert themselves and sociopolitical conditions change.[11] An influx of Persian speakers from other parts of the country, high fertility rates until the 1990s, an effective healthcare system raising life expectancy (starting in the 1960s) and low outmigration (until about 2005) led to unprecedented population increase.[12] Following the last khan's military defeat and demise, Mohammed Reza Shah's land reform (1963–79) was relatively calm locally because few tribal chiefs had legal deeds to land that allowed them to retain their territories and access to labour and products of the tribal people. These continued their economic routines with decreasing pressure for tribute payments.[13] Impoverished, the tribal elite moved into other available economic niches such as business, higher education, the professions and emigration.

After the mid-1960s, strong developmental idealism in the form of 'progress' (*pishraft*) pervaded the country, and economic pressures from rapidly diminishing agricultural resources motivated enough tribal people to aspire to a 'modern' way of life and to change expectations especially for young people who, unlike their parents earlier, had attractive choices, however remote and hard to pursue they turned out to be. Transhumant families settled, villages grew and demanded schools and amenities and the government became an economic source for fulfilling needs and lifestyle ambitions. (The Islamic Republic is called a 'welfare state' by some social scientists because of the many categories of people who can claim benefits from government-linked institutions and programmes. See Harris 2017.) Development came at the price of accelerating the deterioration of the environment and the weakening of traditional, cooperative relationships within families and communities when nuclear families moved out of overcrowded, kin-based compounds and managed their own income. But all things considered, people say that life improved considerably.[14] In hindsight, ordinary people tend to see 'the times of the khans' as a period of oppression, poverty and insecurity, while nostalgic members of the former khans' families emphasize the khans' achievements and heroic, 'truly Persian' lifestyle.

In 1965, two years after the khan's assassination, we met the people of Sisakht as they were starting to assess and choose new alternatives to traditional lifeways.

Literacy and schools had just become a popular choice for connecting to new opportunities. The first teachers – all from local families – were the first men and women with salaries and became role models for their students. A large gendarmerie-post had supplanted the chiefs and local dignitaries as arbiters of strife, including between the chief's relatives and local farmers who successfully claimed the land they had tilled and used as pastures since they had settled there. The gendarmes, outsiders all, were agents of change, introducing, among others, urban ways of conducting religious rituals. As security increased, the first households moved out of the courtyards' stone huts and mudbrick houses with their work-space porches in front and on flat dirt roofs, and built new, similar houses in the surrounding fields. Animals were kept in the courtyards and in stone/mud rooms below living spaces and were herded in communal arrangements among relatives and in seasonal outposts in overgrazed pastures. Life continued to be tough for everybody but especially so for women, who were responsible for the care of children and elders, all household chores (including procuring water and, in many places, firewood), milking and turning milk into products the men sold; for weeding, hospitality, gathering edibles, keeping chickens, sowing and weaving for domestic needs and for men to barter rugs for tea, sugar and some other items. These responsibilities were not options but essential duties that made women chronically undernourished and exhausted. (Garrod (1946: 34), a physician travelling there in the early 1940s, made the same observation.) Depression and suicide among women were high. The mental and physical health of women stayed so poor that in 1981 the governor of Boir Ahmad ordered a study. It suggested that workload, poverty, pregnancies, lack of women's rights within tribal law and violence by husbands and in-laws were responsible for the problem.[15] I agree with this assessment.

Men's chores were not easy either, and men's responsibilities for their nuclear and extended families weighed heavily on them. Their situation was acerbated by the tribal inheritance rule that grants each son an equal share of the father's property. Within a generation of lower child mortality rates, the increase in sons had resulted in insufficient agricultural land to feed everybody and in fights among heirs. However, men had a few options: they could leave wife and children with relatives and work as day labourers in cities or in the Gulf States. A few of these migrant workers came back with useable skills (such as trucking) and savings that provided them and their families with economic comfort; others spent their savings at home fast by paying off debts and helping their struggling brothers, and their families stayed poor. Another choice was to invest in the next generation, ideally by letting sons cover several economic possibilities to benefit the whole extended family: one son as a teacher (or government employee of some sort), another as a farmer, one as a trader in the city and such.

As the traditional family-enterprises and the inter-family cooperative spirit waned in the new cash-based, single-wage earner economy, diversity led to increasing income differences among families and to jealousy. The labour market was limited, especially for women despite their relatively high educational achievements.[16] While a few local women do well in professions such as medicine, most of the few working women have low-paying jobs. Women understand that having no or little income keeps their social position low and limits their status within their families, as this well-worn expression shows: 'A girl has to have her hands in her own pocket'; that is, she has to have control over her own money to have a say in her affairs. In the absence of such jobs, for most women a 'good' marriage still is their best, their only, choice, they say, unless their parents continue to support them at home. Young people have much more say in marital arrangements than their elders who had to marry whoever was arranged for them, but expectations for partners greatly diverge between young men and women: young women are looking for 'rich' husbands who can provide comfort and a neolocal residence instead of the traditional cohabitation with the husband's parents; men argue that they cannot afford to satisfy the demands of young women (and their parents) and, in turn, hope to find as wives good looking, well-off, agreeable service providers. Marital choices are especially problematic when unemployment is as high as it is in Iran. Marital age is rising, alternates to traditional marriages are increasing as are divorce and polygyny, and the birth rate, easily managed with the choices of birth control devices available in Iran, is moving to below the population maintenance level. Differences in lifeways are growing between members of tribal groups engaged in traditional local economic pursuits and those who are able to establish themselves in modern occupations.

The Islamic government, in power soon after the Revolution of 1978, continued the modernization efforts of the shah's White Revolution in education, infrastructure, healthcare and administrative integration of tribal areas into the laws, ways and means of the state. The village expanded spatially and husbandry and agriculture declined. Wildlife and the alpine flora slowly improved when an area around Dena County, our main research area, became a Protected Area in 2008. By 2015 it was in danger from poaching and the newly fashionable taste for 'natural' foods which drove people into the highlands to collect edible wild plants to sell in the bazar (Friedl 2006). The provincial government is pushing tourism and mountaineering in the over 4,000 metre high Dena mountain range along the northern boundary of the province. New economic opportunities sustain the population with income and loans from, essentially, Iran's oil exports. Except for the bazar trade, most jobs in the modern economy are related to the government. This is relevant in a political system that is synonymous with state religion because it encourages people to support religio-political leaders and programmes in exchange for economic benefits and opportunities.[17] (Conservative, poor farmers in central Boir Ahmad supported the Islamic leadership by volunteering for the front in the Iran–Iraq war and since then by participating in organized religious events and demonstrations.) High unemployment and poverty plague people throughout the economically vulnerable province.

In the environs of Sisakht only few people still make a living entirely in agriculture, by farming, herding, tending orchards or growing glasshouse crops. Literacy as well as social and spatial mobility, 'modern' ways of thinking about life, social media, relentless and frustrating lifestyle aspirations, and intra-family dynamics challenge traditional hierarchies and transform the choices people see for ethics, behaviour and gender expectations. The habituated traditional value system and philosophical underpinnings of assumptions about life and transcendental issues that are dealt with in this book are fading, people say, as more choices for being-in-the-world appear. Tribal sociopolitical structures continue to be important for marital arrangements, ongoing disputes about ownership of land and a cooperative spirit among Lurs in general. 'The Lurs all help each other,' said a frustrated Persian government official in Shiraz, claiming that with 'Lurs' in power positions in his agency he could not get promoted. Bilingual now, people can – and do – play the identity card to their advantage, as a well-known physician said in 2006, who cheerfully presented the possibilities as funny alternatives and adaptive strategies in his various environments: 'At international conferences I am a famous Iranian medical expert, as a tourist in Italy I am a rich Persian doctor interested in churches and art, and at home I am a dam' Lur who supports his Lur colleagues and speaks Luri if he wants to play dumb or dress somebody down.'

Despite their manifold problems, people in Boir Ahmad enjoy good company and good, funny stories. It is part of who they are, they say. Their self-deprecatory and irreverent, rude jokes are the salt of every get-together. A quick eye, sharp wit and clever tongue are much appreciated, as are people who can find in mundane situations aspects one can let 'jump and bite,' as a high school student said who was good at it. It is considered religiously meritorious to make people happy, although preachers also forever warn of the sinful and dangerous aspects of laughter and merrymaking, especially for women. Not much has changed in this. A persistent joke-complaint we heard about clerics is that 'first they make everybody sad with constant mourning rituals and then we have to cry to make us feel better'.

Until the 1960s little was known inside and outside Iran about 'the tribes' in this area other than that khans were aggressively defending the tribal political structure and territory and were feuding with each other, and that Lur raiders were plaguing surrounding towns and villages.[18] The aura of hardy, potentially dangerous mountain toughs stays with them to this day, although education and a strong will to make good in this world have put Lur people from Boir Ahmad into high positions in the sciences, teaching and administration in Iran.

We in Boir Ahmad

When Reinhold Loeffler and I, ignoring dire warnings from friends and colleagues, first came to Boir Ahmad, in 1965, we intended to put this unknown area ethnographically on the map. At that time the military governor of Kohgiluye/Boir Ahmad, Commander Alizadeh, his soldiers and gendarmes were enforcing a shaky peace. The area was off limits for foreigners for political and security reasons.[19] Perseverance in Tehran while negotiating a permit, good luck and the assistance of the police in Shiraz (a gateway city to northern Boir Ahmad) brought us to Yasuj, the newly established administrative centre of Kohgiluye/Boir Ahmad. While our friends were worried about us, we felt well treated by our various generous hosts.

Yasuj then was a new settlement with a few small buildings and branch huts along a bazar street providing goods for surrounding villages and camps.[20] By a fortunate coincidence, the annual meeting of the tent-school organization in Boir Ahmad took place while we were there.[21] With one friendly gesture its director, Mr Bahmanbegi, introduced us to all teachers in the area. Wherever we travelled subsequently, teachers knew us and vouched for us. Our children also were helpful by establishing us as a 'normal' family people could easily relate to. With only two daughters at a time when sons were much preferred and women with fewer than four children were pitied, we stirred curiosity but no envy. Eventually, we decided to live in a village on the alluvial plain of Sisakht at the foot of one of the highest peaks of the Zagros range, some 30 kilometres west of Yasuj. With 500 inhabitants it was the largest and most lively settlement in the area, without electricity and water, and accessible with difficulties for a car on a narrow, rutted dirt road. It remained the base for all our subsequent visits. We saw it grow from a tightly clustered, defence-oriented adobe village with a meeting/prayer room, a defunct shrine, two school rooms (one in a former stable), a bath house, a couple of craftsmen and two shops, to a modern small town, the county seat of Dena County with some 6,000 inhabitants, and, among others, several schools, a branch of an agricultural college, two stately mosques, a health clinic, a private physician and a pharmacy, a bank, a lively bazar, several bakeries, two 'women's stores', two beauty salons for women and a coffee shop for young men.[22] (The common drink is tea but among young men coffee is chic.) In this book, 'local' means in, from or near this town.

Further good luck was in local people's appreciation of our work as anthropologists (*mardomshenās*). People understood that we wanted to document and write about local customs and took us at our word. When in a neighbour's house men were negotiating a marriage contract while my husband was away, the chief negotiator fetched me, saying that as an anthropologist I had to watch and write it all down, never mind that I was a woman. A strong 'Sisakht' identity allowed enough people to be proud of their skills and stories, proud to show us what life was like in the mountains and in Iran – 'good and bad and everything' – and to be gratified to get our publications so that we felt understood and supported. In most houses, only politeness, circumstances and time limited our visits. People appreciated that we were serious to learn about their way of life and consented to work with us by their openness and willingness to interact, while we aimed for transparency in dealings with them and with the various administrative control organs. In 1981 the governor of the province, an outsider appointed by the revolutionary government, welcomed us on the basis of earlier reports by various government authorities that had convinced him of our serious academic intentions, he said. Later, especially in 2006, dealing with authorities often was stressful despite our clearances. Police were suspicious and afraid to make mistakes in handling us, and local people were noticeably upset by 'everything' around them, caught in webs of surveillance that also extended to us. Again, our track record, publications and support from local people helped us circumvent difficulties.[23] In 2008 we were denied visas by the Islamic Republic's Consulate in Vienna; I did not try to get to Iran again until 2015, when I spent another month in Sisakht. Altogether, I have stayed in Iran for over seven years in sixteen visits spanning fifty years, between 1965 and 2015. Such continuity makes writing difficult, though, because of the overwhelming amount of information and because there is no fixed time horizon, no 'ethnographic present' short enough to ignore change. This condition easily leads to static 'then vs. now' reports like the one I gave earlier about the growth of the village. 'Then we had donkeys, now we have cars,' a teacher joked in 2015. To acknowledge the very process of change in discussions of beliefs and the ideas behind them is a challenge in ethnographic writing which I felt acutely.

Figure 1 Sisakht, 1995, view towards north. In late fall, the fields, orchards and hills at the foot of the Koh-e Dena are barren. The old part of the settlement and the new graveyard are to the left of the low ridge dividing the plain, and the new part, built into fields and gardens since about 1990, is to the right. The town is growing, while other areas of Boir Ahmad are losing people.

Introduction

The work

When Reinhold Loeffler and I first came to Boir Ahmad, in 1965, it soon became clear that I learnt more about what moved people by listening to them than by insisting on specific topics or data from questionnaires. Listening marked my style of fieldwork from the beginning. Several times I was introduced to outsiders as 'the foreign lady who understands everything but doesn't talk much'. As a woman I was expected to hang out with women and did so but this did not isolate me from men, and neither did women hide from my husband or refuse to talk to him. When, in 1981, I visited an elderly neighbour, an illiterate, reserved man sick with a kidney ailment, I unexpectedly found him alone in his house. By local standards of propriety the situation was a little awkward and improper, but he seemed glad to see me and so I stayed, making friendly noises, when suddenly he broke into a monologue about how the world and God worked, about life and death, good and bad. Clearly, he used the occasion of being alone with me to talk about what occupied him emotionally, sick as he was, but also to instruct me, the foreigner. He obviously felt as good about talking as I did about listening. Similar encounters happened frequently, especially in later visits with men and women I had known since their childhood.

Except in people's cacophonic discussions that kept me silent and often confused, I communicated in a mix of Luri and Farsi, without interpreters and sometimes to people's amusement.[1] A tape recorder documented texts such as folktales. Mostly I scribbled short notes, though, which people appreciated as a sign that I took seriously what they said. In some rare situations people dictated to make sure I got it right for 'the book'. As for short, relevant conversations, I learnt to remember them verbatim long enough to write them down at the next opportunity. When I had questions about words and idioms or needed background information, neighbours helped out. People knew that I would write about life in Sisakht, but they also knew that I kept personal information to myself. Their trust 'opened hearts', as a neighbour said, and often made people vent feelings and thoughts about private matters such as religion. This was fortunate but also a burden because I could not discuss with anybody what I heard. Much to their credit, people rarely asked me about others – they understood and accepted my principle of discretion. For privacy I use fictive names here or identify speakers by sex and age, as 'professional, student, elderly woman, poor farmer' and such. The direct quotes speak to opinions that are generally available options rather than being unique or exceptional; some I edited for clarity and brevity.

Over the years, academic themes of the day worked like lenses, magnifying certain issues without, however, obliterating others. Always, the goal of fieldwork was all-inclusive ethnography. Over the years, between major topics like material culture, children's culture, women's issues, I recorded rituals and folkloric data such as proverbs and songs. The resulting publications are popular in Sisakht as documents of Boir Ahmad's culture and history, people say.[2] From the beginning, I also recorded people's remarks on ethics and religion, contradictory as they often were, and whatever I learnt about people's understanding of their own lives. As time went on, the philosophical tenets that people select and formulate about their own existence and about 'how everything fits together' moved to the centre of my attention.

Reviewing field notes for observations pertaining to such topics I noticed not only how many diverse ancient notions surface in local customs and ideas but also how adaptive the beliefs and customs in the local vernacular Islam were and still are to the people's precarious rural life conditions.[3] Given their past subsistence strategies at the edge of hunger and exhaustion, the range of their beliefs and rituals fits the need for support, for upkeep of small kin groups as well as for ways to minimize the sin aspects in many of their behaviours. The resulting ethics of mutualism and 'necessity' (*majburi*) provided justifications for what others saw as 'bad' and sinful behaviour, such as raiding and violence, and was augmented by quests for assistance from powers considered more potent than humans. The flexible ethics include unconditional hospitality and bitter hostilities; open friendliness and rude assertiveness; polished politeness and aggressive dominance; relaxed, joking interactions and tight-lipped kin groups; open-minded interests and doctrinaire narrow-mindedness; kindness and violence; mild manners and ruthless vengeance; reliance on human agency as well as on autonomous natural forces, all presided over by a powerful ruler, a benevolent but also punishing and revengeful creator-deity who constructs every second yet also appears to be remote, beyond caring. It is difficult to come to terms with these contradictions unless one views them as choices the culture provides, as a frame within which people pick and choose depending on circumstances. Using this wide and loose concept of culture instead of a generalized Local Culture makes it easier for an observer like me to make sense of people's inconsistencies and contradictions. Nevertheless, the fact that people who were feared by outsiders for their violence treated us personally with kindness and sincere goodwill sometimes makes it difficult for me and my husband to acknowledge the darker sides of their lifeways.[4] This is my bias.

Profound changes in lifestyle after the mid-1960s and then in the Islamic Republic have added more choices for people's understanding of the world without discarding all older ones. According to local men and women, life conditions have improved considerably with health clinics, fewer children, better food and lighter workloads as the subsistence economy faded and cash income facilitated buying necessities in the bazar. At the same time, though, lack of jobs and lack of access to resources coupled with a rise in expectations for comfort and status goods created new problems with new potential solutions, and dependency on money and markets led to high debt burdens and increasing discontent. Since about 2000, local women, educated but not actively involved in the post-agricultural economy, live in small households with modern amenities and few children and 'have nothing to do', as they half-joke. They may copy urban lifestyles, elaborate their few leisure activities and complain of boredom. The health problems of a modern, well-fed, sedentary populace are increasing.[5] The few working women (such as teachers and nurses) are in a double-shift bind, routinely expected to manage household and job with little help. Although marital relationships are changing towards more intimacy, differences between the expectations wives have of husbands (generosity, companionship and sharing of responsibilities) and husbands have of wives (beauty, support, continuation of the traditional division of labour) cause discontent.[6] The income gap between rich and poor is increasing and divorce and polygyny are rising everywhere in Iran. Locally, these issues are discussed widely.

As modernity and development added choices to their lifeways, local people readily accepted the new possibilities that formal education and social mobility provided. The town has produced teachers, academics, administrators, healthcare professionals (including some twenty physicians) and several mullahs. Most of the dozen emigrants are doing well in Europe, America and South Asia. In these regards, Sisakht is ahead of other towns in Boir Ahmad but the trend is visible everywhere.[7] Despite setbacks, the spirit of striving to do better and to get ahead has stayed. Sisakht is known throughout the area for its well-educated, well-spoken and successful, if somewhat aloof, people, its pleasant orchards and for being ahead of most other places in matters of 'progress'.[8]

Assumptions

The first supposition in talking about local religion is more of a premise than a mere assumption and regards humans' general tendency to create 'religion'. All cultures offer their members images, rituals and ethics that appeal to humans' universal spiritual inclinations.[9] Likely there are doubters and atheists, deniers of a spiritual life and critics of religious habits in any community, but there is no known 'irreligious' culture. This assumption allows me to look at religious life in Boir Ahmad beyond the norms of Shia Islam as preached in Iran today, although experts in Islam and orthodox believers may be disconcerted about the amount of 'superstitions' and 'wrong ideas' documented here for a Muslim group. If so, they are overlooking that social scientists ought to report 'what is' without evaluating it by authorities' definitions of 'what ought to be'.

Second, for understanding local religious life, low-keyed or ostentatious as it might be, I base my observations on the assumption that culture provides its members options for behaviour and beliefs, including contradictory, incompatible choices, within a frame of possibilities that is accepted as possible, as common-sensical. As time goes on, some options lose attraction while others are added. In Boir Ahmad, this common-sense frame includes, for example, a creator-deity, extra-human powers, authoritarian relationships, patrilineal groups, a social hierarchy that puts males over females, and wide ranging humanist ethics.

In small social groups culture is shared in the sense that everybody is familiar with the choices: they belong to the vernacular language and cognition (Bauman 2008). Although individuals may prefer, accept, disagree with or reject other people's choices, they understand them, no matter how different they are from their own. For example, there is no point in counting how many people in Sisakht believe in jinn, the often mischievous extra-human shape-shifting powers thought to harm people. Even those who reject this belief know about it: jinn are part of the cultural inventory. A local teacher who pushed rational arguments and science wherever he could answered a jinn challenge by his mother with, 'Nonsense. There are no jinn. This talk is stupid superstition. And anyway, a cat is just a cat, and a jinn instantly disappears if one says, "*bismillah*", even if it is a cat.' He could talk about jinn perfectly well although he did not 'believe' in them. Similarly, a committed adherent to Iran's official Shia Islam will expect to be in paradise eventually but nevertheless can understand people who say they do not believe in heaven and hell. However, he would be bewildered if a neighbour claimed to be a reincarnation of a worm or that his house was haunted by grandfather's ghost. Neither ghosts nor reincarnation are part of the local understanding of life after death. Finally, the local common-sense ethical frame includes personal generosity and hospitality but excludes large-scale philanthropic acts such as leaving an inheritance to a social (in contrast to Islamic) charity, thereby depriving the heirs of their legal property.[10]

Looking at variants in beliefs and rituals as equally valid and cognitively present prevents academic construction of the Local Religion. Such essentializing inevitably loses minority practices by either privileging statistical data or reflecting the norms of a local power group such as proponents of present-day 'government Islam' in Iran.[11] Rather, in my interactions with people I deliberately acknowledged different opinions and interpretations, ideas that looked idiosyncratic at first but widened the horizon of what is taken as possible in this seemingly simple culture. People construct their religion from available cognitive building blocks, depending on purpose and circumstances. A person may negate the possibility of a jinn being a cat when arguing for an enlightened world view but the next moment may throw a rock after the cat just to be safe or to follow a common-sense habit because there is a baby in the house, vulnerable to harm from jinn.

In the course of the Islamization of Islam[12] with vigorous proselytizing by the Islamic government, choices of what it means to be a Muslim are shrinking and crowding out some religious customs. At present, though, these continue in local religious imaginations, adding to explanatory and behavioural choices. Before the Revolution (1978) a local, pious woman from a Seyed family quietly said a customary 'bismillah' ('In the name of God') whenever she handled food, to shoo away hungry jinn who would eat, too, causing a shortfall of food. After the Islamic government had established itself, she still said 'bismillah' when serving food but her explanation left out the jinn: now it was a plea to God to make the food plentiful so that nobody would be hungry, she said. In 2015 she still said 'bismillah', but now 'in order to remember God'. Over a span of forty years, she had added two options to explain the habit in a nod to the changing religious customs; other women stuck to the jinn explanation.

After the universality of religion and choices a culture provides, the third assumption is that people defend but also evaluate, judge, criticize their own culture's choices. They identify with some ideas and are troubled and exasperated by others. They talk and argue, joke and quarrel about them. Tribal inheritance customs, for example, led to disputes 'in every family', people say, especially among brothers. (Women did not inherit at all.) When Sharia law in the Islamic Republic gave women the right to half of their brothers' shares of the inheritance, it opened new ways of thinking about women and tribal customs in God's purported justice. The law meant that women now could take brothers to court over this issue, thereby challenging (God-given) family hierarchies and risking (sinful) hostilities within the kin group. It took years before some women in town dared to sue for their inheritance, and more time until young women, inspired by the new choice of 'Islamic feminism', dared to discuss the half a brother's share rule as an injustice. How people use their own culture's possibilities and what they think of its features is a theme that newspapers report on, such as on protests against modest dress in public in Iran, but is writ small in the ethnography of Islam.[13]

These assumptions focus on ideas, on philosophies of life as lived and expressed in actions and talk, in rituals and songs, indeed in all behaviour. Staying as close to the vernacular aspects of life as I do here means that I prefer the emic, experiential side of ethnography: it helps to visualize people's total frame of possibilities, the great – and unexpected – variety of choices for thinking about existential premises and one's place in the universe. Access to this 'thinking' and to people's movements in widely different, even contradictory, schemas is made possible by the generous vernacular logic people employ in arguments. In scientific logic most arguments are unacceptable, but for people who use them in order to come to terms with their world, they are popular, handy choices.[14] Rather than dismissing the logical fallacies they produce, I list some examples for vernacular logic in lived religion here without further elaboration: teleological explanations; propinquity turned into causality; opinion turned into 'truth'; intention and purported cause as justification; means justify the ends; function as raison d'être; generalizations based on anecdote; wishful thinking as prediction; prejudice informing judgement; post hoc ergo propter hoc; intentionality equals causality; reference to an inscrutable superhuman 'Will' of a deity beyond people's reach.

Religion

About 90 per cent of people in Iran and nearly everybody in Boir Ahmad are Muslims of the Twelver Shia group, adherents of the political and spiritual authority of the twelve divinely ordained early Muslim leaders, the Imams, who are accepted as the legitimate successors of the Prophet Muhammad.[15] In theocratic modern Iran, a religious elite directs the political life of the nation and watches over the exegesis of canonical texts, the application of Sharia law and the morality of the citizens. It is a powerful 'government religion'. To be a good citizen is to be a good Shia Muslim. This causes dissent.

Local people insist that they always have been good Muslims, even though their circumstances and isolation from centres of religious learning and activities did not encourage demonstrative piety, grand myths and elaborate rituals characteristic of large urban or agricultural communities. Instead of pomp or fertility rituals, for example, ethics (summarized as 'humanism', *ensānyat*) and rituals were about averting hardships and managing relationships in small groups where strong interpersonal ties make members stay true to shared practices even when these are challenged.[16] The recent missionary efforts by the government have added mosques, clerics and more rituals to the town and thus to local people's choices but also have made many believers doubt what they see and hear. Statements like 'We didn't know Arabic when we were living in black tents but we were better people then' undermine new, fervent believers' assertions that only through obedience to doctrines and the government could one please God. Locally, such *hezbollah* (Party-of-God) zeal may be viewed with apprehension, especially so as the economy of Iran no longer can provide basic necessities for the millions of citizens who have no access to the sources of great wealth open to a small moneyed elite. Repeated references in this book to discontent, criticism and signs of severe stress are supported by global indicators. If anything, there is less misery in Boir Ahmad than in many other areas in Iran.[17] Iran's stressed social contract is expressed in the traditional saying, 'If the king is bad, people will suffer' (*shāh kharāb, velāyat kharāb*). (Turned around, it declares poverty a sign of bad government.) It is popular again, a choice that renders piety and the Islamic government's claims to provide superior, divinely guided leadership hollow. When believers no longer have the sense that God is working for them, trust in religion and religious authorities will fade (Heelas and Woodhead 2005).

The umbrella of Shia Islam covers a variety of religious behaviours. Mostly I will use local people's vernacular, overlapping categories for differences in theology and practice: 'Mullah-Islam' means what people hear from preachers in sermons and on television. Tone and messages of these sermons range from common-sense ethics that even doubters can appreciate to 'fundamentalist' and political Islamic topics. 'Government Islam' is what happens in public life under the banner of 'Islam', such as in law, public rituals and demands on the faithful.

'Hezbollah' (Party-of-God) refers to militant, intolerant, 'fundamentalist' adherents of 'government Islam', including many Revolutionary Guards, and implies zealotic commitment to a political programme.[18] It appeals to lower classes and the poor in the province's capital and in central Boir Ahmad more than in Sisakht, where such fervent piety is looked at with distrust. But its tenets and activities are well known, and adopting them at least outwardly constitutes a choice for disenfranchised, poor men (more than women) who want – or keep – jobs or other benefits Party-of-God leaders can grant. 'Orthodox' and 'traditional' are my words for believers who prefer traditional, understated, quiet rituals and religious activities to the more demanding, loud and energetic versions of government Islam. Most people in Sisakht belong to this loose group, including younger people with years of doctrinal-fundamentalist religious education in school.

Literature

Most of what is written about religion in Iran lies either within Shia exegetic and proselytizing texts and sermons for the faithful (e.g. Lankarani 1999; Qummi 1999) or within a historical or sociopolitical frame (Arjomand 2016; Bausani 2000; Davis 2015; Fischer 1990; Foltz 2013; Foroutan 2017; Hegland 1983, 2014; Keddie 1972; B. Lewis 1988; Moaddel 2005; Nachman 2018; Richard 1995; Sakurai 2012; Widengren 1965). Donaldson (1938) counts some folklore as 'Mohammedan'; Massé (1954) relegates rituals to folklore; Kriss and Kriss-Heinrich (1960/62) discuss religious topics as 'folk-belief'. In the 1980s ethnographic approaches added other thematic angles and insights to the study of religion in Iran, including to the 'lived religion' of ordinary people.[19] However, ethnographic studies in Iran are difficult to do, and studies on lived religion even more so. Bromberger (2018) gives a short overview of ethnographic fieldwork conditions. Anthropologists Kamalkhani (1998), Vivier-Muresan (2006) and Shirazi (2009) write about how women move within Shia religious rules and prescriptions. The most insightful studies are about women's shrine visitations in Shiraz (Betteridge 1985, 1993, 2001; Honarpisheh 2013). For other, narrower topics see articles in Ansari and Martin (2002), Aghaie (2004), Brooks (2002), Flaskerud (2010), Friedl and R. Loeffler (2018), Hegland (2014), Kalinock (2004), R. Loeffler (1988), Moaddel (1998), Shirazi (2005), Torab (2005, 2007), Wellman (2018), Zahedi (2018).

Studies of west Iranian tribal people's religiosity, of beliefs and rituals (in the widest sense) available to them, are rare. Brooks (2002) describes Bakhtiaris' visits to shrines; R. Loeffler (1988) described the great variety of beliefs of men in a tribal community; Friedl (2001) elaborates aspects of women's religiosity there. The earliest ethnographic account of tribal life in southern Iran (Barth 1961) unfortunately set a negative tone about twentieth-century tribal religion with the remark that the Basseri in Fars Province gave little, if any, thought to transcendental or spiritual sides of existence. In the literature this turned into the stubborn prejudice of the tribes' purported 'irreligiosity'. Where anthropologists working in tribal communities address religion at all, they mean standard, urban Shia Islam, with emphasis on the handling of important Shia rituals and prescriptions. (See Beck (1991) about the Qashqa'i in Fars Province; Black-Michaud (1986) and Demant Mortensen (1993) about the Lurs of Luristan; Bradburd (1998) about the Komanchi in Kerman province;[20] Suzuki (2011) about the Doshmanziari in Kohgiluye/Boir Ahmad.) Tribal graveyards get some attention (Alehassan 2017; Khosronejad 2014; Demant Mortenson 2010), as do shrines (Haerinck and Overlaet 2008)[21] and death, generally (Khalili 2010), but their discussions suggest little about beliefs and death theology. Other features of religious life are ignored, mentioned in passing as folklore (Amanolahi 1975, 1986 on Luristan), as women's customs (Beck 1986), or are treated as 'superstition' (Demant Mortensen (1993) about Luristan; Shahshahani (1982) about the Mamasani, neighbours of the Boir Ahmadi). This neglect is as much a function of the prevalent professional interest in sociopolitical topics in the academic anthropological community during the respective research periods as it is a function of Islamic prejudice: 'religion' means 'high' religion, and in this regard 'the tribes' are found to be 'only nominally religious' (Beck 1986: 322) or to have 'limited knowledge of theology' despite being 'most devout' (Bradburd 1998: 52). Thus found wanting in their expressions of 'true Islam', tribal people's actual beliefs are easily overlooked.[22] Yet, ignorance, restraint or reluctance in the observation of standard Muslim rituals in itself do not amount to 'absence of religion' (as Bradburd (1998: 51) also observed). As negative statements prevent insight into what low-keyed tribal people in Iran actually believe and practice, I changed the focus and took a closer look.

Looking closely, purported differences between the religious and spiritual lives of men and women shrink. Men present themselves as more rational and better informed than women and as more dismissive of anything beyond their hands-on agency, but as R. Loeffler's presentation of twenty-one men's handling of Islam and ethics shows, men are well informed about what their culture offers regarding religion. The present text enlarges the frame to include what women make of religion and extends the time frame to the present. Gender differences appear to be less about beliefs than about gender-indexed duties. Thus, for example, men used spells, amulets and sacrifices to prevent a wolf from striking a herd or locusts from destroying a crop, and performed burial duties required from Muslims. Women, in charge of their dependent family members' well-being, used rituals deemed necessary to keep everybody safe. Men and women know of each other's rituals. Moreover, a husband readily provides funds for a votive sacrifice for a child's health but his wife will cook and distribute the food. Likewise, an eldest son is responsible for 'feeding' his dead parents by offering food to graveyard visitors at the obligatory Thursday-afternoon visits or at mourning events but he delegates the actual work to his wife. I suggest that to dismiss such 'popular religion' activities and thoughts as 'superstitions' or as 'women's religion' is taking an uncritical position in line with the local androcentric gender structure.[23]

Furthermore, the low-keyed, community and subsistence-oriented Muslims' sparse and terse philosophies and nearly stoic aims matched their hard life. People emphasized reliance on 'knowing how' (Pavese 2016), on personal skills, strength and experiences, on personal responsibilities for actions and on the communal ethic of mutual assistance. Locally, a label of 'good person' and 'humanity' (*ensānyat*) remains high praise and reflects social ethics. Given contentious, impatient human ways, though, people say they expect conflict; the ideal of harmony and support is not a reliable motivator of behaviour. One has to be on guard against hostilities. For dealing with unavoidable problems people have the option to perform various traditional rituals tempered with basic Islamic beliefs designed to protect them from harm, promote good experiences and help with daily difficulties and with catastrophes. Such rituals range from invocations, blessings, curses and sacrifices to managing a host of extra-human powers, personified diseases and efficacious saints.[24] A Creator-God rules 'everything', but looking back people suggest that He was easier to approach in the past and now is becoming increasingly remote and difficult to engage. Itinerant preachers and purported descendants of the Prophet Muhammad (called Seyeds) living in the area occasionally taught basic Islamic tenets, performed prescribed Islamic rituals and collected religious taxes. These services and the preachers' descriptions of a personal, moralistic God provided different options to relate to the transcendental sphere but did not challenge ideas people held about how their tight, difficult world worked.

In the 1960s, after the collapse of the tribal sociopolitical hierarchy, small, pastoral communities had to adapt quickly to Iran's complex society and overarching government institutions. The organizational powers of kin groups, pasture-camps and chiefs faded against the new political rules and the features of 'modernity' and 'progress'. The Islamic Republic added religious specialists, sophistication in theology and rituals, and architectural and aesthetic symbols as well as the assurance that all was watched over and directed by an all-important 'Big God' (Whitehouse 2019). This God is understood to act like a powerful king-ruler who guards and controls a large, complex, unruly populace. These developments added choices to local people's understanding of themselves and to their religious lives.

Over the past decade, a lifestyle revolution towards libertarian hedonism especially in urban middle classes has produced options that have little to do with traditional ethics, religiosity or morality. In Boir Ahmad, strong social controls work against these new lifestyles but among young, somewhat jaded, city-oriented people, an apparently global development away from doctrinal moralistic religiosity is noticeable, as, for example, in a blurring of 'liberated' sexual relations, internet-based dating, time-limited marriage and prostitution.[25] Religious authorities say they try to accept some trends, knowing well that social change tends to undermine religious leadership if the guardians of religion won't or can't accommodate them. The manifold ideas and practices, the contradictions and seeming idiosyncrasies described in the following chapters can be understood as a reflection of what happened, cognitively and in practice, at the historic juncture of small-scale tribal communities and a large-scale, complex, bureaucratically administered society. One can safely assume that similar developments happen in other parts of Iran, too. However, there are no ethnographic studies of lived religion with this focus from elsewhere in Iran that would allow comparisons.[26]

1

Religion and gnostic realism

People express assumptions about life, philosophical notions and spiritual matters in casual comments in vernacular language and with vernacular logic. With this term I summarize the various patterns of arguing which people use outside of scientific logic to relate to this – and any potential other – world. My observations cover a long time and considerable sociopolitical upheavals that necessitated adaptive changes in people's daily routines and philosophies but did not wipe out traditional pieties. These pieties tend to get filtered out in ethnographies that use the matrix of orthodox Shia Islam, and much is thereby missed. Most noteworthy in local theologies are a deeply rooted leaning towards empirical knowledge and its attainment (proof, experience) that opens all belief to doubt as a matter of unstated principle;[1] neo-platonic ideas such as transcendent divine authority, the power of the mind (*aql*), light as an emanation of God;[2] and Zoroastrian dualist notions that urge people to take the 'right path' and to uphold order and peaceful communities by following the Golden Rule.[3] The range of traditional philosophies people use to guide theology and behaviour can be summarized in simple principles with emphasis on experience as the best form of knowledge and doubt about most else. But doubt and a reluctance to talk about transcendental issues do not amount to religious indifference, as is sometimes claimed in the literature.[4] As local small-scale tribal Muslim groups integrated into the complex Iranian state in the mid-twentieth century and into the Islam of a well-trained Shia clergy a generation later, they had to come to terms with new options for beliefs and actions as they adapted to Big Government as well as to a moralizing Big God ruling a large, diverse population.[5]

In low-keyed local life, people place essentially vulnerable humans in a materialist physical universe with regularities and a world animated by extra-human powers, all created by God. They express a strong need for assistance to make it in the difficult world, and tend to see God and various powers as potential helpers in a form of moralistic therapeutic deism. Vulnerability leads to 'magical' thinking, a logic of cause/effect that precludes falsification, and to habituated, durable rituals rooted in tradition. The combination of powerful words and detailed prescriptions in scriptures opens a door to the next life, too, for those who believe in it: methodical doubt, the possibility that what one is told to believe might be false, is ever present. This empiricism is not dogmatic but based on personal experience and trust in one's observations and judgement in matters of living in this, a real and rather unforgiving, world. The acceptance of the existence of God on principle, the experience of a structured material environment, doubt about what is outside one's experience, and acting daily on one's knowledge and tried-and-true habits amount to what I call gnostic realism.[6]

Gnostic realism

The basic argument in people's quest for first causes is this: we *know* that all that exists must have a beginning. This beginning is called God. God is the ultimate origin, a powerful, inscrutable creator-king who has no beginning and no end. God created an orderly universe (or created order in a chaos) with dependable regularities. It includes humans and whatever is useful, inconsequential or dangerous for them, such as nature, extra-human powers, ailments and their remedies, rituals for warding off dangers. As all this is based on observation and experience, it is reasonable.

For navigating through this difficult life people say that God has given them reason and intellect (*aql*) with which they ought to acquire knowledge through observation, trial-and-error, experience, learning from others, and following tried-and-true traditions (*ādat o rozume*).[7] People have to learn the rules, the order by which things around them move, the laws of nature God established; they have to figure out how to make things work for them, how to counter ever-present disintegration, disorder, chaos.[8] This is hard work but possible. Impossible for humans is to understand why God made all this, the purpose of the cosmos, including earth and life on it.

Likewise impossible to understand is to what purpose resources and circumstances in the world are distributed unequally and encourage oppression and domination: males dominate females, the wealthy oppress the poor, aggressors violate the meek and death eliminates life.[9] God willed all this, obviously, but it is beyond human understanding, and lets one experience God in many ways, from an active autocratic ruler who creates or wills every moment of existence to a creator who now rests somewhere, taking only sporadic interest in what happens on earth.[10] (This is an increasingly popular choice for imagining God.) People may insist that all they 'know for sure' is that they are born without being asked, struggle through life, take care of their obligations (*vasife*) and then die and go back to dust. The before and after is unknown, a matter of belief. Trusting their own experiences, they tend to be suspicious of anything beyond their control. Such basic assumptions fit small-scale, subsistence-oriented societies, where everybody knows everybody else, making ever-present eye-in-the-sky observers redundant.[11] Religion and science both assist in figuring out the why and what-for of existence for those who ask such questions.

This is the beat a nearly otiose deity is drumming for life on earth, audible in most local talk about religion and philosophy. Much of what people are told by the Islamic Republic's Shia authorities to accept on faith thus does not quite fit experiences and reason.[12] An elderly local man bothered by injustices in this world explained:

> There is a power – God, we say – that makes the seasons, rain and snow, day and night, makes a date-palm different from a cherry tree and puts us people into all this. We move and hustle as best we can, and then we die. This is the end of all problems. Heaven, hell, prayer, all this is beyond what we can know. But to think that every thief and scoundrel will go free – this is hard to imagine.

Conundrums, fault lines

In Iran, including its hinterland, forty years of intense efforts by the government to develop 'correct' piety have quieted (but not silenced) many critical thinkers, doubters and traditionally pious people.[13] The state religion gives rise to adaptive, opportunistic and dissimulative strategies people may choose who want to get ahead economically or avoid drawing attention for fear of harassment. Especially dissidents, agnostics, atheists and religious minorities need skills for living below the radar of guardians of 'Islamic principles'.[14] The strategies also inspire sinuous (*pic pici*) arguments and religious justifications for just about any behaviour, said a devout and frustrated physician in 2018. When politicians bend religious texts and dogmas into restrictive rules, social and ideological pressure produces qualitative shifts in attitudes towards religion and rituals of piety. Authorities who have the power to formulate ideas can persuade or force people to agree to a fairly uniform and exclusive vision of an ever-present ruler-God demanding obedience and rituals of submission in a watchful relationship with people. Doctrinal hardliners ascribe the ills of Iran to people's reticence in embracing this 'true Islam' and point to the social and professional successes they themselves earned by choosing the right path. The tug of war between them and 'liberals' over control of behaviours they deem morally suspect is less obvious in small towns than in cities but such polarizing leads to distrust in politics and in theology everywhere. In Sisakht, when government agents in the name of religion persecuted local dissidents after 1981,[15] an elderly, pious man was so distressed that he loudly vented his (and others') suspicion that the Imams and early heroes of Islam probably also had been sowing distrust and pain instead of demonstrating the ethical superiority of Islam.[16] The assertion that the 'time of the mullahs' has a bad influence on people's character by weakening 'humanity' (ensānyat), especially kindness and empathy, by making people self-serving and blind to injustices and the needs of others, and by weakening reason, has become a much-cited trope. When a local Party-of-God adherent told of a martyr's severed head speaking while impaled on a sword, a young, conventionally pious listener was offended: 'How can the mullahs spread this nonsense,' he said, implicitly defending rationality and progress, and relegating such religious pronouncements to the superstition bin. 'Thinking about things' and critically observing the goings-on have become popular options to deal with religion, all the way to voicing the suspicion that any religion is 'made by men for men', as an elderly woman said. Her God did not make such an imperfect religion.

On the most general level, local people used to handle transcendental issues and assumptions about cosmology, God and the vagaries of life by combining their knowledge of Islamic theology and so-called popular beliefs into *din* (religion). Both hinge on knowledge orally conveyed from one generation to the next with some input from the outside,[17] on trust in a more or less remote creator-God, and on practical, work-based experiences. 'Islam' included most local beliefs and rituals that promised advantages for conducting one's affairs. Urban, educated Iranian critics of villagers' purported backward mentality like to say that this mix of 'superstitions' (*khorāfāt*) and 'true religion' (*mazhab*) came about when mullahs had to present religious concepts to rural illiterates in terms of local customs in order to be understood at all, and that religious understanding will improve now that everybody can read the Quran.[18]

Since the late 1960s, however, *din* is diverging from what people believe and do. With increasing modernity followed by Islamic reforms, many local assumptions and practices moved from 'true religion' to *khorāfāt*, that is, to superstition, idle talk, ignorance, fanciful stories and vestiges of old habits, as a teacher explained, while the rational, experiential side of local religion that is based on knowing, tradition and self-preservation is moving to science (*elm*) and to modernity/progress (*pishraft*). Science and progress, however, do not provide a strong ethical foundation supporting local values. 'Enlightened' (*roushan*) people root these values in Islamic and modern humanism, but the essential, ubiquitous Persian concept of *ensān/ensānyat* (human, in the sense of polite, cultured, good conduct) is even stronger. The first local government-appointed physician, Dr Dibazar, a dedicated, empathic and competent man from Tabriz, is remembered still as a 'real human being'. Without *ensānyat*, piety and religious rituals are nothing, neighbours said of a local Seyed who was known to mistreat his wife; and in the meaning of civility, *ensānyat* is the opposite of 'wild' (*vakhshi*, uncultured, boorish, violent), covering animals as well as rude, belligerent people's conduct regardless of religious affiliation.

Clerics and adherents of doctrinal piety insist that formal aspects of religion are necessary for promotion of the greater good. 'Without religion people would kill each other like wolves,' is a standard assertion. Yet, older people say that over the past four decades instead of improving ethics, religion has been shrinking to belief in scriptures and their exegetes, and has expanded mosque-centred rituals and actions that guardians of religion encourage and expect people to attend.[19] Both opinions have adherents. Although mosque-activities attract many men (and fewer women, confined to the balcony),[20] outward signs of religiosity alone do not guarantee ethical behaviour, people say. Rather, the popular critique of modern times is that morality and traditional Persian ethics are dwindling. In their stead, people can choose to act on a quite elastic understanding of morality.[21] Critics say that *din/mazhab* now is elitist in the reliance on written sources, on interpreters and guardians, on prolonged study to understand God's word 'properly', on designated, expensive spaces, on practices that are difficult to align with rationality, science and lifestyle aspirations, much to the disadvantage of especially the young and the poor.

This constellation encourages anticlerical sentiments when unpopular clerics claim political power. (The slogan, *zālem va ālem* means 'Oppressive power plus clerical moral authority spells trouble.') When a little girl asked about a mullah's large white turban, her uncle said, 'It used to be a short shawl Arabs put on their heads against the sun. Over time, the less the mullahs had to work outdoors the longer the shawls got, and with each new turn they bound up a thousand hardships for us.' People in town point to zealous (*ghaliz*) outsiders urging them to participate in rituals they organize, and to one of the village's earlier mullahs, a stranger who became so wealthy in this poor town that he had to make the hajj to Mecca and often was called 'ignorant'.[22] The religion of the pious newcomers was based on formulas and rituals, on urban bazar sensibilities of people who were spared manual labour. In the diversifying local economy, their religiosity provided a further choice, attractive to people who could use 'piety' to further their socio-economic aspirations. In the climate of clerical authorities' heavy-handed rule over all aspects of life, making fun of leaders became popular as well as dangerous, and cynicism regarding leaders' behaviour and messages increased to the point where listeners to sermons called many pronouncements 'lies' and 'superstitions'.[23] People who closely adhere to 'mullah-piety' may be said to have 'fallen into religion', meaning they are neglecting reason and social duties, or else may be suspected of using religion to advance their prospects. Opportunistic religious behaviour is called, 'dry religion' (*mazhab khoshk*) by critics who, in turn, are accused of maligning Shia Islam. Quietly religious people, though, assume that the government benefits clergy businessmen and is hard on everybody else but say that this is no reason to give religion a bad name. The Islam they know is a good religion and its demands on people are easy, their fulfilment beneficial for those who keep the faith.

The widening range of possibilities to think about religion includes traditional, well-used ideas as well as extreme orthodox and critical options now. Despite contradictions people often use them simultaneously, depending on the occasion and the pressure or necessity (*majburi*) they feel. In 2015 a psychologist in Shiraz suggested that the status quo in modern Iran fostered misgivings, psychological problems, depression and existential difficulties, and thus did not provide a healthy spiritual and ethical foundation for life.

Din and people

In its original meaning, Latin *religio* implied people's obligations towards and care for the gods (Rüpke 2013: 7). Applied to God, obligation and care are major ingredients in the popular understanding of religion in Boir Ahmad too. In vernacular speech, the term *din* is used in expressions such as *din-e mā* (our religion, followed by a rule or order, or to highlight differences to another religion); *din ige* (the religion says, followed by a dictum); *dine mā Eslam* (our religion is Islam, implying religious, philosophical, ethical and political identity).[24] But in practice it also includes the belief in Quran-based extra-human powers (jinn and demons), in the powers of saints and of magical formulas, powers in plants and minerals, in time, diseases, sounds and such – all validated by the conviction that God created everything, including these powers.[25]

Furthermore, *din* covers philosophy, ethics and assumptions about life and relationships. This is of importance today. Local people may say they have been Muslims 'always', and good Muslims at that: they knew what to hold dear and what to avoid, and always found somebody (mostly itinerant clerics) who read the Quran and performed death prayers. They honoured the important rituals in the Islamic calendar and supported relatives. They did not need yet another conversion, and certainly not by a government they blame for many problematic changes in their lives.[26] In 2006 a well-regarded, old local farmer, deeply committed to religion, upon returning from a pilgrimage disparaged much of what he had taken for granted earlier:

> Until the revolution I believed everything, prayers and amulets and votive promises, just like everybody else. But when I heard that Ayatollah Khomeini, a mere Seyed, now was called the thirteenth Imam,[27] doubts grew in my mind, and now, after visiting this big shrine I am sure that everything is a swindle except God. Only God can create life, God is power and will, and people cannot influence Him – not with prayer, not with sacrifices or promises or pilgrimages. God does what He wants. We cannot reach Him. Everything else we believe and are told by the mullahs is just to keep us busy, to entertain us. If a sick man gets well at a shrine it is because the journey lifted his spirit and made him feel better, and because he really believed in the saint. But how can one believe it is the saint who helps? The early Imams and their descendants, that is, the saints, could not help themselves when they were in trouble, and God could not or would not save them either – so, why should God or the helpless saints help me? I see just the opposite: a thoroughly despicable woman goes to Kerbela and not only does not get a nosebleed but now is a '*Kerbelāī*',[28] rotten to the core still and richer every day, while other people, good people, go there and remain sick and poor. All this is one big lie. Religion should make one's life good. Ours doesn't.

Islam is more than a syncretized cult of a monotheistic deity, though. Authorities insist that cooperative submission puts people on a path to a God-pleasing and therefore successful, good, peaceful life rich in merits and poor in sins, with chances for continuation of bliss after death. If asked directly, most local people will readily agree to these benefits of Islam and argue that without religion's checks and forceful guidance the naturally violent and unreasonable human beings would destroy the world.[29] Yet, off the record, people of all degrees and kinds of religiosity like to throw at this piety one or another of six arguments that amount to options for viewing humankind and religion. They may be mixed and matched according to the occasion.

One is rhetorical and theological: It is hard to believe that God made humans weak, unreasonable and aggressive, and afterward ordered them to be submissive to religion to prevent the consequences of His creation. Related is the problem of asserting God's Will for everything that happens but then insisting on rewards for and punishments of people's actions.

The second is political: Muslim countries either are poor (as in Africa) or ruled autocratically (as in Saudi Arabia), or else they are at war (as in many places in the Middle East).[30] How does this square with Islam as a path to peace and a good life?

The third is historical: The creation and elaboration of the Shia-Sunni differences point to the political, man-made parts of Islam. Who knows what else is man-made?

The fourth is an economic cui bono-argument: Islam in Iran works for the rich, the mullahs and those around them, not for ordinary people. Religious schools are filled with students who see theology as a path to a good job in an otherwise dismal economy.[31]

The fifth argument is social, based on the firm expectation that scientific, economic and technical progress (*pishraft*) will facilitate 'freedom' (*āzādi*), health and a good life. In periodic demonstrations and a steady brain drain, people who focus on progress complain that Islam as enforced by the government thwarts their God-given abilities and aspirations because it is focused backward on the time of the martyrs, not forward to people's needs and abilities.[32]

The sixth argument is psychological: The belief in the mercy of God and the possibility of earning unlimited merits during one's lifetime undermines obligatory (*vājeb*) religious prescriptions and creates moral wriggle room for slackers and scoundrels.

People who ponder such issues see the logical and practical problems contained in the arguments as 'wicked problems', as resistant to solutions because of contradictory assumptions and goals. Good Muslims do well to ignore such troubling thoughts, they say.

The good Muslim

Local people expect the good Muslim to be married, have children and to be a caring, wise family member and neighbour. Celibacy is seen as unhealthy rather than as a moral virtue. Unmarried adults stand a bit outside the God-ordained place for their age. A college-educated, single man in his early forties with a good job said he could not find a wife who shared his inclination towards hard work, a simple life and taking care of his ageing parents. He fashioned himself into a dervish (*darvish*), the socially and morally acceptable alternative to a good Muslim householder: he lived frugally, shunned festivities and loud rituals of piety, cultivated a humble, quiet demeanour, read Islamic mysticism (*erfān*), was generous with his time and money and became a trusted counsellor to men and women around him. Another local young man renounced the world, work and people after wild teenage escapades, and lived with his parents, studying religious books. A third 'dervish' had turned his back on marriage after his parents had vetoed his choice for a wife. He had a job but otherwise cultivated the demeanour of a very private, pious, self-contained wise man, much to the chagrin of his parents.[33]

To get along with kin and neighbours, to be helpful and show empathy (*mehrabuni, delsuz, ātefe*), to fulfil one's responsibilities (*vasife*) and work hard, and to meet joys and hardships calmly and patiently, all top moral expectations.[34] People are appreciated who talk and behave like stoics, keep strong emotions in check and project a well-balanced, unflappable outlook on life as masters of the art of living. However, fulfilling plain duties won't earn one the merits to be had by performing government-organized rituals.

Here is how a young mother (S) answered my (E) rare questions, in 2006:

E: What does God want from people, from a good Muslim?

S: Well, to take troubles, to do one's work and eat a piece of bread, to feed the children – eh, of course, the children. To sit with the neighbours, talk with them, help them, ha, for sure. To be good, no stealing, no fighting, no bad words. No lies, huh! [*She laughs*]. It won't happen! [*Laughs again*].

E: What if one falls ill or is poor?

S [*quickly*]: This is God's Will. That's it. Nothing more.

E: What about the other world? Paradise, hell?

S: *That* world? What about it? What can I say? Nobody has come back from there yet to tell us how it is there. [*She shakes her head, smiles, shrugs her shoulders.*] People say this, they say that – I don't know what to say.

E: And the Day of Judgement?

S [*chuckles*]: Oh yes, the Hidden Imam will return, they say. We'll see, for sure. We all die. But for now we are alive – so what can I say? Thanks be to God! We'll see what happens then, what?! In *this* life I have to see that I do my chores, that everybody is kept alive, night follows day, sun-up to sun-down, or maybe not?!

For local people like this woman – the 'silent majority' or else those who set the tone in the humming undercurrent of philosophy – religion is a code, a God-given, sensible programme for making it in this world. An usually kind elderly woman criticized her neighbours, a hard-working, successful family, for being so eager to make progress that they were herding their animals in the highest mountain pastures all summer long and did not meet anybody or take a bath once. For her, God demanded cleanliness, to feed the hungry, to speak well of others, respect everybody and be reliable. According to her paupers' ethics, the neighbours had taken themselves out of these commitments for weeks on end and thus had failed important moral obligations. By contrast, whoever honours these social commitments likely is declared good no matter their possible doubts about mullahs or God's powers or beliefs in life after death. A grandmother remembered a day when she was young, pregnant and carrying a heavy back bag way up to the summer pasture camp:

> I got there so hot and exhausted from the long climb in the sun that I thought I would faint. And when I came to our branch hut I found the water-bag empty, a dead fire, no food. I was so discouraged and weak that I fell down and slept. And when I woke up there was a pot with soup on a fine fire, the water bag was full and firewood was handy; the other women in camp had done my work – not for religious merits but to help me. Good people, God approves of them.

Some men (more than women) may become 'addicted' (*mohdād*) to a severe, unyielding form of piety that lets them neglect their worldly duties and earns them disapproval from others. In the early years of the Islamic Republic, girl students were especially susceptible to demands of modesty that made them 'crazy (*kelu*), sitting in a corner wrapped up in veils, memorizing the Quran'.[35] In a neighbouring town a man with this piety affliction oppressed his family so much that the wife killed herself. 'He was full of religion but not a good man,' said a shopkeeper. Good people have their peers' respect and have nothing to fear for life after death either. For them the mullahs' emphasis on honouring *din* in order to accrue benefits for the afterlife is superfluous. A good afterlife – such as there might be – comes automatically as long as one behaves right. While the code of this worldly ethics includes – or does not exclude – honouring prescriptions of rituals, prayers, cult-obligations, fasting and taking care of the dead, people may choose to treat piety as a private affair entwined with daily chores, and to treat cultic aspects as limited by circumstances. In the past, public performances of piety were confined to grand occasions such as funerals and Muharram.[36] Few people had the money or leisure for the pilgrimage to Mecca or to the big shrines in Iran. As long as they took care of their obligations, worked hard, thanked God for their livelihood and prayed and fasted when circumstances allowed, they counted as good Muslims. A local old man's story highlights the criteria:

> A poor man from a village on the other side of the mountain came across the pass to beg for food here.[37] It was late fall, cold, snow – he never made it back home. Next spring, I and some other men found him up there. He was decomposing in his clothes, and we slid the body down to where we could dig a shallow grave. The stench was bad. We put him in the grave, clothes and all, and heaped stones on top. Back home we asked a mullah to do the prayer for him. He refused because the corpse had not been washed properly, he said. I said, 'How can we wash him – he is half mush!' But the mullah said no, impossible. 'Very well', I said, 'We'll go back, dig him up, bring him down in a pail and you wash him.' Now the mullah prayed!

People who excel in public shows of piety are readily derided for lapses in their social obligations. A local Seyed merchant, an outsider who for decades had enjoyed commercial success and the people's esteem, was criticized harshly when he took a second wife, and harsher yet when he neglected his first family. Likewise, public opinion discredited recruiters of tribal men for the Iraq–Iran war: the boys they 'caught' ought to obey and help their parents, not be swindled by 'false promises and a plastic key to a fake paradise'.[38] And when a quiet old couple died, the neighbours' opinion was that they had neither harmed nor helped anybody. Nobody was angry about them but nobody missed them either; they would be forgotten soon.

The long Iran–Iraq war, government agents' extensive and intrusive control of people's modesty and, later, Iran's expensive engagements abroad were carried out in the name of an increasingly moralistic and formalistic religion. The new ostentatious religious behaviours made so many people weary of authorities' claims of Islam as a religion of humbleness that the suspicion arose that from the very beginning Islam might have been more about fights for the glory of political power than for the welfare of the souls of the faithful. (The counterargument is in the option to declare the global success of Islam to be a sign of Islam's superior message.) Participating in government-arranged religious events could take on a cynical tinge. 'I have to go shed tears of mourning for some stranger, what choice do I have?' said a professional man explaining a lengthy absence from his office. A joke we heard first in the 1980s was relevant thirty years later: 'We used to pray at home and drink in public. Now we pray in public and have no fun at home either.' The strategies people may select to make the system work for them turn *din* into a tool for demonstrating political loyalty. They require skills of dissimulation and of bending conditions to one's advantage. In 2015 local people told this story:

> A sand-hauling truck with two local men got stuck upriver, and three men from there, before lending a hand, wanted a contract for paid work in compensation for the sand the Sisakhtis 'stole' from the river. The negotiation ended with the three river men beating up the truckers. In front of the judge, however, the rivermen swore that they had punished the truckers for maligning Imam Khomeini, whereupon the judge praised them and admonished the Sisakhtis to repent.

Other versions have the same messages, namely, that one is forced (*majbur*) to use 'religion' when circumstances make it expedient, and also that a system that allows people to use religion to lie, is a bad system.[39] (Yet, in the next breath, a critic commented that given their sticky situation the river men had lied well.)

A similar case supported traditionalists' warnings of the dangers arising when men and women share a workplace:[40]

> A nurse in the local health clinic, a city-woman who treated her rustic patients with contempt, was reprimanded by the male doctor after patients had complained. The miffed nurse went to the clinic's supervisor and falsely accused the doctor of drinking alcohol and harassing her sexually – grave moral offences, both. The supervisor moved the doctor to a remote village. Local people were upset but there was nothing they could do: the nurse had mobilized religion to make life easy for herself, they said. 'Bad for the doctor, good for her.'

Since about 1981, people say that whoever has professional or socio-economic aspirations better choose the government-created options for behaviour, dress and talk. Depending on purpose and location, one's persona differs at home, in school or work, in front of neighbours, teachers and guardians of morality and political reliability. Outward signs of morality (such as in dress) and religious engagement are measures of political loyalty: a good Muslim supports the government. This makes local realists weary of morality claims, lofty ideals and demands by the government, and supportive of the idea that religion ought to be a personal affair, not an order.[41]

Governmental orders are easier to enforce and behaviour is easier to control in rural places than in cities because everybody knows everybody else's opinions and allegiances. Nobody wants to be conspicuous. Thus, while modernity has brought options for styles of dress beyond tribal costume to Sisakht, just about all local women choose to dress in black-veiled anonymity outdoors, more modest than God demands. Conformity makes life easier, said a student. A well-regarded woman famous for her colourful tribal costumes in the past, in 2015, careful to toe the government line, dressed in black and assured me without a hint of sarcasm that the current all-black women's wear reflected the globally preferred colour of fashionable women.

Despite socio-economic and political ups and downs over the past three decades, locally the qualities that make a Muslim 'good' have held steady. A good Muslim continues to profess belief in and obedience to God, to honour the Prophet and the Imams and to organize affairs so that people can be at ease and at peace. When a young couple's quarrels annoyed their neighbours, the local mullah asked me, a non-Muslim, to intervene, arguing that as peacemakers 'we are all Muslims'. In 2006 a teacher defended the new custom of letting young people choose their spouse by arguing that if later they had problems, they could not blame parents for an arranged marriage, the dispute would stay indoors instead of dragging relatives in, and this would make everybody a better Muslim. Yet, people also insist that holding the peace is as hard as avoiding lies, and quote a famous local storyteller who said that good stories are about bad behaviour; nice, quiet people did not make a gripping story. A man passing the new mosque had a similar sentiment: 'The mullahs tell us what should be; we have to face the world as it is.'

The moral foundation of Muslim life

Beyond belief in God's power, benevolence and justice, in the Prophet Muhammad and the Day of Judgement as cornerstones of Islam, people routinely mention the Muslims' duty of doing good. Doing good means to satisfy demands that closely conform to the 'Five Pillars'.[42]

(1) Faith (*imun*) means to recognize God as creator and ruler. This is how most people see God anyway.

(2) Prayer (*namāz*): the obligatory five prayers per day/night at fixed times are meant to honour God. People who work hard in manual tasks often squeeze prayers aside out of necessity, they say. This excuse may bother and anger some but also fits the comforting thought that God does not really need people's words to know their hearts and will forgive their irregular or faulty prayers. 'Prayers are very good, but what counts with God are deeds, not mumblings,' sums up the sentiment. A further popular option is to promote prayers (and God's other orders) as a path to a good life here and after death.[43]

(3) Charity (*sedāqat, kheirāt, khoms, zākat*) is seen as the duty to take care of the poor and ailing rather than as a religious tax obligation. Alms are said to benefit the

receiver and the giver: the needy get help and the donor can ward off a misfortune or earn merits for the afterlife. The poor feel left out, though, although they often hear that giving 'one single date' would do and that their poverty enables rich people to earn merits through generosity. Critics call it an injustice. Mullahs talk about this on television, people say, but the issue of wealth and merits is not settled.

(4) Fasting (*ruze*) from sunrise to sundown during Ramadan[44] is said to show compassion, build character and improve one's health and spiritual well-being if done in the spirit of obedience to God. A routine remark to a fasting person is, 'May God approve your fast.' To abstain from food and drink is a difficult command, especially in the summer. In the Islamic Republic, morality watchers control infringements in public. People who don't fast at home without a valid reason (such as sickness) keep quiet about it. Fasting against doctor's orders counts as especially meritorious among some women. ('The real martyrs are women,' said a student of sociology. 'They work at it!')[45] In 2015 fasting was so popular that women challenged each other, declaring that it was 'good', that 'everybody does it,' and that 'losing weight is healthy,' that is, they touted here-and-now benefits. A young Hezbollah woman declared such reasons invalid. 'Fasting is God's order, not a sport,' she said.

(5) The hajj, the pilgrimage to Mecca, is an obligation for the wealthy who then enjoy the honour of being called 'Hajji'. A poor pilgrim who cannot afford the travel commits two sins: neglecting dependents in order to facilitate aggrandizement. People who choose to stay at home may argue that pilgrims' expenses earn more merits if applied to one's social obligations. A story with a local twist follows a group of Mecca pilgrims, a professional thief among them:

> Resting one evening they heard children cry. The thief left to look and learned that a kettle on the fire in the next house had only water, and that everybody was hungry. He went to a sheep pen, stole a lamb, cooked it and fed the children. Meanwhile the others had left, but as they arrived in Mecca the thief was walking in front of them. His good deed of feeding the poor had made him a hajji without being in Mecca personally.[46]

Around the year 2000 local people acknowledged the religious aspects of big pilgrimages (to Mecca, Kerbela, Mashhad) but also emphasized political pressure to do pilgrimages, and the fun of travelling.[47] A wealthy developer, 'too busy to go to Mecca more than once a year', he said, sent his wife 'to every nearby shrine I can think of', thereby demonstrating his religious fervour and the political allegiance that brought him lucrative contracts. Fifteen years later, this frenzy of religious activities had subsided a bit, if for no other reason than most people had become 'too poor to travel'.[48] In 2015 a limping woman declared that if she ever had enough money for a hajj, she would spend it on a hip replacement.

People treat the Five-Pillar obligations as identity markers for Muslims generally, and in particular emphasize the benefits they bring for everybody in this life. When no such benefit is obvious or when life conditions make neglect 'necessary' (*majbur*), God's mercy can be counted on to minimize the potential sin of ignoring the order.

Summary

The tribal agro-pastoral Shia Muslims' views of themselves, nature and God reflect basic, realistic requirements and offers limited options for living in this world. Economically and politically stressed and struggling to provide necessities, people's deep-seated self-reliance fosters doubts in anything outside their trial-and-error-based experiences and know-how. Coping efforts and longing for reliable structures inform a life philosophy emphasizing knowledge, experience, agency as well as mutual support from people, God and purported extra-human powers. Elevated to a moral basis, the motif of personal engagement fits a small-scale society with close personal relationships. Beyond this, nearly all people declare the tangible existence of life and the universe to be proof of a powerful, if remote, creator-God who established regularities and 'laws' in nature for people (and animals) to adapt to and use. The acceptance of a creator-God as a Necessary Being and ruler over an essentially rational world, together with doubts about esoteric aspects of Islam, locally amount to gnostic realism. Requirements and values of modern life in a complex society and the demands on the faithful in the Islamic Republic to satisfy a moralistic God add to the traditional choices people see in the scope and uses of religion. At the juncture of their own traditions, 'progress' and the nation's Shia doctrines and rituals, people may choose to proclaim orthodox and fundamentalist notions to identify themselves as 'good Muslims'; they may alternate between doubt and acceptance of these notions in trying to define the basis of human existence; they may rely on rituals and religious habits to improve health, or else pick and choose, modify or reject ideas and rituals to manage daily challenges; they may use piety as sociopolitical tool to achieve a better life; they may fuse anticlericalism and doubt about doctrines with keeping up the appearance of a faithful citizen; and those who feel unbearably constrained by a moralizing government in a bad economy may opt to leave altogether, in spirit as well as bodily.

Figure 2 Sisakht, 2006. After the Friday prayer, the resident mullah poses with some men inside the new mosque, built by a wealthy urban man and an expatriate Iranian woman in Kuweit.

2

God

The essential choice in Boir Ahmad regarding God is binary and straightforward: either one accepts God as the uncaused First Cause, which by far most people do, or one does not. More choices appear in details of God's powers and qualities, and in relationships with His creation. People mix and match them to fit circumstances, thereby creating contradictions, swift changes and turnarounds[1] at a time when traditional life-supporting imagery and imaginings met up with doctrinal, moralistic religious structures. These started before the Revolution of 1978 and accelerating especially after 2000. Over a span of about fifty years, choices became narrower and polarized. The two terms used for 'God' in Iran provide an example: Persian *khodā* (*khodāvand*) and Arabic *allah* officially mean the same, but in the contexts of their uses *khodā* may appear as God in general and Allah as God in Islam.[2] Emphasizing the closeness of Christianity and Islam, people asked, rhetorically, if there wasn't *one* God (*khodā*) for all people (*ma na khodā yeki*?). But answering 'Yes' to the question, 'Do you believe in Allah?' brought one close to Islam. In exclamations such as 'thanks be to God' and 'God may grant health,' *khodā* likely is used, while 'Allah' in exclamations of *bismillah* or *mashallah* will banish malevolent powers, thus affirming the superiority of *allah*'s might. Luri *khodā bekhā* (may God will it) is a blessing, while *inshallah* (if Allah wills) supports a wish but is also a pious way of saying, 'maybe' or 'I hope so.'[3] When a school principal gave a teacher a vague promise that ended with *inshallah*, the irate teacher accused the principal of bad intention.

Judged by local people's talk, the following are God's most popular attributes.

God is the creator and cosmic authority

Muslims must believe in God because religion, identity and loyalty demand it. There is no choice. Most local people, however, turn the argument around:

to believe in God is reasonable, it makes sense, and therefore Islam and to be a Muslim make sense.[4] The cosmological argument rests on the logic that everything that exists has a beginning, and that therefore a creation must have brought about humans, animals, plants the cosmos. It is an 'ex nihilo nihil fit' (nothing can come of nothing) argument, locally expressed as '*bi hič, hič*', meaning 'without nothing there is nothing'. The three syllables with three negatives and no verb pack a lot of persuasive power: only the eternal God has no beginning and no end and can create something from nothing.[5] A local elderly man put it like this: 'God created everything, knows everything, will end this world, may make another – this is not for us to ponder. We only live one life, right now, and do not know what will come next.' Thus, 'God' is not a belief – people say they *know* God exists, that the cosmos is proof. For people to make sense of existence, God is absolutely necessary.

Yet, doubters and critics of religious beliefs and habits exist in any society.[6] In the Islamic Republic belief is a political issue, and as people fear reprimands if they vent agnostic or atheistic ideas too loudly, doubters uphold religious conventions and customs in public. In private talks, however, doubt and criticism about God's powers and intentions (but rarely about God's existence) surface.

In 1980, shortly after the Revolution, a wave of accidents, suicides and deaths of young people put Sisakht into mourning mode. A crying woman who tended to see God as a powerful but remote deity fell into a harsh lament:

> God kills people without discrimination, left and right, old, young, here, in Tehran, everywhere, so many. But God was especially cruel when he let the two boys drown here and killed my neighbour's son in Tehran and a teacher's son in a car crash and my brother's daughter in suicide. All these young people! What oppression (*zolm*)! Nobody can say, 'Thanks be to God!' Thanks for what? For tyranny?

A distraught woman's comment in 1981 on a relative's suicide over the incessant fights between his wife and his mother illustrates these issues:

> It is all God's fault (*takhsir*). Had God wanted them to live in peace He would have given them enough to build a house away from the mother. The man wouldn't have died. But God didn't. God makes one woman miserable with ten children and gives me only one daughter and she died. We always argue and fight and kill ourselves – all God's fault. If God would give to everybody equally, be it a lot or nothing but the same, there would be no discontent, no envy. God wants us to be unhappy.

Further proof of God's existence is seen in the obvious, observable, reliable cosmic order. A local weaver philosopher once put a complex idea into simple words: 'Until God told them what to do, the stars were just bumping into each other and didn't know where to go.' In this logos theology, divine reason gives order and meaning to the cosmos. This order is beautiful and good, and so is God. The good order can be seen in 'everything natural', people say: birds and goats moving in formation, grass growing straight up from the soil, tight-fitted peas in a pod, a snowflake, a suckling calf, a crackling fire under a pot with food, the stages of life, an inspiring verse, a pleasing garden,[7] an orderly house, a good tool, a woven rug, a well-arranged life – all these show God's order. People can wax poetic about 'how everything fits together', as a farmer said with satisfaction while viewing his orchard. Confusion and disorder are ugly and have several terms, all negative and hinting at moral shortcoming.[8]

The 'nothing-from-nothing' argument points to signs, as in the laconic saying, 'Water is shown by mint' (*ou ve piden*). Just as the orderly cosmos points to God, miraculous help at a saint's shrine indicates the saint's power and makes it true. (If there were 'nothing' at the shrine, no miracle would happen.) Persistent hints about corruption point to a scoundrel, sudden wealth points to bribery, dark gossip points to something bad. A legend is explicit:

> The Prophet, his wife and servants once stayed in a caravanserai. In the morning his wife missed her necklace and found it only after the caravan had left. When the Prophet asked about her, a servant said she had stayed behind, talking and laughing with the host of the caravanserai. The Prophet knew this was a lie. He sent for her and she and her maid told him what had happened. He believed them, but the people were talking. 'Nothing comes from nothing,' they said, 'there must be something to it.' The rumour turned loud and ugly and the Prophet divorced his innocent wife to keep the peace.

The belief in a creator-God does not, in itself, determine God's relationship with the creation but lets people imagine and elaborate it.[9] A popular image pictures God as an otiose deity who once set everything in motion within the rules of nature that force people to figure out how to live. An educated woman said, 'God's place is comfortable now. He has no business with anybody and only keeps watching us like we watch television.' A related option is to see God sitting on a throne in a remote corner of heaven while his angels do the administrative work: two keep track of everybody's good and bad deeds, one collects the souls of the dead, one decides if and when souls will go to heaven, others guard the door to heaven. A radically spiritual choice is to experience God's presence vaguely in nature, when no loud, busy, anxious people are around. The natural order also includes dangerous powers such as diseases and accidents that people experience as autonomous agents or as sent to test or punish them. All these fit the remote creator-God idea.

At the other extreme are orthodox interpretations of scriptures that have God, 'the cause of every heart beat', as a physician said, act like a micro-managing, autocratic paterfamilias, a suspicious ruler who wills and controls every second of everything with orders (*hokm*), wilful wishes (*meil*) and promises of mercy (*rahmat*). In everyday situations people combine the options, even contradictory ones (such as immutable fate and free will), as the following remarks by an elderly craftsman show during a measles epidemic:

> God gives a child the soul when it first moves inside the mother, and writes its future on the forehead. This plan cannot be changed, ever. As the child grows up, God knows everything it does, but it seems that He is more interested in some children than in others, that He won't look at this child here burning up with fever but looks at another child so it won't die of measles. After children have acquired their full reason, it is up to them to decide if they commit sins or acquire merits – God further has nothing to do with it.

God is all-knowing and all-powerful

People see this as a sine qua non for God, but in the daily 'mill of hardships', as a tired old man said, the question arises why an almighty God creates so many difficulties? This is a popular sentiment in crisis situations, especially for women buckling under their workload or heavy-handed treatment by husband and in-laws. In a well-known saying a woman summed up her woes, in 1974: 'God makes everybody within His power miserable and poor' (*khodā – harkes ke zuresh mirase, badbakht o fakiresh ikone*).[10] Here, God is an uncaring or even mean deity but implicitly with limited power. In 2006 a hard-put woman felt powerless: 'Do I maybe have any power over God?' (*ma zurom ve khodā irase?*). In 2015 God's power was the issue when a woman was musing the hard lot of Afghani road workers in the noon heat:

> Everything bad and difficult, God (*khodā*) put on Adam's descendants. Bears do not need food during winter. No gazelle needs clothes. No worm has stomach aches. Yes, indeed! But then again, animals cannot defend themselves well. We step on worms, snakes have no legs – but they can't break a leg either. It is

difficult to think this through. There is the story of the bees. They went to God to make a deal. They said, 'We will make a lot of honey but any person we sting shall die.' God heard them but turned it around, and now bees make as much or little honey as they wish but will die if they sting a person. God does not like people much, and not bees either.

Likewise, men and women in a philosophical mood often ask why God puts people on a 'bad path', as criminals, corrupt politicians, warmongers, drug dealers, thieves, neglectful parents, all ending up in hell to nobody's benefit. 'Does God create them just to watch them stir things up like some gossipy women in a crowded courtyard?' asked a woman. The pious answer that suffering tests people's loyalty, gratitude and faith is no consolation for discouraged or poor people or those who tend to look at things critically. Rather, suffering links power (*qodrat, zur*) to respect (*ehterām*) and fear (*tars*). Preachers and their followers stress the obligation to obey God on the pain of punishment. 'God has become a god of fear,' said an angry young dissident in 2006. Although God also is said to be so generous and merciful that no good person has to fear Him, to see fear as an organizing principle of His world order is a much-used option. A deeply pious, outspoken woman suggested that God made heaven and hell on a whim but then needed people to populate both, so He makes good and bad people.

The natural order (and thus, God) requires people to work hard and take responsibility for their actions. Thus, rosy health in a baby points to the mother's skills, circumspection and diligence in doing her duty. ('If the baby cries I cannot say, "God's Will" and do nothing!')[11] A father ascribed his young sons' misbehaviours to their 'wild' Lur disposition he was unable to manage. A miscarriage was blamed on the weak uterus of the mother who had been married off by her unwise parents when still too young to bear a child. Great physical and ritual efforts may bend a woman's humoral condition towards producing the preferred boy. The proverb, 'The cat won't get the mouse just by thinking of God' (*gulu ve fekr khodāna moshk nigire*), speaks to the necessity of hard work, as does the saying, 'Exertion from me, blessing from God' (*az man sahmat az khodā barākat*), known throughout Iran. It is a long way around human deliberations and agency until one arrives at God's Will as an ultimate cause.

People use 'God's Will' readily and gratefully after a danger has passed. When a three-year-old boy got up without a scratch after a stampeding cow had kicked him, his aunt explained that God had not wished his little slave to die. Witnesses to a car accident ascribed the lack of casualties to God's Will. Such cases prompt people to accept an averted misfortune as a sign of God's omnipresent, benevolent power, and to thank God quickly.

God's will is inscrutable

This dictum fits local sensibilities and experiences well. God obviously did not equip the human mind to fully understand His creation and intentions. All theological arguments end here, be they about theodicy, social inequality, the misery of innocents, the purpose of life – people think critically and ask many questions about existence and philosophical matters, but the argument of God's intellectual superiority stumps them. Expressions such as 'Unless God knows – I sure don't' (*gheir a khodā midune*) acknowledge human limits and are convenient final words in any argument. Inscrutability also implies that people ought not to dig into God's mysteries. This irks some university students who point to the much-quoted exhortation to Muslims to seek knowledge wherever it can be found.

God's Will as a concept to give meaning to whatever happens may fade into unquestioned acceptance and surrender over a lifetime of problems. A grandmother described this process:

> When my second child was yet another girl, I said, 'Why, God? What have I done that you punish me?' And when my sister lost her mind, I said, 'God, why are you doing this to us?' And when my brother died, I said, 'Eh, God, what is in it for you when we suffer?' And now that I am old I only say, 'So be it, whatever it may be.'

A middle-aged farmer expressed a similar attitude while watching his sleeping grandson:

> Some people say that if I step outside and fall down the steps it is my doing, I was careless and hasty. But I say, God wants it that way although we don't know why. Nobody has come back from God to tell us what really is going on. Only hearsay, books and words – the preachers, eh! Now, take this baby here. You see him, can touch him, hear him, talk about him. But about God's reasons we cannot say anything.

This attitude is not good enough for a pious argument that rests on Muslims' duty to thank God for everything, good or bad, desired or dreaded, given or taken. Especially the elderly end stories often with *shukr khodā* (thanks be to God). 'Without gratitude there is no path to the other world,' said an old woman who patiently had carried 'one heavy load after the other' all her life. Answering the greeting, 'How are you?' a woman said, 'Eh – we thank God. This is life – good or bad, we have to agree.'[12] About an accident, people may say, *meilesh bi* (it was God's wish), whereby *meil* has a hint of pleasure, as in 'it pleased God without a discernible reason', but in the same breath also may insist that God 'wants us to be grateful', or 'is testing us', implying that God uses hardships to probe people's humble, grateful acceptance of their lot.

A nearly unquestioned aspect of God's Will is in the conviction that one's fate (*qesmat*) is 'written on the forehead' (*pishuni neveshte*). Having survived since antiquity, as a post hoc explanation of events this concept is always 'true'.[13] It is used routinely for a woman's marital situation, good or bad, implying that nobody can foresee or change it. A local father said about his daughter's maltreatment by her husband, 'Why does God punish me with this program on her forehead?' It was easier to ascribe his daughter's pain to God's punishment of his own sins than to try changing her 'fate'. A story links fate, sexual misconduct, misogyny and God:

> An angry man threw a rock at his wife. A script appeared on her forehead, saying that she would be a prostitute. The man's mother scolded him for his violence but shut up when she saw the writing. She sent the wife for water, and somebody grabbed her and took her to a brothel. Her husband did not look for her because he knew her destiny. After forty days she returned. The old woman asked her this and that and how and why but her son silenced her, knowing that it was not his wife's fault but her fate, that God had wanted it that way.

In some versions he then 'quietly divorced' her, indicating that God's Will and fate have little to do with guilt and innocence implied in social norms and conventions.

As local people recently came to understand that in new urban ways of life prostitution could be a lucrative activity, the choices for judging this immorality expanded: instead of seeing it as a fate willed by God or a personal choice of sin, it now could be seen also as a way to live well in times of scarcity.

God is benevolent and merciful

A popular option in the God–people relationship is to insist that God created everything so that people can have a good life. Proof may be seen in the useful qualities of plants, for example. The local folklorist-historian Ghafari (n.d.) lists dozens of medicinal plants used in the traditional pharmacopoeia of local herbalists.[14] This tradition is fading because preparing medicines is cumbersome and doctors' drugs are effective. When I commented on a famous healer's diligence in preparing *celdāri*, a concoction of forty-six ingredients, she answered, 'God does not reward laziness.' The obvious limits to God's human-centred generosity in nature (such as the existence of wolves or poisonous plants or dangerous rivers) are kept out of conversations in pious company but not out of the range of options to see God's creation.

God's benevolence also may be seen in hints about impending calamities in dreams and in known effects of certain dates or times. Throughout Iran, Saturday, the first day of the work week, is said to be bad for starting anything important.[15] A local student missed her bus back to her faraway university because her grandmother's foreboding dream had necessitated an hour of almsgiving. Countless domestic quotidian rituals such as blessings and curses, pausing after a sneeze or ejaculations to shoo jinn, rest on expectations of benefits put into them by God.

This goodness leads to the option of seeing God as a salvific power. Pious people insist that whoever follows God's orders as laid out in the scriptures will have a good life and afterlife. Experience again contradicts this piety, though, if for no other reason than the human tendency to disobey God, which begs the often-asked question how God's decision to create people as moral weaklings fits His intention to give people a good life. Moreover, people may argue that given their (God-given) situation they often 'have no choice' (*rāhi nist*; *majbur*) but to disobey God in order to make a life at all, let alone a good one. With this shift in moral ground, lying and stealing, corruption and violence, even suicide, become sins diminished by necessity. Adverse circumstances brought about by the wheel of time or by God's inscrutable Will makes one sidestep good intentions at many turns. A hungry man stealing food, a child lying to avoid punishment, a chief forcing his people to work hard to make the village prosper are sinful but still make good sense.[16] In the end, most people's backs are bent with the weight of sins, but there is the consoling choice to count on God's mercy (*rahmat*), on His understanding of the motives that drive people to sin. God will forgive, especially if the sinners repent. Saying 'Repentance!' (*touba*) opens a handy, quick path to forgiveness.

God generously keeps another 'wide, easy path' open to forgiveness by balancing sins with religious merits (*savāb*) such as for good deeds. They accrue throughout one's life, documented by the scribe angels. Most people will have more merits than sins when all is said and done, said a kind grandmother. For people like her God's love is implied in the assumption that 'God is not mean, will always help me, either here or in the next world,' as she said. A local mullah once complained that tribal people were more afraid of the khans than of God. Although Sisakht has no Sufi lodges, Sufi principles are known, such as that rewards and punishments, heaven and hell are not important for people on the right path, or that submerging oneself in God's love assures mercy and forgiveness. These are important choices in local people's traditional, complicated relationships with God.[17]

More in tune with experiences, though, is to see God's help as a rather remote possibility. In 2006 an unmarried ('unprotected') woman physician, after describing her bad experiences with male landlords and supervisors who had cheated her yet fared well despite her fervent prayers and pleas with God for help and justice, joked that from now on she would praise such scoundrels loudly so as to let the evil eye punish them: the 'salt-eye' might help more than God. God was 'too far away' to hear her, she said. A pertinent quote from a woman in Mamasani, a Lur-tribe adjacent to Boir Ahmad, puts such remarks into a developmental frame that also was familiar in Boir Ahmad:

> In the beginning, God was nearby and small like us. He saw us and we saw Him. He heard us and we could touch Him and He helped us when we asked Him. But people were bad and He moved away, farther and farther, out of our reach. (Shahshahani 1982: 69, summarized)

With this observation the image of God transitioned from a nearby, accessible helper-deity in a small-scale society to a remote Big God in a complex one, creating a theological difficulty. Although omniscient, in practice God first has to notice a plight in order to do something about it. In the past He met people on their level but now that He is a remote ruler it is difficult to catch His eye. One may implore God, perform rituals of submission, make promises, pray, 'be noisy' (i.e. publicly pious), but if He keeps looking elsewhere, the petitioner or a whole nation will remain vulnerable to harm from dangerous powers and enemies. During the Iran–Iraq war people said, 'God has averted his eyes from us and probably from all Muslims.'

God is truth

God's revelations have to be accepted as truth, including the Quran. While anything written carries weight for illiterate people, it also carries doubt because it is man-made. People usually prefaced mullahs' assertions that martyr-soldiers go straight to paradise with, 'according to (*ba qoule*) the Quran'; it was a shaky fact. This expression is popular, as is reference to a vague 'they' such as in 'they say that a woman who dies in childbirth has all sins forgiven'. An articulate, pious woman summed up her opinion:

> Of course I agree with the Quran, surely, the book is right, I believe everything that's written in the Quran. It is written! But when I look around me at all that is wrong, deep inside I think maybe the talk of the mullahs is just as much a lie as is everything else in the world. Maybe they only want to make us obedient and quiet to earn their keep. How everything really is we will know only when we see it ourselves.

Being all truth, God cannot, will not lie and confuse. 'With trust in God' (*bā omide khodā*) is a much-used blessing and exclamation of hope. But humans and some human-like powers such as jinn have a problem with truth. Lying is sinful in terms of morality, but in terms of having to make it in this world, the ability to lie well points to a sharp mind and to success. A young teacher and master of self-deprecatory jokes said that a Lur who did not tell at least one good lie a day would get a stomach ache. To be able to discern between truth and the many shapes of non-truth, God has equipped people with *aql*, a term covering mind, reason, understanding, discernment. It is said to develop in children as they grow; young children are endlessly exhorted to use their God-given brains to avoid having to lie and to believing a lie. The most popular variants of truth come under the umbrella 'I know' (*dunom*) and range from a mere opinion to what counts as proven truth.

In conversations, *dorost* (accurate, as in two and two equals four) and *eshtebār*, *qalat* (error, mistake) judge a fact, and, with different overtones, polite agreement or disagreement. The opposite of these truth-expressions is *duru*, a deliberate untruth, a lie, an intentionally false statement or deed.[18] A *durugu* is a habitual liar. Folk tales, too, are a kind of 'lie', made-up stories rather than accounts of true happenings. 'Lie' is an extraordinarily potent and popular word, central to local ethics. Just about anything one does not want to hear can be called 'lie'; doubt is ever present. It is implicit in standard phrases such as 'they say' (*igon*), 'it is written' (*neveshte*), 'I heard' (*eshnoftom*) and 'according to [. . .]' (*ba qoule* [. . .]) that shift the burden of verification onto other people or a book. Except for the Quran and the hadith,[19] any knowledge is open to potential negation unless it is vetted by one's own reasoning and experience or an authority's testimony.

Believing a statement or promise quickly is considered foolish, a bad choice. Parents worry about how to teach children trust and suspicion together with skills of dissimulation (if not deception) they will need to make it in a deceitful world while demanding truth from them at home. Truth often is buried beneath layers of talk, hearsay and self-serving assertions, and the resulting insecurity and mixed messages stress children, psychologists say. Truth, indeed, may be declared dangerous; white lies that hide upsetting bad news are ethically in order, even meritorious.[20] Means justify a good end:

> In two families living next to each other in a courtyard, the woman in one and the man in the other were friendly cousins. All was well until the woman's third child looked 'exactly' like her cousin's children, people said. Gossip bloomed but quickly was smothered by all grandmothers in both families who swore to everybody's innocence. The issue was buried to prevent it from turning into a poisonous 'truth' provoking a scandal, a divorce, motherless children, a stigmatized little boy and heartbreak and hostility. Even if the denial was a lie, people said, it was a good lie that saved the peace, the husband's face and the children's wellbeing.[21]

The conviction that a white lie is good extends to prominent religious figures such as the Twelfth ('Hidden') Imam who legitimizes the lie of a poor man trying to fulfil his fatherly duty:

> A poor man with seven daughters promised the king he would show him the Hidden Imam if he gave him enough money to provide for his seven daughters until they were married. The king did so. When the poor man returned alone, fearing to be executed for lying to the king, a dervish-boy joined him – he turned out to be the Imam.

For pragmatic people preoccupied with making it in a difficult world, the most valid proof for sorting out what to rely upon, accept tentatively or dismiss is one's own experience. Once a medicine has cured me I'll count on its potency. The credibility of accounts depends on authority: a physician's opinion of my ailment has more weight than my neighbour's. Dreams, too, provide proof: I doubt stories about the afterlife, but when my dead mother tells me in a dream that she lives in the other world, I will believe it. Likewise, if I dream of a felled tree or of teeth falling out, I better give alms or make a votive promise to ward off the misfortune that such dreams had announced before.[22] The calamities following a dream as well as those that a sacrifice obviously prevented are taken as proof of the dream-as-omen truth.

God and justice (*haqq*)[23]

Among poor people living in a sociopolitical system marked by authoritarian relationships, violence and limited access to meagre resources, justice on any level is dear. Experience suggests that God's order also is unjust, is 'palace and stone hut' (*kākh o kukh*): kings live in opulence and we, the people, live in poverty. A system of patronage, influence peddling and forced submission to a father, a tribal chief, the police, the revolutionary guards and whorls of power encompasses all aspects of life, from childrearing and family relations to governmental institutions, and as a popular choice also to relationships with God.[24] Many coping strategies are seen as a sin and a scourge, yet as necessary to make it in this life.

People who won't see God as an otiose, remote deity who keeps out of His creation's daily struggles have two options regarding justice: they can see God as an absolute, transcendent authority who judges the behaviour of His subjects and doles out rewards and punishments in a platonic afterlife, or else as a powerful, forgiving ruler. Depending on what side one sees as expedient or necessary to keep one's head above want and woes, one likely counts on benevolence-justice for oneself and on punishment-justice for enemies. A local man who lost his fiancée to a wealthy suitor declared he would believe in God's justice again only if God would punish the rival. When the rival and his family died in an accident, the story became 'proof' of God's retribution. A farmer quoted a laconic proverb: 'If you sow barley, you'll harvest barley,' meaning that every sin will make God angry enough to send a fitting hardship, a *muqāfāt*, for the sinner soon. Such clear cause–effect situations are rare, though.

Except for doubting what cannot be proven, few people have a problem imagining rewards and punishments in the afterlife. Considering that hardships mostly pile up on the innocent, the lack of justice in this world is a proof-by-necessity for justice in the other world. 'If justice does not happen here and now, it must happen there and then,' concluded a woman, fuming about what she saw as her in-laws' ill-gotten gains. However, the other world is a lifetime away, too far to worry about now. God's punishment in this world has several problems. For one, it rarely follows a bad deed quickly enough to satisfy people's wish for retributive justice. A woman who swore that she would not pray until her father's killer was executed called this an attempt to force God to speed up the punishment. Another is that, on principle, people see themselves as innocent, falsely accused or else driven by circumstances to behaviour that others declare sinful. It can be explained and excused. Furthermore, hardships may be taken to be one's fate, beyond explanation, unavoidable and presumably God-willed; or they may be due to some chance-encounters with adverse powers such as a measles epidemic or the evil eye. The mishap might be God's punishment for – well, for what? For sins? Am I not innocent or forgiven? Do my accrued merits not balance my sins? Am I punished for an ancestor's sin I know nothing about? Such questions are ubiquitous. Theodicy frequently poses emotional and intellectual problems.

The punitive *muqāfāt* is a misfortune likely sent by God when He is angry or offended. People use the term frequently when describing a big trouble. Gossip called the impotence of a local woman's sons a *muqāfāt* for her sin of having tried to blind her co-wife. Even sins committed unwittingly may be punished. If old, sick or neglected persons cannot die, people may murmur that this calamity might be a sign for some unknown sin of their own or of an ancestor. A woman suggested that settling a sin with a swift punishment will prevent it from 'walking to the other world on its own legs' to be punished there, maybe severely so. However, loudly declaring somebody's mishap a punishment is second-guessing God's intention, a potential slander and a sin.

Qossa is a similar hardship: God may send one for whatever reason, but mostly it comes by itself like a malevolent force, but often after announcing itself in a dream. Some people are more likely to get such foreboding dreams than others. The dream allows one to make a preventative sacrifice (*rafe qossa*), as a woman explained:

> I dreamt that I was lighting our lamp but it would not burn. I woke up troubled and realized that the dream announced a calamity. So I took a bowl of wheat to a poor woman to ward it off. In the evening a lamb was missing and we never found it. Clearly, the *rafe qossa* had diverted the calamity away from us onto the animal. That's how it works.[25]

Such non-sequitur, slight-of-hand linking of unrelated items into a cause and effect relationship that resists refutation is a feature of narrative logic and embedded in local rhetoric.

Protective sacrifices open the choice to wonder if thereby people have not crossed God's plan of sending them a hardship. This is the unsolvable dilemma of God's stacked plans: God wills a hardship; sends a warning dream; lets the person make a sacrifice; removes or deflects the hardship. 'So', a peeved woman said, 'What was it all about?' God's purported anger about a misdeed such as suicide poses a similar dilemma. God willed it to happen (because it did happen), and now is angry about it. 'One cannot get anywhere with God,' said a craftsman who had this troubling thought. A young, childless woman saw her infertility as God's wish and refused any intervention. Her people lauded her piety and scolded her for not using help that God made available. And about the customary blood sacrifice of a chicken[26] when the door is hung in a new house to accident-proof it, an irreverent joker said that thereby God's intention (potentially to send a misfortune) was voided, that God had lost, as in a game.

What God wants from people[27]

Acknowledgement of the supremacy of God, Muhammad as God's messenger and the Quran as God's word appears as the sine qua non for any Muslim, and as so reasonable that even doubters and critical thinkers will agree to it, people say. What public opinion finds most reprehensible about communists is not their political agenda but, in the poetry of a children's ditty, 'Death to the communists, why do they say there is no God.'[28] In 2015 a medical student was explicit: 'So much nonsense has been heaped on religion (*din*) that one can have doubts about everything. But to say that God does not exist is like saying that air does not exist. We would not be alive without either.'

God's self-evident existence demands unconditional gratefulness. Beyond this, God demands obedience to the rules laid out in the Quran. Illiterate people whose language is fundamentally different from Arabic have to rely on their memories for prayers and on translators and exegetes. Man-made sermons and pamphlets, however, fall squarely into the doubt-category, especially so if they do not agree with each other. But even well-educated people's understanding of original texts is limited. The stunning calligraphy of a popular Quran verse on a wall in the home of a local couple with years of study of Arabic and the Quran was simply 'good and beautiful', they said. They could not read it.[29]

What God wants most from people, though, is easy to grasp: to be peaceful, hard-working and sociable. 'Take troubles, eat a piece of bread, sit with your neighbours and thank God,' a farmer advised his grandson. One must accept one's status and the responsibilities and behaviours that go with it. A good father is as God-pleasing and necessary for everybody's welfare as are a good carpenter, a good teacher, a good king. Whatever hinders these goals is easily declared bad and sinful, from alcohol to lies, from theft to slander, from curses to murder. Except in orthodox circles, polygyny can be seen as a man's sin because it is 'impossible' for co-wives to get along and for a man to treat them equally.[30] The 'best' people are appreciated for their wisdom, their reliability and helpfulness, their industry and for keeping their affairs in good order. This makes them morally good even if their observance of rituals may be patchy. About a couple whose lackadaisical habits prevented their progress, a relative said they behaved 'as if there was no God': laziness resulting in lack of success was a sin. A local migrant worker called the Kuwaitis 'best Muslims' because they were trustworthy, they prayed and their many blood sacrifices provided meat for poor people like himself. The local generous and peaceful people in town are held in esteem, too, but most people fall short of God's wishes, people say. 'Sinners left and right', said a woman about herself and her neighbours, but then counted on God's mercy to mellow His judgement of people pulled into sin by necessity.[31]

Merits, sins and the afterlife

Although earning merits (*savāb*) is handled as a personal choice in real time, merits also happen because God wills them. God lets people sin but also, mercifully, provides opportunities to redeem even notorious sinners, as an elderly man said, 'A hungry scoundrel saw a piece of bread on the ground. He picked it up and ate it, and for the good deed of saving it from being stepped on, God pardoned his sins.' As in this example, in everyday life merits are more likely a bonus for a good deed than a motivation for doing one. On top of people's lists of merits are generosity, taking care of the poor and sick, giving alms and hospitality. Kindness towards people and animals ranks highly, too, and children learn this early on when their elders add, 'it has merits' (*savāb dāre*) to many requests. 'Help your little brother climb the stairs, take apples to grandmother, feed the hens', all likely have the promise of merits tagged on. The link to God's approval is understood.

Merits for observing God's rules are less clear. Most rules are taken to be obligations, duties without special merits. Thus, tears for a dead parent earn merits but for a parent to cry for a dead young child is a sin.[32] Fasting is a plain duty and therefore carries no merit but not fasting is a sin under any circumstance except while sick or travelling. For a husband to order his wife to fast has merits for him; if he forbade her to fast and she fasts nevertheless, her disobedience is a sin. Arguments can turn scholastic easily, and people tend to formulate their own choices regarding merits and sins. There is widespread agreement that the wealthy have more chances to get do-good merits than the poor. In the mullah-religion merits for good deeds within the social ethic are played down while merits gained by supporting mosques and financing Islamic rituals increase. This draws the criticism that now 'any rich crook' can get merits by covering the mosque floor with rugs while a dutiful, good person (in the quiet social-ethics sense) gets no merits. As to God's motive for providing merits at all, one can see it as an act of God's mercy, a sign of God's inscrutable Will or else as a reasonable managerial rule. A trader's wife spoke for all who see God as a manager: 'Poverty, wealth, sickness, misery, good and bad are in the world so that everybody can earn merits and thereby God can separate good people from bad ones.'

'The religion' declares young children to be free of sin (*gonā*) no matter what they do, but human nature and the ways of the world make adults sin. Even if God did not want people to sin (which may be questioned because God wishes all that happens every second; yet why should a merciful God wish people to sin?), God's creation is such that in order to live and honour one's duties one can't avoid discomforting and harming others. Of all sins, those against God, such as neglecting prayers or fasting, are taken to be less grave than sins against people.[33] People joke about it to make light of their spotty praying and to give moral weight to offences by others against themselves. The sins mentioned most are fighting, maligning others; neglecting children, work and duties; swindling and lying 'too much', and being lazy. A proverb goes, 'Women sin by walking around (in public), men by sitting around (doing nothing).'[34] The worst sins are fornication, adultery, harming others by cheating or violence, oppression and theft.[35] Compared to the khans' times, murder, a capital sin, is rare now.[36] Men also commit a sin if they mistreat their wives 'without good cause' and for refusing wives' reasonable requests, while a woman sins if she disobeys her husband and fights with her in-laws. The grave sin of suicide is decreasing especially among women. People's realistic view of suicide made the verdict of 'sin' difficult, though. Women died because they did not see a way out of poverty, overwork, ill health, fights over necessities and because of an overwhelming need for *rāhati* (comfort, stillness). A dead woman's biggest sin was to leave her children motherless.

Traditionalists and orthodox believers like to declare that women commit more sins than men because they are morally weaker and less rational than men. A more practice-oriented reason is that women are caught daily in 'a hundred' frustrating chores, while men go about their jobs outside with interesting diversions. Yet, before God women's sins count the same or more than men's. Why this is so, 'only God knows'. Young women question such gender assumptions. In 2006 a local high school student became angry when her aunt said that of a hundred women only one is admitted to paradise while only one of a hundred men ends up in hell. 'How do you know?' she said, 'Dumb old men make up these lies and superstitions. They don't help us at all to get ahead.' In 2015 'old beliefs' were popular still in Party-of-God circles, while the popular choice was to credit socio-economic progress (*pishraft*) for the improvement in women's lives.[37] More food, space and resources, less hard work, better health and fewer children prompted many expressions of thanks to God for progress but added the option to doubt God's providence because He had not provided these earlier.

Summary, a give-and-take

The following conversation, in 1981, is one of many similar ones I had over the years. In 2006 such exchanges were even more laconic. In 2015 they split into sermon-like assurances of orthodox, government-sanctioned beliefs by people who saw a fervent demonstration of religious convictions as necessary to call themselves 'Muslim', and into customary assurances of the 'only God knows' kind by most others. Here, a wife (W) had been complaining to her husband (H) and myself (E) about her in-laws. Her husband tried to lighten the mood with a joke:

H: Don't you know that the first thing God's angels ask after death is how well a woman got along with her in-laws?

W: Lies, all lies.

E: Everything is lies?

W: What am I to say? Nobody has come back from God to tell us what is happening. No, no – all this they make up so that we will be quiet.

H: This means that all Seyeds and all mullahs are liars? What?

W: Yes, lies, liars. They tell us all this so that we will put a piece of bread into their mouths. All lies. Nobody knows except God.

H: Well, good that God is not a liar—

W: No, no, God is true. Thanks be to God, God exists. God made everything. But God will not clean these lentils on my tray – I have to tell my hands to do it. Or maybe not?

H: Yes, you'll go to heaven!

W: What heaven? What hell? What is this supposed to mean? Who has come back to tell us about it? God alone knows. We say, 'Heaven'?! 'Hell'?! It does not exist.

H: Yes, who knows? We'll die, for sure, but then? Thanks be to God.

E: Well, what does God want from people?

W: To wash our skirt, to bake a bread for the man, to put a piece of bread into my own mouth, to take troubles, the house, his old parents, my sick father, the children, of course. Eh, that's it. Morning, evening, night, dawn again. Thanks be to God.

E: Sins? Merits?

W: We all are full of sins, for sure, but who has merits? What? One gives a neighbour a piece of bread and then turns around and says, 'I fed this poor wretch – ?' I help a woman in the morning and in the evening I brag about it? This has merit? No, none of this has merit. And it gets worse every day.

H: Mudslides, water, once half the village was swept away.

W: Yes, but then it was better. All of us, from morning to night, work, tobacco weeding, poppies, no bread, acorn-mush, children, and they died all the time, all of us work, work, hunger, dirt. But good prayer then, no bad talk, no wagging tongues, no sins. We had no time, too busy, too tired – God's Will, we say! Now we sit around and talk and talk.

H: Wait! Men—

W: Men have fewer sins – they work hard: wheat, water, harvest, threshing, tired, quiet. But women sit and talk, and one says, 'she said and he said,' and one says, 'my neighbour's skirt has ten yards of fabric,' and that a cousin went this way and came that way, and what not. And when the man comes home and says, 'I am hungry, cook me some rice,' she says, 'I am tired, leg hurts, headache, I can't, eat some bread.' It's like this. Good? God likes this? What?! [*She laughs.*]

E: And nobody is afraid of God and the Other World?

W: Oh Amir al Momeni![38] The Imams be my witness, God is great! We'll see what God will do with us, then. We all will die, that much we know – after that, only God knows.

Figure 3 Sisakht, 1997. People say that God's presence may be felt anywhere in nature, such as when one is in good company at a family picnic at a spring in the mountains. The author is sitting with the women.

3

Theology, extended

The salient shared features of the origin-myth as told locally are that God made everything, from the cosmos and universe(s)[1] to the smallest bug, and that the first human being got the life-soul (*jun*) from God in paradise but then offended God by listening to the devil and subsequently was thrown out with his wife into or onto our world. Here people have to work, suffer and die after an allotted lifetime (*ajal*) but why and what for is unknown. God also made other life forms, and people use some and not others and in turn are used by them. Like animals and people, the devil, too, may have multiplied. It is a difficult existence for most life, not only for humans, and God wanted it that way – God is almighty. These are the outer parameters of the theme 'God's creation'. It leaves ample room for people to choose, combine and elaborate specific notions.

Life and death

There is overwhelming consensus that life comes from God by way of a life-soul (*jun*) at the moment when a pregnant woman feels the child move for the first time. This is a matter of experience and therefore of knowledge, people say. But beyond this certainty, life and soul are complicated, as the three different terms for them show.

Nafas locally means breath.[2] Absence of breath is the sure sign that a person is dead and that the heart (*qalb*) has stopped pushing the breath. Breath is a visible sign of life or is life itself.

Jun is life, spirit. Measured by its prolific use, *jun* is the most important concept, a life-soul located anywhere in the body but mostly in the solar plexus (*del*), the heart (*qalb*) where it ticks like a clock, and in the head.[3] It is the vital organ. In a tired or lame person, the *jun* is weak or may have left a little bit. If one dreams, the *jun* may do the travelling and observing. If one is being pestered and at the end of one's patience (nagged by a child, for example), one may combine life and breath, saying, 'You are pulling my life out through my nose' (*jun ve noftom ikeshi*), while as a heartfelt term of endearment, *junom* (my life) means the addressed person is as dear as one's own life. 'He has no *jun*' (*jun nadāre*) may mean unconscious but not dead, while death means that the *jun* left for good (*jun raft*). In this case it is assumed to stay around for three more days before going through the routines of the afterlife. But as nobody ever has verified this ephemeral stage, it may be taken as an unjustified belief, more a possibility or a hope than a certainty, especially for women. Doubts about the houris in paradise are similar: like dead people, houris might be just *jun* without a body, and if so, then what would male and female *jun* want with each other? It is like with food in paradise. Allegedly there are figs there and milk but it stands to reason that souls don't need to eat – or do they? The woman who asked these questions summed the issue up as 'hodgepodge'.

Nafas and *jun* are fundamental concepts in the sense that even firm doubters agree to them and agree that they must come from God – where else from? God created life, and at the end of life *nafas* and *jun* disappear and the person is only a corpse. Everybody knows these assumptions, but they are especially popular with people who opt for sticking to the obvious: whatever might happen after life is intangible and doubtful because it goes against all experiences and observations; because there are no facts, no eye witnesses; and because it begs questions such as what happens to animals with apparently the same life in them as people, and the same end.[4]

Ruh. The Arabic/Quranic word *ruh*, meaning the divine spirit imparted to humans, that is, a 'soul', locally is not used much and often is linked to *jun* in talks about the afterlife. After the *jun/ruh* has left the body, it might be the *ruh* that is being questioned in the grave. Asked directly, most people say that *ruh* and *jun* are just about the same, but in vernacular use *ruh* is a person's moral compass, the part of a person that eventually will go to heaven or hell, the Quranic 'soul', while *jun* is what makes one alive and spirited. *Ruh* is in the *del*, the seat of emotion; if one is angry or depressed, the troubled *ruh* will swell up the *del*. *Del ruhi* means mind, psyche.[5] 'Disquiet soul' (*narāhat ruhi*) is the umbrella diagnosis for psychological problems. The radically simple option to view this is that every person has one *jun*, that is, one life and thus one soul, and upon death it disappears together with the breath (*nafas*). Its existence is proven by the state of living and of death, while *ruh* has no tangible quality and therefore what happens to it after death has to be taken on faith as something that is unknowable and thus shaky. *Ruh* belongs to the language of *din*: important, hallowed and difficult to think.

Similarly difficult to think – and rather confused and confusing – are thoughts about what may happen to the *jun/ruh* after it has left the body at death. A semi-literate, pious mother of five children, fascinated by her religion and trying hard to pull all she learnt and heard about it together, explained her options for the afterlife to me twice, twenty-eight years apart.

> (1976) It is said that the *ruh* stays nearby until a dead body is in the ground in order to see who comes to the funeral, how much the relatives cry, what they say. It is said that each bad word about the dead is a blow for them, and each good word is a soft wind. But I say that how one is buried and how many people show up and all that is only for the mourners and for those who think of their own death. If a dead person has no ritual washing (*ghosl*), if one is shattered falling off a cliff or is killed in battle or water carries him away – it makes no difference for the *ruh*. What happened during life is important, not what happens to a corpse. After a burial we say that the *ruh* of a bad person is in a lot of trouble but the *ruh* of a person with many merits has a comfortable place. The prayer for the dead (*fateha*) is a pleasant wind for them; food given away in their name is good, too. The *ruh* stays there until the end of the world. That's what we say.
>
> On the Day of Judgement there will be a huge earthquake, the earth will split open and everything will disappear in the chasm and Mahdi will come to be the judge.[6] Every *ruh* will be alive again, and the people's sins and merits will be known. Good people will go to paradise, bad ones will go to hell to stay there forever. It is said that a man and his wife will meet again in paradise if they have the same amount of sins and merits. If not, they won't ever meet again. But, well, we also say that 'sheep are hung by their own feet and goats by their feet' – they are different, and so are people, and therefore I think a husband and his wife will be separated in the other world.[7] The signs for the coming of the Last Day are described in the Quran. Children will disobey parents, will insult and curse them, and people will no longer pray and make ablutions. Well, it seems the next Day of Judgement is near! After that God will make new beings – they will grow out of the earth like grass, and it will be a good world, the mullahs say. Who knows how many worlds and Judgements were already before us?

Her 2004-version stayed on the theme of 'the end is near', with doubts about the shape and meaning of the Day of Judgement, and shifted emphasis from the afterlife onto what is good for her in this life and to millenarian anxieties. She did not mention paradise at all.

> (2004) We understand things better now, and we know that following the Quran and the preachers is good for us. We live better also – better houses, clothes, food, a mosque, schools, but the corruption and the lies and the running after money

here in this world are getting worse. So much sickness! So many young people die! So many people addicted to drugs! The end is near, surely. A good thing is that travel is easy so that we are able to visit the Imamzadeh at their shrines and can tell them our problems. I have visited Bibi Hakimeh[8] three times, and next year I will go to Mecca with the help of my sons and the government, in a big group from town. We do not know what God will do with us next, we just are grateful for what we have, and when I die I know I will not suffer, God is merciful. As to the Day of Judgement – of course, this is important for Muslims, and everybody has to believe it – we just believe it, it is the truth, for sure, and we will see, but I won't tell you because I won't come back!

On the Day of Judgement (*ruze qeiyumat;* Arabic *al-Qiyāmah*), the Last Day (*ākherat*), life, death, souls, God and time come together at the grand finale of Reckoning and Resurrection. One can expect that souls will be resurrected from their graves or from wherever souls are after death, maybe even from hell and paradise, and the final judgement will sort them into good and bad, stay and leave. People, especially men who see a grievous lack of justice in this world, often mention retribution and reckoning. 'Day of Judgement' is a popular term, taken to mean to frighten people away from sins, the pious insist, but as the event is in the future it loses scare-function easily. When the Last Day came up in a discussion among women, one cheerfully spoke for many: 'Oh well, by then I am no longer alive! Right now I better worry about living.' Another joked, 'Why get worked up about it now? I'll find out soon enough.' And when the speaker at a sermon for women talked about the Hidden Imam (the Mahdi) walking among the people, an elderly listener quietly commented, 'Doesn't he have anything better to do?!' Women's knack for pitching esoteric thoughts against their everyday experiences tends to turn the former into pretentious piety. Yet, the promise of a resurrection of all good people for populating a new world is a pleasant thought for believers and doubters. 'It means that the new world will be all good and easy,' said a widow who was said to have seen more hardship than was reasonable. A radical and rewarding option for thinking what may happen to bad people is that they will burn in hell and thus be gone for good. For an old widow, never again meeting violent enemies, angry husbands, cruel relatives, corrupt masters after they had burned to ashes was a much more satisfying image than the Quranic and pre-Islamic-Zoroastrian notion of a cleansing by fire. The connection between the Day of Judgement, heaven (or paradise) and hell, though, is muddled. 'I leave this to the mullahs to sort out,' said the mother of a seminary student, and a sincerely pious local male physician dismissed the issues as unimportant: 'All this talk is like a myth to give people something to think about. Talking about angels (*maleke*) and devils (*sheitunal*) does not make anybody a good Muslim.'

This echoes an elderly, illiterate woman who nursed her ill husband in an exemplary 'good Muslim' way not for religious merits but as her duty as a wife, a human being and a Muslim, she said. She dismissed merits and most ideas about the afterlife. Her minimalist religion centred on an almighty God who reigned like a remote king, punishing some, rewarding others, at will. Here is a summary of what she said at different occasions.

> As long as God knows what He is doing – I sure don't! Not if I see what is going on in the world. Heaven and hell and the Last Day and such things are very good stories but they are made up by the preachers. Prayers, alms, mourning and pilgrimages are true, though, they are beneficial. The Quran is true, too, God's word, but written in a language nobody here can read. What I see is that people live and die, are buried, and then other people live and die: a hole in the ground, earth on your head, that's it. The other world, souls, paradise, hell are useful to teach people how to behave. But we know how to behave anyway! The difficulty is in doing it! Whatever one does for one's own *del, ruh, qalb* [seat of emotion, soul, heart] or whatever you call it, is to keep oneself at peace. One has to live for whatever is important right now, not for some story-time. One has to be on one's toes, use all that God provides, my herbs, prayers, beads against the salt-eye, dreams about calamities. Before my husband fell ill I dreamt of a tiny light standing among his new little apple trees. As I got nearer the light got smaller and smaller. I was afraid of this dream. I did not know what it meant. Just to be safe I gave alms but probably not enough. Obviously the light was his life, in his orchard, slowly burning down. Suddenly he fell ill, and now his life is just a flicker. I let him down because I did not know what to do about the dream.

She did not mention fate or God's Will here: her own lack of knowledge had caused the calamity; her personal sense of duty made her care for her husband, all watched over by God.

A thirty-year-old illiterate mother of four, with a sunny disposition and a heart problem, liked to listen to Friday sermons. Curious about the world, bright and outspoken, she touched on several choices popular in the community about religion and human existence in the following statement. It is in her own words, cobbled together from several talks, mostly in 1981, two years after the Revolution. Since then her views have changed little but her misgivings extend to the economy. The quality of a government is shown by how well people are doing, she said in 2015 (and many others said, too), and on this count the mullahs' rule is bad.

> God made people because He wanted to, but I don't know what for and what God wants of people, really, nothing – we just live! [*Laughs*]. God makes sure that we carry a lot of burdens, though. The reason for this and for pains and accidents I don't know either. But I know that good people suffer more than bad ones. God wants it that way – it is *qesmat* [fate]. There is no point in asking why. After death we bury the corpse. It is said – it is only said, mind you! Who knows? – that they take a good person to paradise and a sinner to hell. That's what they say. [*Laughs*]. I don't believe it. Whoever died is dead, gone, under the earth. But I'll find out after I'm dead. It also is said that a man and his wife may be together again in paradise, but I think that whoever died is gone, and that's it. The Mullah says no, there is the *ruh* – well, we'll see who is right, he or we? Paradise for sure is better than what we have here [*laughs*]; why else would anybody want to go there? Lots of flowers and fruits and everything. Hell, it is said, hell is dark, dark like the darkest night, and I am afraid of the dark. Our Mullah said that hell is there so that people will be afraid and do good in order to avoid it. Well, this may work for some more than for others. It is said that women who commit suicide leave their children destitute and go straight to hell, but I can't say this. The women do it not because they are bad but because they see no way out of their difficulties, hell or no hell. They want to leave because for them this world has nothing left. They kill themselves and are gone, this is all we know for sure.
>
> I don't pray much – how can I? With little children I am always unclean. But I know that if a bad person prays, it is of no use, and if a good person does not pray, it is no sin. I can't fast either – I am sick. When I was little, many people fasted, but now very few do. It does not matter, though – most people here are good people, they don't meddle in others' affairs, they are grateful for what they have, they work, have warm feelings for the poor, for their children, they take care of them, take care of the house, they keep the peace. We make vows (*nazr*), pledge something to a saint for making a sick child well, but the one I made I still owe. The saints have power just as doctors have power. Both help if they want to.
>
> We do all this because this is what is needed; it does not bring merits for the afterlife. When somebody is hurt, we say, '*muqāfāt*'[9] and 'God, what have I done that you punish me?' But this is just talk. A *muqāfāt* simply comes, mostly to good people. God might send it – God does what He wishes, but since the revolution more people say that probably there is no God, things just happen. But no, no, God is the highest, and we call on him when things are bad. 'Oh God, help me', we say.

Good, bad and sin

Theologians and clerics maintain that God gave humans the ability to be good. Locally, being 'good' is seen as any behaviour that supports social harmony, even if the act itself may be sinful, such as, for example, a white lie that prevents sadness. Kindness, generosity, being helpful, working hard, taking care – all are 'good' even if in the course of such actions somebody may get angry or hurt.

In everyday talk, though, people express a dim view of human nature. Based on observations of the behaviour of others and of themselves, they assert that it is much easier to be bad and sinful than good. 'Stolen walnuts taste better than those from my own tree,' people say when they see boys coming from the orchards with bulging pockets. One can do little to make human nature better. However, relativism often complicates the judgement. A person who appears 'bad' to a neighbour by stealing water for his field is helping his own plants and thereby his children, which is 'good'; a woman may be demanding and unfriendly in her daughter-in-law's opinion and the best mother in the view of her own children.

Furthermore, it is easy to be good if one is not challenged, people say when making light of sins. A wife with a reasonable, just husband will be a good wife; a man who never meets a herd of sheep will never be tempted to steal a lamb; a blind man won't have sinful desires when meeting a beautiful woman. Parents and upbringing can steer a child either way. A scoundrel likely will father (or nurse) a scoundrel because his seed (or mother's milk) is morally rotten. A thief's son likely will be a thief; a polite house likely will produce polite children; a boy in a rough peer group will be rough. A middle-aged farmer explained individual good – bad differences with an agricultural image: people are like a patch of soil that produces trees and flowers but also weeds. Few people, though, opt for optimism about basic human inclinations. 'Look at children playing to know human nature,' said a retired teacher watching some children slowly kill a bird.

On top of basic nature, 'seed' and upbringing, there is the individual mandate and responsibility to do good and avoid everything not-good; for this, pious people insist that religion is of importance by defining sins to avoid and meritorious acts to emulate. Less pious people point out that these are self-evident, that they belong to being 'a good human' (*ensān*), a person polished by education, manners and good reasoning. Duty and responsibility again figure prominently, clearly defined by custom and by the expectations people have of each other. Fulfilling them is right and good but not necessarily religiously meritorious, while committing a sin out of necessity (*majburi*) is of little, if any, bad moral consequence. Necessity overrides moral and ethical principles when it appears as the only or most promising choice. In a crisis, people may argue that by sending a misery, God forces people to neglect reason or a religious duty in order to survive. The wife of a seriously ill man who against doctor's orders worked all day in his orchard said, 'He knows it is bad for him but he has nobody to help him, he is *majbur*.'

As to why people are located here or there on the good–bad scale, the easiest answer is that God wanted it that way because otherwise humans' so-called free will to do good would be a lot stronger than it obviously is. This pious way of saying, 'I don't know,' includes a warning against second-guessing God. But thinking about good and bad often leads to choices informed by frustration and disillusionment that may topple into doubt about God's benevolence, if not His power. A woman articulated her sadness about a relative's unshakeable drug habit, saying, 'Maybe God wants us to be good but doesn't have the power to make us good.' And a young man concluded about unruly jinn and devils that God was unable to make them obey Him. Although vigorously opposed by preachers, seeing God's powers as great but limited is a choice when one tries to come to terms with the ills of the world.

While 'good', 'bad' and 'sin' are popular words, 'evil' has no term. The much-used word, *bad* (bad), as in bad smell, bad behaviour, bad pain, bad storm, lacks evil intent and a firm moral component. A thoroughly despicable person may be called 'dirty' (*gand*), 'totally bad' (*aslan bad-e*) or vile, rotten (*past*). Not even the devil is all evil – in some folktales he helps a miserable person after God and the saints failed to do so, and there is the proverbial comparison to one's own hardship, 'How much worse can the devil be?' Adults more or less affectionately or proudly may call uncontrollably frisky, lively children 'devils' (*sheitunal*).

The devil (*sheitun*, thought of as male like other celestial beings) is mentioned rarely, mostly as the voice that talks weak or disheartened people into committing suicide. Adults are not much afraid of the devil and rarely blame him for things that go wrong. They say that in paradise the devil was an arrogant angel God banished to earth where he tries to corrupt people. Lately, he merged with jinn, the malevolent spirit-beings that vex and harm careless people. An elderly woman weaver, one of the most prolific local thinkers and storytellers, had this to say about him, in 1971:

> Sheitun was a prophet. He lived with the other prophets in paradise. The smell (*bu*) of paradise nourished them and they did not need to eat or shit. One day they had nothing to do and said, let's make a dirt-person. But the earth did not want to give them any soil and started to tremble. The prophets said that they

needed only a handful of dirt and that the person soon would turn into soil again. Earth gave in, they made Adam and Eve, and the two sneezed and God's *jun* (life-soul) went into them. The prophets greeted them but Sheitun refused to bow. The prophets complained, and God told them to build a room with a low door to force Sheitun to bow his head when entering. They did so but he entered butt first, and this was really bad, and God punished him by making him ugly and putting him into a deep hole. He pleaded with God, and in the end God heard him and let him live in the belly of Adam and Eve. The first thing he talked them into was to eat wheat, which they were not supposed to eat, and they liked it but it made wind (*bād*) in their bellies, and God saw it and threw them out of paradise. Gabriel put them on his knee, hard, to make a hole in their butts to let the wind out so they wouldn't burst. The devil left with the two, and now is inside all their offspring and tries to talk everybody into doing bad and stupid things.

The devil does not explain all that is bad, though. Local 'students of human nature', as an elderly farmer said, tend to see nature itself as basically violent, God's order as heavy on pain and light on comfort and benevolence, and God as simply not caring much. And when people cannot understand or explain why bad things happen to them, they may keep God the benevolent separate from God the cause of misery, often in the same breath: 'Oh God, help me – why do you bring this misfortune on my head?' Aside of the inscrutable 'God's Will', reasons for what happens in everyday life, good or bad, are bundled into various forms of 'fate'.

Fate

In order to explain the cause of a happening, there is a choice of several 'fates': preordained fate (*qesmat*); lot, allotment (*ruzi*); writing on the forehead (*pishuni neveshte*); chance, luck (*shans*); luck (*bakht*). All are said to be God-willed but except for 'written on the forehead' and 'allotment' they are treated as independent agents. In theological theory the all-powerful, personal God can change anybody's luck/fate, but in practice rarely does so. People may appeal to God frequently in sighs and ejaculations such as 'May God wish; Whatever God wants' (*khodā bekhad; meile khodā*), 'God forbid' (*khodā nakone*) and 'If God wishes' (*inshallah*) throughout their busy days but misfortunes happen nevertheless. Yet, people do not hide behind 'fate'. Rather, they see their own actions as most consequential for good and not-good happenings and for solving everyday problems. No shape of 'fate' is a good excuse for letting things go, for not trying, for not applying oneself. The saying 'From God the blessing, from me the effort' guides this work-philosophy. When a young local woman died for lack of a blood transfusion, relatives who called it 'fate' were reprimanded when it became known that none of them had donated blood – the death was her relatives' doing. That the relatives' refusal also must have been the woman's God-willed fate is an argument doubters may use and is buried quickly by evoking the inscrutable ways of God.

Pressed for an important decision, some people do an ad hoc ritual of assurance by quietly asking 'Excellency Fatemeh' while opening the Quran at random to find an answer on this page.[10] They expect to receive a mystical hint 'in the head', a spark of a thought illuminating the future. The reference to Fatemeh and the use of the Quran link this ritual properly to 'religion'. A well-wishing ritual on the evening of the solar New Year mixes a pre-Islamic ritual with the lunar calendar of Islam, when the mistress of the house goes into her courtyard, faces the direction of the Qibla in Mecca and asks for a blessing for her family.[11] A local student of economics called her urban classmates' fortune-telling rituals 'superstitious insider trading', and when I talked with a retired teacher about such 'theologically questionable behaviour', as he called it, he shook his head and said, 'Bad, bad but it works'. Experience trumps doctrine.

Qesmat (kismet, preordained fate) is mentioned routinely. Whatever happens is 'kismet', willed by God and doled out to every being. Experienced as discrete event or the absence of expected events, it ranges from the monumental to the trivial, from dying or not dying in a car accident to having or not having a good night's sleep; from being mountain or water to being beautiful or plain. In serious circumstances the word defines an ultimate cause. A fatal accident is *qesmat*, as is the death of a sick person who died despite the best care. In both cases the allotted lifetime was up. However, only after everything possible has been done about a condition will kismet, together with 'God's wish', be summoned to explain an outcome. A neighbour half-joked about it when she found a piece of meat she had left out overnight, saying that had it been the meat's *qesmat* to be eaten by the cat it would have happened even if she had locked it away. A beleaguered mother who was called to some emergency just after sitting down to a glass of tea, joked, 'Not even a single tea is my *qesmat* today'. At a traffic accident, when victims and bystanders could not establish a cogent cause for the crash in a lengthy discussion, they summed it up as, 'it was *qesmat*.'

Logically, responsibility for one's own deeds and the deeds' consequences does not sit easily with kismet. Either one's life is mapped out by God in details that cannot be changed, or else one has to make decisions in life, said a young woman. Practically, though, the incongruity does not pose a problem because everybody is obliged by reason, God and the religion to exert oneself. One has to work to get food; one has to consult the doctor to recover from illness. Thus, personal engagement is placed in the zone of free will where sins and merits happen, and in the zone of reason. Effort, application, reasoning are moral obligations as well as sensible ones. Kismet, on the other hand, in casual uses of the word explains difficult or fait accompli situations, especially one's own. It stands outside the moral frame.

Pishuni neveshte translates as 'written on the forehead' and in vernacular speech means the same as it did in antiquity: one's life events, one's 'fate' is written on one's head, permanently. The expression is well known and well used for covering women's marital situations, especially problematic ones. If and when a girl is going to marry and how she is treated in her husband's house are her immutable fate. Used to explain or justify a woman's unwanted but insistent and successful suitor or a married woman's sad marital life, it underscores women's lack of agency: a woman's life is mapped out indelibly at birth. 'Whatever will happen to me, I have to say, "Thanks be to God,"' said a high school student betrothed to a relative in Canada she had seen last when she was six years old. Men, who have more choices for action than women, rarely explain their circumstances with this concept.

Shans (from French, chance; perchance, luck, fortune) is more popular and closer to experience than the religiously heavy *qesmat*, although how *shans* deals with individual people is part of their kismet. People talk about it as an uncontrollable, disembodied agency reminiscent of Luck's deity origin in antiquity: it may come or not and be of advantage or disadvantage regardless of a person's moral standing, wishes or piety. As a causal concept it is easy to work with. Being born into a wealthy family is due to good luck; by chance finding a pot of gold, by chance meeting somebody useful – all these are *shans*. The driver in a fatal car accident called the death 'bad luck', thereby negating evil intention on his side but also denying responsibility and his potential obligation to pay blood money. The young son of poor, incompetent parents (bad luck) was taken on by a truck driver as a child servant (good luck) and ten years later was a well-to-do chauffeur (more good luck). And, on the light side, a local herder, Ali, who had 'no luck' with his animals, lost so many that his brother joked that the hungry wolf obviously always asked the shepherd politely to point out one of Ali's sheep in the village herd for the next meal.

Ruz, ruzi, ruzegār means daily allotment, lot.[12] One's daily challenges are preordained, to be mastered or endured. 'Let's see what the day (*ruz*) will bring' sums up the attitude, as does the proverbial complaint, 'I have no life and no life-program either' (*na zendegi dārom na ruzegār*). If one got more than what is taken to be a normal, reasonable amount of good (such as several twin births in a herd), or bad (such as several accidents in a family), a likely imbalance ought to be rebalanced by giving alms or making a sacrifice. In the expression, 'The day is toying with me' (*ruz vam bāzi kone*), a sick woman complained about not feeling well, giving *ruz* personified agency.

Bakht ('fortune, luck') is a popular expression and handled as a personified power. The way it is used suggests that every person has a companion kind of luck. If the companion is young and strong, the person is well and successful. If the companion is old and tired, the person is weak and unsuccessful. 'My *bakht* is asleep' or 'has left me' (*bakhtom ve khouë; bakhtom vellom kerd*) explains why things go wrong for me at the moment. 'Bad luck' (*badbakht*) is the much-used expression for an unfortunate, miserable person, and as a verb *badbakhti kardan* covers all menial or unappealing, stressful work. Although said to be made by God like everything else, people may relate to it as an independent force beyond anybody's control.

The assumption of such active powers challenges the theologians' assertion that God wills every move.[13] It provides the option to assume that God delegates some movement as a chore to intangible entities. To make this clear, a middle-aged man pointed to a bush pummelled by wind: 'We don't see the wind but we see what it does. It comes and goes. It exists by itself.' Such images lead to various strategies for dealing with these powers. Thus, submission to the demands of the all-powerful ruler-God does not void people's ability to manipulate whatever has a bearing on their lives. Rather, emphasis on God-given reasoning and intellect (*aql*) and people's obvious survival duties strengthen human agency.

Sacrifice

The most common option to influence powers and events is sacrifice, based on the conviction that anything given away in good faith and with sincere hope will benefit the donor. Attracting the attention of benevolent powers with promises of money and food is as popular as warding off dangers with alms to the poor. Offerings range from simply 'thinking of God' to gestures of submission and propitiation.

Least firmly embedded in orthodox religion are sacrifices meant to ward off hurtful events such as a *qossa*, a personified disaster. It may announce itself in a dream, thereby giving the person time to deflect it by giving alms, a *rafe qossa*. If no misfortune happens, the apotropaic sacrifice obviously was successful in restoring order and balance; if there is a mishap nevertheless, the sacrifice may be declared to have been insufficient or else the disaster to have been stronger than the sacrifice. Such reasoning, resting, as it does, on the attribution of causal relationships between actions and events that cannot be disproven, convinces most people of its veracity.

A blood sacrifice (*khinrizi*) is considered to be especially potent because meat is 'stronger' and more expensive than other food. Done for a sick child, for example, the recipient of the meat will say a prayer for the child, which amounts to a veneration of God as well as a supplication. Done for the joyous birth of a third or fourth son, when building a new house, or after many sheep survived an epidemic, a blood sacrifice is less a sign of gratitude than expected to prevent harm from people's jealous talk and the evil eye.

The 'more-than-my-lot' sacrifice (*navaruzi*) reflects a similar mindset. Anything above and beyond a 'normal' allotment – such as rapid growth, a big wheat harvest, a fat baby – is an imbalance that may bring problems for the owner, such as the evil eye. Alms may restore the balance and prevent harm; an amulet against the evil eye (*nazarband*) or a spell such as 'throw it on yourself' (*bezanesh ve khot*) is taken to be more reliable, though.[14] A mother remembered:

> Our first child was tiny and weak; the second, a boy, was big and feisty. He was clearly *navaruzi*, different from all other children his age, and so we hung an amulet and a blue bead and a salt crystal against the salt-eye on his shirt and on the cradle, and I burned wild rue. And we said, 'Throw it on yourself!' so much that before he could talk he yelled it at me when he was angry. It worked, though, praise be to God.

Vows and votive promises (*nazr*) have become the most popular religious rituals in town with a great many choices. They range from the promise of a pilgrimage, that is, a visit to a saint's shrine, to special meals cooked for the poor or for participants in religious public rituals; from promising a daughter to a Seyed to cooking soup (*āsh*) for one's neighbours in memory of a dead relative.[15] Such activities often are connected to an 'if' proposition: 'If my child gets well, I will give money to the shrine of Saint X; if my son gets accepted at a university, I will give alms to the poor.' Mostly, though, the less specific vows ('for the health of the house') are made routinely to ward off a bad happening or attract a good one. A local woman described a bull sacrifice at the Feast of Sacrifice (*eid-e Qorbun, eid al-Adha*)[16] when she was a child. In her well-to-do father's house a yearling bull was stuck with a knife, bled to death over a hole in the ground, the blood covered with soil and the meat given away, all for religious merits for the afterlife. Locally nobody can afford to kill a bull now, she said.

Firmly anchored in orthodox religion is the *vaqf*, a forever-dedication of a field's or orchard's harvest for financing Muharram performances or meals for worshippers in the mosque, or for feeding the poor. Its aim is to create religious merits for the spender. About a man's dedication of the income of a row of his vineyard to the mosque, his wife said, 'We will see what it will do for us in the next world!'

Regarding expected benefits and motivations for other donations (*sadeqeh, kheirat, khoms*) in food or money to the poor, a shrine or mosque, there are choices, depending on occasion. They may be based on empathy for poor people befitting a 'true human'; they may be done to earn religious merits or to make a public statement of goodwill and piety; and as a gesture honouring God, they may be expected to motivate God to aid and protect one's family.

These rituals and customs have long been part of local people's identity and ideology and are thoroughly habituated, as are expectations for their effects. For believers, they combine faith with actions that people trust as being tried and true, whether they be called religion or magic or superstition. Deep believers rely on them and even people who are critical and suspicious of traditional pieties perform some or keep quiet when family members do them. 'They won't do any harm,' said an outspoken critic of 'such nonsense', and a pragmatic merchant said that at the very least they put one at ease. The efficacy of rituals is judged in an empirical manner, but as the purpose of the ritual gets intertwined with the performance, doing the ritual is rewarding in itself. Crying at a funeral feels good and so does having fun at a votive cook-out or giving a bowl of rice to a poor neighbour. Disappointing results can be dismissed as being due to the insufficient size of the offering, mistakes in the performance of the ritual or due to God's Will.[17]

Negative terms such as 'magic' are chosen mostly to degrade old rituals to 'superstition' (*khorāfāt*) for religious as well as enlightenment reasons. The Farsi term *jādu* (magic, spell) in the past was used for sinful black magic, for formulas or acts meant to hurt. A woman may use a black spell to prevent her husband from taking a second wife, for example, or to make her husband dislike the other wife. A few people in the vicinity were known to make and sell such spells; they may be useful at times but also be called morally questionable, if not wrong.

In crisis situations, magical thinking proliferates and may result in obsessive attention to details. When in 2004 several unexpected deaths in town left unsettled people groping for explanations, somebody dreamt that the cause was the incorrect interment of a man who was not born in town.[18] To stop the death trend, he should be reburied where he had come from. A visitor in town advised to put a pair of shoes and two eggs with every burial in order to prevent death – any death – from 'pulling more death after it'. For this urban outsider, 'Death' was a powerful agent but its power could be broken by eggs and shoes, items that locally had no traditional symbolic significance but now added an option for dealing with death.

Altered states of consciousness such as spirit possessions, the Zar-cult, Sufi mysticism, trance-experiences and techniques to achieve them are known but provide no options for action locally. People say that jinn make troubles but not that they invade a body; that the devil tries to persuade a weak mind but won't 'take over' a person. The dead are no haunting ghosts. Even deep believers treat spirit-beliefs and meddling in the occult as going against reason (*aql*) and therefore as likely false. They are not what God wants people to be, namely, guided in their actions by reason and God's orders. None of the popular rituals encourage the pursuit of revelations by altered states of consciousness.[19] Rather, they are grounded in everyday awareness and experiences, and mostly are seen as aiding people to get through life.

Summary

Most locally popular religious concepts and religiously motivated choices have in common the aim of managing life for people in this, a difficult, world. As keen observers of harsh living conditions, people opt to rely on their own, experience-based ways and means to manage life's problems. These are based on communal ethics, a strong sense of duty and self-reliance, and accepting responsibility for dealing with challenges, whereby the ends often validate the means. Rarely is 'fate' (in several forms) invoked as immutable cause of happenings before everything possible has been tried to master a situation. A somewhat remote God is asked – and thanked – for help routinely but to prevent bad things from happening, to explain why things happen or to ask for assistance in difficulties, people have the choice to manipulate a rich universe of extra-human powers to their advantage. Insisting on a firm link to the creator-God prevents locating these powers cognitively in a spiritual universe different from that described by

Shia Islam: all powers are created by God and can be used freely by people; all belong to religion. Indeed, a strong anthropocentric view offers the option to assume that God created the powers to benefit people. The many unexplainable issues surrounding life on earth inspire options for thinking and acting that range from blind adherence to doctrines and rituals to doubts and agnostic distancing from orthodox truth.

Figure 4 Sisakht, 10. Moharram, 1970, in the courtyard of the old mosque. The most important day of mourning for Shia Muslims is celebrated with processions, chants and self-flagellation by men. Women watch from surrounding flat roofs of houses.

4

Saints and clients

Appealing to saints for help is an option anytime but especially when God is seen as too far away to listen. A father drew comparison to schools: 'It is easier to ask a teacher for help with my son's learning problem than the minister of education in Tehran who won't even answer the telephone.' Furthermore, saints are said to need people more than God does. They like visitors and need to be remembered to remain powerful.[1] The cult of saints is popular and ubiquitous in Iran even among people who call it superstition or swindle. The following discussion highlights the choices local pilgrims have for engaging saints' assumed powers, their spiritual energy.

In Islam, the customs, beliefs and theological arguments regarding saint veneration were established by the Middle Ages. The saint complex we see in Iran today extends across Abrahamic religions just as it has done for centuries, modified to fit changing ways of life.[2] In 2005, when an elderly, pious Iranian Muslim woman who never before had been in a church, visited catholic Saint Xavier in Arizona with me, she not only understood the meaning of tomb, relics, candles and pilgrims' prayer performances but expected help from the Spanish saint herself. For her, all saints shared the same *baraka* and *shafa*, the same blessing, grace or benevolent power, the same access to God regardless of religion, place and language. In this transnational/trans-faith case as well as in Boir Ahmad such hybrid identity depends not on diffusion or unilinear historical connections but on pilgrims' pan-human search for help and consolation in places emanating good vibes, charisma, energy or power (as, for example, from a 'saint') that produce strong emotions or an 'experience' (Melotti 2019) in the visitor.

In Boir Ahmad, most saints are dead people with a patrilineal genealogical link to the Prophet Muhammad that carries the title Seyed. Descendants of an Imam, one of twelve leaders in the Prophet's lineage in Shia Islam, are called Imamzadeh.[3] Their God-willed spiritual energy, the power to change living people's circumstances, emanates from their names, bodies and tombs. People honour and supplicate the saints, assume that they obey God and are inclined to strike bargains with people by providing help – unpredictably so – in exchange for signs of esteem. Such signs are invocations like 'Oh Ali'!, 'Oh Highness Fatemeh!', visits to tombs and offerings of food or money, and approaching them with a trusting, open heart. All saints are assumed to be good; differences lie in the strength of their power as demonstrated by their efficacy and their willingness (or ability) to look at and listen to supplicants. To get attention people try to establish personal bonds with particular saints.[4] These ideas and their practical and cognitive dimensions are in evidence for the Near and Middle East throughout the millennia (see, for example, Athanassiadi and Frede 1999). The ancient (Roman) notion of a religious group's duty to care for their deities (Rüpke 2013: 7) also fits the relationship between ordinary humans and saints in Boir Ahmad.

Words

The oldest saints' places in Boir Ahmad are called *pir*, generically or followed by a personal name, and meaning a wise elder as well as a person who has portentous dreams and other abilities that show that he (rarely, she) emanates spiritual energy (*baraka*). A *pir*-'saint' links the pre-Islamic notion of the resting place of a charismatic person whose help and counsel is sought to the Islamic notion of grace and blessing vested in some Seyeds, and to the tradition of mystical connection with a helpful spiritual master. Predating Islam, some shrines are prefixed with 'Shah', connoting a great, famous, exalted person.[5] In pre-Islamic contexts divine beings, the predecessors of some local saints, were said to have direct influence on people's lives and in turn to need people's care and attention. Muslim male and female saints have similar functions and purported needs but with the difference that most are taken to be descendants of an Imam.[6]

God's grace flowing through the Prophet's patrilineage[7] does not have to be bolstered by exceptional piety or by feats of religious fervour. Martyrdom, however, helps. Most shrines in Boir Ahmad trace their legendary origin to the interred saint's murder while fleeing enemies. Not all descendants of the Prophet have power, though.[8] Most Seyeds have ordinary human capabilities. Thus, 'Sey Mahmud' the neighbourhood store-keeper is just a Seyed by the name Mahmud who sells dry goods, while the shrine of 'Sey Mahmud' in the next village is the old tomb of a saint by that name who exerts a pull on pilgrims by his purported efficacy in solving people's problems. The few shrines of women in Boir Ahmad are called Bibi (Lady) followed by the name. The biggest shrine in the province is that of Bibi Hakimeh.[9] A Bibi may also be a 'Seyda' (*Sayidah*, daughter of a Seyed). Locally Seyda is used rarely and likely is taken by others as an attempt to elevate one's status in the Islamic Republic. Descendants of the Prophet honoured in a shrine may be addressed and referred to as *hezrat* (Excellency, Highness).

A miracle story told by a young female descendant of a saint buried in a small shrine in Boir Ahmad shows how tightly this power is linked to the genealogical Seyed status. The narrator's father, Seyed Ali, was a pious and well-off herder.

> A boy in our summer camp had nearly drowned in the river and was in a coma. After a month in the hospital in Yasuj, the doctor said he could do nothing more, that God and a saint would have to help. On that day, by chance my father had sent the boy's mother money for her living expenses at the hospital, and at that moment the boy woke up and was well. It was a miracle.

Local people explained this miracle as coming from the saint via his descendant, Seyed Ali, without a pilgrimage and a votive promise. Rather, Seyed Ali's generosity had opened his saint ancestor's flow of healing power.

Little, if anything, is known about the saints' lives, and pilgrims don't seem interested in hagiographies. Not the saint's life but the tomb, the cult activities and the saint's efficacy legitimate shrine and pilgrimage. As to why exalted Imams' offspring came to the remote mountains in the first place is not of much interest either. People say about most of them that they were martyred by the conquering Mongol khans' armies (in the thirteenth century) that chased Muslims into the hinterland. Most saints are remembered as victims who had suffered greatly and therefore understand the suffering of the petitioners who present themselves as victims of circumstances, enmity and the vagaries of life.

For want of a better word in English, and keeping in mind the above-mentioned connotations, I use Imamzadeh or saint when talking about these hallowed personages, and call their places by the local designations, Emamzada, Pir and Bibi.

Places

Local people estimate between thirty and 'a hundred' shrines in Boir Ahmad, and 'thousands' in Iran. This is not far-fetched. Varjavand (2011) reports between 300 and over thousand shrines in Iran because every village has or wants one (see also Kriss and Kriss-Heinrich 1960). Some Emamzada are based on open-air pre-Islamic tree-and-water cult places and may not even have a grave. Visitors to these kinds of Emamzada may hang small strips of fabric into the trees for 'binding' their wishes, and may light candles on walls surrounding trees and a water source. They murmur a greeting/prayer together with their petition during this low-keyed, quiet ritual to catch the attention of the saint. In 2015 a local friend whose job takes him all over Boir Ahmad, described several sites with old trees local people call Pir. People store household goods at the site when they go away, trusting that the Pir-saint would protect them and punish a thief. When a few years ago such a Pir-oak was felled during road construction, workers were startled by a loud wind-like noise emanating from a hole in the trunk and left, refusing to work there. A spring in north-western Boir Ahmad is called 'Qadamgāh Hezrate Suleiman' (Footstep of Excellency Salomon), and its water is said to ward off locusts.[10] Government authorities declare these places illegitimate and heathen because there is no tomb and thus no buried saint, and therefore expressively discourage pilgrims, candles and rags by building cement platforms among the trees as 'picnic' places. One such place, Shah Qāsom in northern Boir Ahmad, near the village of Khungāh, consists of a few old trees next to a spring-fed brook surrounded by a low stonewall with dark smoke patches.[11] In 2006, when we visited last, visitors hung their rags high up in the trees to keep them out of easy reach of government agents and lit candles in holes in the trees before spreading picnic rugs and tea utensils on the platform. There are few visitors now, and those who do come seem to connect to the purported saint in ways close to mystical ritual visualization of the saint (Fenton 2019). Sufi principles are known locally, and a vaguely mystical bond between people and saint is an option in the relationship. These ancient places are doomed through neglect, disuse or destruction according to local people and a historian at the Cultural Heritage office in Yasuj.[12]

In 2006 a physician in a remote village in central Boir Ahmad showed us a similar cult place at a rock-wall facing a brook, consisting of remnants of several cave burials in the rock face, cairns and pieces of fabric in tree branches. It is known as 'Bibi Bānu Geshasp', which local people translate as 'The Kind Lady'. Likely it is of the Zoroastrian origin they claim it to be.[13] Local people mentioned danger from looters and from Revolutionary Guards who might destroy the site. Other Sasanian rock tombs also attract unwanted attention, although they are not places of veneration unlike some Achaemenid and Sasanian sites in the province and elsewhere.[14] A few Emamzada are based on cairn-like piles of stones marking the graves of purported saints. This pre-Islamic burial practice appears in folktales (Friedl 2014: 169), in remarks by early travellers[15] and as a remnant of old practices to this day among transhumant pastoralists in neighbouring

Bakhtiari (Alehassan 2017), where small cairns mark some children's graves.[16] Stone-piles, too, come under scrutiny by authorities in Boir Ahmad if they are called Emamzada and attract pilgrims.

Such ancient cult places aside, most local Emamzada consist of a square or octagonal room with a tomb in the centre which usually is surrounded by a lattice fence. Pilgrims walk around the tomb enclosure, touching and even kissing the lattice to partake of the *baraka*, the grace, said to emanate from the (saint in the) tomb. The room likely has a dome-shaped roof, and the buildings range from small, unadorned mud brick structures in graveyards to the large pilgrimage centre of Bibi Hakimeh with an elaborate shrine in a big building embellished with tile work and a shiny dome, surrounded by hotels and markets for the pilgrims. Every shrine has a caretaker who, in most cases, claims to be a descendant of the saint believed to be buried there and who gets paid in money or in kind by pilgrims' votive offerings. It is a hereditary vocation.

Most shrines are built near or atop a water source and in the shade of trees. People say – and 'prove' it with anecdotes – that whoever fells such a tree or destroys a shrine will die soon, that a saint's power can be dangerous or else that God will punish anybody who dishonours a saint. One such story is about an old, small mudbrick shrine in Sisakht, built in the late 1800s and never blossoming into a place of power and healing. It was dismantled some sixty years later, and the man who struck the first blow into the crumbling wall died soon afterward in an accident.

The making of an Emamzada

Burial places – one body per grave – usually last as long as memories of the buried person are alive in a community. Grave markers extend memories, but not forever. When the old graveyard in Sisakht with headstones engraved with gender markers and figures had been abandoned for some forty years, the authorities selected it for a new religious meeting place (*hoseinië*), a new shrine (to replace the old abandoned one) and an Islamic cultural centre. In 2000 the old graves were levelled and bones and headstones hauled off unceremoniously by government agents. For a grave to remain alive in the cult community more is needed than commemorative care by relatives. For a Seyed such permanence can be achieved by building a small green dome over the grave, marking it as the place of a dead relative of the Prophet and thus inviting a special kind of attention; the dead Seyed might, just might, turn out to be efficacious when petitioned, and then the tomb could be used as a new Emamzada. In the 1950s the sons of the dead resident Seyed-mullah, an outsider, tried this but without success. The little mausoleum is sitting in a small, forgotten graveyard squeezed between two new roads, and hardly anybody in the younger generation cares about it.

The standard and more promising way to create a shrine is by a notable person dreaming of a lion circling a particular location. Men then dig there, and if they find a burial, they'll know that it is that of an Imamzadeh. Identifying such a saint is a problem, but it seems that somebody always can remember or has heard or read somewhere that a certain Seyed died in this area. This triggers activities for turning the grave into a tomb with a domed building, the Seyed's house, people say, where he or she lives. If then petitioners honour the saint with visits, vows and thanks for help, the Emamzada is justified and will bring pilgrims, money and distinction to the community. It needs quite a bit of work, public relations efforts and political will to create a new shrine, but the same effort may be needed to prevent a grave from becoming a political embarrassment. Since about 2010 the imposing tomb of Cyrus the Great, the founder of the Achaemenid Empire, has attracted ever larger crowds of visitors from all over Iran.[17] By 2017 the authorities had built fences around the area to block access, declared the visitations illegal gatherings and arrested visitors. Guardians of the Islamic Republic do not wish to have nationalist groups with Zoroastrian agendas use the tomb as a focal point for potentially anti-government sentiments.

Throughout Iran people tell anecdotes about the creation of shrines. A story about one near Sisakht is about a tribal chief eager to have an Emamzada in his realm but unable to locate a convincing burial despite a dream and great efforts. He finally ordered his men to build a shrine over an empty grave pit, declaring that surely the fickle saint would move into the nice, new grave-'house' on his own (Friedl 2018b: 80).[18] A visitor to the open-air cult place described earlier made a point of the fact that people found help and solace there, which showed that a saint was present even without a 'house' but could not convince the authorities. The most detailed account of the recent creation of an Emamzada (in northern Iran) describes it as an invented tradition, a deliberate, politically motivated act by religious authorities and relatives of a young soldier-martyr in the Iran–Iraq war (Ayaz 2012). In 1989 the body of Ayatollah Khomeini, the Republic's venerated leader, first was kept in an inaccessible repository surrounded by stacks of shipping containers and a band of young men. While we were watching in a large crowd, a bystander told us that the men were there to prevent (without success) mourners from touching and kissing the containers. The Ayatollah's hidden body instantly was used as an Emamzada based on the belief that it was emanating blessings and grace even before a 'house' was built.[19]

In Sisakht, one day in 2015, without forewarning, government agents razed the crumbling fort of the late shah's gendarmerie on top of a hill overlooking a new neighbourhood at the site of a purported Sasanian settlement. They interred two nameless fallen soldiers there, started to build a shrine and organized regular prayer meetings. People predicted that this would become an 'artificial' (*masnui*) Emamzada, organized by a local government functionary, a Seyed who thereby wanted to ingratiate himself with Party-of-God officials.

Some old shrines in Boir Ahmad are located along ancient trade routes in the ruins of settlements of an earlier population in the Zagros area whose culture and lifestyle were quite different from those of the pastoral, semi-nomadic Lur tribes living here now. Nevertheless, the ancient cult places, Pir and Emamzada, make perfect sense to the present inhabitants; many places retain their original names although nothing else may be known about them.[20] So-called living Pir, wise elders with purported healing powers, are known to exist but not in Boir Ahmad, where many people opt for calling them swindlers. Reports about one such living Pir, a Lur from Boir Ahmad living in a village in neighbouring Fars Province, greatly amused people in Sisakht in 2015. He had fled his own village after a family fight, arrived in Fars cold and hungry, found out that people admired his vivid dreams and believed in the healing power of his saliva and his amulets, and soon 'was sitting at the foot of a rock, with women lining up to consult him'.[21] When a visitor from Sisakht said he did not believe that the women the 'Pir' treated had no more problems, the fellow allegedly said, 'I don't either but now I am eating well.'

Religious authorities in the Islamic Republic probe the legitimacy of old shrine structures by examining written documents that may refer to the saints allegedly buried there. When an Emamzada is declared legitimate it may be renovated, even rebuilt in a modern cement-and-tiles style. The wells and springs will be concealed 'for hygienic reasons', as a Revolutionary Guard told us, but clearly also to discourage any potential water-deity veneration. At a visit to such a refurbished shrine the pilgrims I travelled with were critical about the new look. They hardly recognized 'their' shrine, they said, and missed the sulphurous spring and, most grievously, the light that used to appear Thursday nights on the cupola as a sign of the saint's presence.[22] A doubter from Sisakht took the popular option to declare the light a swindle by the shrine's wardens who wanted to attract more pilgrims to increase their own income. Caretakers may be held in esteem by pilgrims or, at other occasions, declared to be self-serving crooks. To believe in saints' powers but disapprove of the 'shrine-business' is a popular choice for people. Yet, despite criticism of the new look of these Emamzada, the opinion that the new, shiny shrines are signs of progress, 'good, modern' improvements in the area, is equally attractive. Ancient as well as new Emamzada are featured in travel brochures published by the Tourist Bureau in Boir Ahmad in order to promote the beauty of the area, to attract visitors. Officials appreciate the irony behind the government wanting to eliminate the old mudbrick shrines with their 'holy' trees and waters yet needing them to lure tourists in search of historical monuments.

Some Seyeds in Boir Ahmad link their families to one or another shrine, declaring the ancestral saint buried there to be 'their' saint, a relative. They expect that by honouring the saint with visits and paying the custodian for upkeep services, they will get preferential treatment from the saint. They oblige the saint by their show of fidelity just as they would try to oblige a powerful administrator with presents and performances of deference, humility and admiration to granting a request. Saint veneration and the uses of saints run parallel with social practices of manipulation of authorities. Indeed, if a saint won't help despite all expenses and efforts, the petitioner may abandon the shrine and try another. A man singing about his fear of being drafted, threatened, 'I am a descendant of Seyed Mahmad. The military is on my heels. If my ancestor won't do anything for me, I won't call him my leader' (Friedl 2018a: 162). And a lovelorn young man sang of his resolve to try another shrine if 'his' saint would not help him get the girl.

Saints and clients

In the veneration of saints, a strong *do ut des* principle is evident in vows: 'I promise the saint a lamb so that – or if – the saint will heal my leg.'[23] Such vows are made throughout Iran, and people go to great lengths to fulfil them. The motivations for vows span the range of human problems.[24] Women make vows in order to conceive;[25] a young woman in Tehran told me of her promise to a saint for help to get a husband 'in Canada' to escape pressures to marry her 'good for nothing' cousin; young men make vows for jobs; a father in Shiraz made a vow for his daughter to recover from brain damage brought about by a medical error;[26] a woman in Isfahan was asking a saint to help her daughter get a safe place to live at a faraway college. So many young people and their parents make vows for a good grade on the university entrance test that a young man in Sisakht said that the saints in Iran get belly aches from all the votive meals the students' parents were feeding them.[27] A local eight-year-old girl to everybody's amusement hoped a vow would get her annoying eldest brother 'out of the way, into a city-job'; and a woman blamed her husband for the saint's failure to keep her son nearby during his military service because the husband had substituted a cheap young rooster for the expensive lamb promised to the saint (the shrine keeper, that is). On the dark side, we heard that a public servant in Ahwaz promised a hefty gift to the family's saint if his competitor, a 'scoundrel' who had bought himself a promotion, would die in an accident. Fatal car crashes are so common that the man assured the saint he would not even have to exert himself much to bring one about. This example shows that as long as petitioners honour the vow conventions, saints are expected to help without judging the morality in clients' intentions.[28]

Saints become famous for their success, and the success is linked to their powers as well as – or even more – to their personal engagement, case by case. People act on the assumption that just as they decide how much or little effort to put into any endeavour, so do saints. A neighbour had this example:

> I can help my younger brother and my old father with their firewood but I will help the old man more because I am grateful to him or I like him more or I feel sorry for him or because my brother can work without help but my father can't. The saints surely think so, too, when deciding who gets their help.

This may lead to hope, expectations, exertions and gratitude in people but also to deep disappointment. And just like whimsical life in general, the saints have no obligation to provide justice for their supplicants. Like their clients, they are pragmatists.

A bit of the energy that makes saints successful is said to rest in some ordinary people, too. There are men and women whose counsel, whose very presence makes tired people feel lively and sad people consoled; others can heal wounds with their saliva or create protective amulets by writing words from the Quran on little pieces of paper.[29] On the sinister side, people are afraid of curses (*nofrin*) from a disappointed beggar-dervish[30] and avoid people whose sheer presence is known to make others sad or sick. Anybody can talk and listen, anybody can spit or curse, and anybody who can write could make an amulet, but only a few people's efforts are efficacious, for better or worse.

The power to influence human conditions, to 'find inoffensive intrusions into the order of things' (Rüpke 2013: 9), is strongest in saints. Ultimately, people see it resting in God, channelled either by God to saints, for them to use as they see fit, or else by God listening to particular saints' petitions on behalf of clients more than to others. In a strictly monotheistic religion this is a difficult theological issue because all power rests in God. Answering a direct question, believers in the saint-cult say that 'of course' the saints' power comes from God because everything comes from God, and will explain unequally granted help from saints with God's inscrutable Will. In daily usage and in common-sense expectations, though, the saint 'has' the power;

it is part of him/herself, at the saint's disposal, just as a strong man has his strength ultimately from God but it rests in him, for him to use. The practical problem with this power is to get the saint to look at the petitioner's plight in the first place. After a saint extended help, people may say, 'The Saint supplied the requested,' but also, 'The Saint listened to (or looked at) my request.'[31] At an abandoned shrine tomb in town that never turned into a pilgrimage place, a friend said, 'The Excellency (*hezrat*) here did not listen.' An elderly visitor to a small shrine near Sisakht said, 'The Saint here has good ears, if he *wants* to hear me.' The communication is one-sided, though: saints may hear and see but do not usually talk to their petitioners; at most, they may get a message to people via dreams in a roundabout way.

One can try to get a saint's attention anytime and anywhere by promising a visit to the shrine and imploring the saint in a convincing, heartfelt way. A pious widow who had raised her children by herself (instead of remarrying and leaving them with their father's relatives) used this formula 'with great success' when supplicating her preferred saint: 'Oh Abulfasl[32] I face you, and you face God (*khodā*). Give your blessing to my son.' Such pleas accompany a votive offering of food or money for the poor or of a gift to the shrine keeper. A donation to the shrine keeper may range from foodstuff and money to – in the past – a daughter, for him to decide which relative (if not he personally) will get her as a wife without paying a bride price. One may argue that the greater is the promised gift, the more and sooner the saint will be interested to help, and this is what some people say – one can opt for calling it, half-jokingly, a 'bribe' (*reshve*)[33] – but hardly anybody doubts that saints also have empathy for poor people and may help without a gift. The saints' accessibility to petitioners who are far away from a saint's tomb is more problematic. It is taken to be either due to the saint's spirit that is free to roam, similar to part of a person's soul during a dream, or else a swindle. In other words, not everybody participates or 'believes' in the cult of the saints, but enough people affirm the saints' efficacy to keep the cult a prominent and popular choice of religious activities.

All visits, offerings and promises are said to please and honour the recipient saint just as they honour any recipient. A friendly visit elevates and gratifies a host, while for the visitor it amounts to a show of subordination as it entails an effort, a kind of sacrifice. Host and visitor alike benefit from the patron–client ritual. Pilgrimages to shrines in Iran range from casual daily greetings to saints commemorated in small neighbourhood shrines built into house fronts (Betteridge 1985)[34] to travels to big shrines that are thriving commercial enterprises offering pilgrims elaborate aesthetic and emotional experiences.[35] The most coveted, once-in-a-lifetime pilgrimages are to the shrines at the spiritual centres of Islam, to Mecca, Medina (both in Saudi Arabia) and Kerbela (Iraq). Government agencies arrange and subsidize these pilgrimages, making them affordable for many. For most participants, pilgrimages have become the only travel entertainment available. A well-off local man said he was taking his wife and children on visits to all saints 'far and wide' because his family liked the diversion so much. Pilgrims to the famous shrines feel obliged to buy many gifts there (such as sweets, prayer rugs and clothes) for relatives back home. A recipient of such a gift joked that the returning pilgrims are generous because they liked being addressed with the honorific titles, 'Hajji' or 'Kerbelai' by the grateful relatives. In 2015 an economically struggling widow returning from Kerbela with a 'big bundle' of such gifts said she had taken a loan to pay for them, more money than she could ever pay back, but she was not worried: her son would pay the debt because it earned him religious merits. In 2006 an elderly pilgrim to Kerbela, an orthodox believer from a Party-of-God family, at her post-pilgrimage lunch party 'for two-hundred guests' praised the government's arrangement of 'everything' during the eight-day journey. (Her grandfather, she said, had made the thousand-kilometre-long pilgrimage on foot and was buried in Kerbela, which is believed to assure acceptance in paradise.) For her the highlights were visiting Ali's house and seeing the spilled blood of slain Husein in the sand under a glass-top. This caused heated arguments with her children who called her bereft of reason for believing such swindle.

Pilgrims thus can take a pilgrimage as a religious ritual and an obligation, a necessity of piety; as a heartfelt visit to the saint; as an occasion to earn religious merits and an honorific title; as a way to get support from the saint; as an opportunity to travel and bolster one's well-being; as an appreciated gesture of generosity by the government; as a show of support for the government; as a shopping trip; as an established custom of the group one belongs to; as the government's attempt to make people 'stupid', and as a combination of all options. Most popular, though, is a quasi-rational experience: supplicating a saint brings proven results.

The more visitors a saint has, the more honoured and famous the saint will become. In this sense saints need people (as visitors and supplicants) who will validate their status as tutelary spirits. At an abandoned small shrine in Boir Ahmad my local companion said that the saint most likely had left his 'house' when nobody was visiting any more. Such thoughts make sense in a vernacular logic but are theologically difficult: if the potent part of a shrine is linked to the body buried there, what happens when the body disintegrates? Does saintly power disintegrate, too? This is an unpleasant thought for believers and a ridiculous one for critics. People may choose to argue that the soul of the saint or a quality of personhood ('the saint himself') remains near the body even after only the bones remain. Yet this, too, is confusing because the souls of dead Muslims are said to leave the body at or shortly after death and go somewhere to wait for the Day of Judgement rather than 'hanging around a stinking corpse', as a resolute local woman said. And if the souls of saints stay, what about those of other descendants of the Prophet? An elderly, illiterate weaver with 'a lot of time to think about things' while sitting on her horizontal loom, was puzzled. Nobody, she said, had given her a reasonable answer, not her student granddaughter and not the Mullah either.

In any case, the cult of saints rests on the assumption that like any dead person, a dead saint is not all gone and that therefore it stands to reason that he or she retains some needs such as for company but also for food. Votive meals, offered to neighbours, the poor, participants in religious events, either fulfil a vow to a saint or honour a dead relative. Votive soup (*āsh nazri*) has become popular in Sisakht, a *mod* (fashion) in the absence of entertainments for women, a devout woman doctor said. My host joked about recognizing the cooks of every votive soup in the neighbourhood by the different tastes, and a neighbour said she could stop cooking altogether with all the soup delivered to her door.[36] Votive meals benefit the spender socially by the public demonstration of loyalty to a saint or dead relative and morally by the dutiful attention to their memory; they are said to earn religious merits (*sabāb, savāb*) for the host as well as the recipients who accept the food and will bless the honoured dead by saying the *fateha*, the first chapter in the Quran.[37] Materially the food benefits the recipients who get a good meal.[38] A busy woman whose sister had brought her an excellent soup thanked her, saying that while she only could hope that it would benefit the dead, she knew for sure that she and her family would benefit. Women cook votive meals in big pots with the help of neighbours and relatives and cherish the cooking parties for the opportunity to meet 'in person, not only on the phone', as a hostess said. Everybody brings 'cooking tools and patience'. The utensils inevitably get mixed up in the wash up, and it takes many polite phone calls and sotto voce curses until pots and knives are sorted out again. Young members of the *nazr* (family) deliver the food to various houses, on foot or in cars. When a six-year-old boy learnt that his favourite aunt, a famous cook, was making votive soup, he planned to go there by himself for an extra helping. His mother was less enthusiastic. 'I am tired of eating other people's *āsh*,' she said, 'I like my own food better.' For her, accepting and eating votive food was a duty, a neighbourly and religious obligation. One can feel touched, amused, put-upon and virtuous about it.

The duty of accepting offered votive food can have social consequences. A neighbour who bears a grudge against the giver's family may refuse to accept it, thereby depriving the intended dead beneficiary of spiritual benefits and also telling off the giver without so many words. A woman from another village who had married locally refused a bowl with votive soup, telling me later that she was offended because she had not been invited to the cooking party. In fact, nobody had been 'invited'; she knew this but wanted to point out that she felt left out in the women's circle. In 2015 this food ritual had diminished in favour of the option to give 'a quiet sum of money' directly to a poor family in lieu of cooking expensive votive soup that would go to relatives who didn't need it anyway.

Stories of help, even miracles, brought about by votive promises proliferate in Iran and make some critics doubt their own doubts. An educated young woman who had reservations about many religiously motivated customs, including vows, nevertheless once justified votive rituals by relativizing her own culture: 'I do it because I belong here, where it is an old custom. Had I been born in Italy I would go to Lourdes.' A young man from a mullah family reported a string of positive experiences. He had made a votive promise to Imam Reza for a good wife – and got one; a votive promise for a job brought a job; another healed his baby's diarrhoea. His brother's lame leg, though, stayed lame despite several vows, he said. This was God's Will.

The purported benefit of votive food for a dead saint or for dead relatives is theologically problematic for critics as well as some pious thinkers because a tenet of Islam holds that death is a border that cannot be crossed back and forth. The dead have to fend for themselves in the other world with the good and bad deeds they had collected while alive. Living relatives cannot help them. On the hither part of the divide, the living cannot expect favours from dead people either. There are no intercessors or mediators between God and a person, the faithful learn. How, then, is a votive-effect for a dead father in the other world to be explained, or a vow to a dead saint in exchange for help in the here and now? These are unanswered questions for those who ask them, even if preachers address them occasionally. They prompt proclamations of trust in God's inscrutable ways. As in other circumstances, 'God's Will' can be used as a kind of safety hatch, an escape preventing one's incomprehension from leading to doubt and confusion.

Summary

Most shrines of powerful saints in Boir Ahmad are graves of members of the patrilineage of the Prophet Muhammad. Some others are pre-Islamic sites said to emanate 'power' and 'blessing' from visible burials or from special trees and waters, likely places of ancient tree-and-water deities. People propitiate saints with visits and gifts and in exchange expect from them help in difficulties. Saints may be thought to appreciate, even need, the attention of the living and to be grateful for it or else to have to be persuaded to look at a visitor's problem. In vows and sacrifices, the cult of saints fuses with the cult of the dead generally. Pilgrimages to big, famous, faraway shrines have increased in the Islamic Republic. Old local shrines may be rebuilt and enlarged if verified, while those of undocumented 'saints' are razed by the government to discourage 'heathen' ritual elements. The cult of saints is popular among firm believers in the saints' powers as well as among doubters and critics who enjoy pilgrimage travels as a pleasant diversion or a hallowed tradition. Doubters may argue that saints and their relationships with clients are theologically problematic as it is not clear to what extent they operate independent of God and because in Islamic doctrine there is a strong border between the living and the dead. Deep-rooted pre-Islamic memories flicker here in the realm of lived religion, notions about a community of the living and the dead, about deities and their entourage and powers, about the needs of the dead and of divine beings, about tutelary qualities of the departed, and even some faint fear of ancestors.

Figure 5 Khungah, North Boir Ahmad, April 2006: Trees and a small brook (flowing through the wall), together with the location near Sasanian ruins, suggest a pre-Islamic heritage. Few such open-air pre-Islamic cult places have survived. Visitors burn candles in the wall's crevices and hang pieces of fabric on tree branches, 'tying' their wishes for the deity or saint believed to be there. The government demoted the 'Imamzadeh' (descendant of the Prophet Muhammad) to a 'picnic area' because it lacks a saint's burial.

Figure 6 Imamzadeh Mahmad, Central Boir Ahmad, May 2006. This small, ancient (Achaemenid) shrine surrounded by graves is being renovated. The government and pilgrims' votive gifts pay for repairs of authenticated Imamzadeh, that is, for shrines with graves of historically documented descendants of the Prophet.

5

The end of life

Death and its causes

According to a common-sense tenet in Boir Ahmad philosophy, human life is part of nature, predictably unfolding from birth to death like any other form of life. Time itself appears as an agent of ageing and decay.¹ Pious people assert that nature and life are God-willed and God-made, and it stands to reason that this includes the natural unfolding and limits of life. Yet, according to preachers and scriptures, God wills every single movement of everything. This assertion is hard to align with the experience of reliable regularities without which nobody could make a living: night follows every day, winter follows every summer; plants, animals, people grow and decline in reliable increments, time rolls on relentlessly. People who find it difficult to see an instantaneous act of God in each and every moment of these regularities routinely soften the theological conundrum with ejaculations such as 'God is great' and 'God wills it'.

Planning one's livelihood on the matrix of expectable conditions, from the movement of the stars and the four seasons to the reproduction of life, is not seen as a choice but a necessity. In discussions about such matters few people denied that God created everything, including cosmic regularities. Agnostic and atheistic arguments are options for talking about conditions in this world rather than about God the creator. A popular reasoning is that the regularities people count on for their livelihood show that God created this order to make human life possible.² In this homocentric theology, death has a logical place because without death the overcrowded earth would burst, as a local man said, trying to console himself when his father was dying. Ageing that ends in death thus is a natural process supporting the natural order and does not need further explanation: all people lose abilities and usefulness as they age and in the end finish their life (*omr tamum ikonen*).³ There is a straight line from the beginning to the end of life, and nobody ever has escaped death. Indeed, not being able to die when one's time obviously is up is called a hardship for the old and their caretakers and may be considered God's punishment (*muqāfāt*) of sins. These ideas are not treated as optional beliefs but as proven truth. Any kind of death other than from old age begs an explanation, though.

The high infant mortality in the past also had a ready explanation, based on the experience that like any other weak thing, the very young die quickly, be it lambs or birds or children; there was little one could do about it. Young children died when an illness swept through communities every spring (such as diarrhoea) or every few years (such as measles or whooping cough), 'hitting' many.[4] It happened so frequently that it was nearly normal (*normàl* is used), and mothers were told not to cry because their tears caused the dead children pain. Dead infants were buried quickly without a public mourning ritual. Only the fact that an epidemic killed one's own child and not the neighbour's was beyond human understanding and needed a Will-of-God assurance.

The untimely death of children who had survived infant-perils and of adults is not labelled 'normal'. It needs reflection because it goes against God's natural order that relies on adult people to work, to marry and take care of children who, in turn, are needed to carry life into the next generation. Such death is seen as a consequence of something extraordinary. The most popular explanation is personal failure, one's own lack of knowledge and judgement, or the failure of the person instrumental in the death (a suicide, for example, or a speeding driver causing a crash). Another is a lack of reason, such as in people ruining their health by overwork, or in lack of good sense when in-laws mistreat a young daughter-in-law and she kills herself. Personal failure is the first, quickest choice in explaining misfortunes, a choice that emphasizes agency and personal responsibility, with blame found on the human here-and-now level: the driver was going too fast when he hit a pedestrian and will have to pay blood money or go to jail. The Will of God, the glib, final cause of any death, is not a satisfactory explanation for individual cases. As an expression of resignation it is used even by critics of religion who scoff at it and by ardent realists and pragmatists. Although handy when one is stumped for a reasonable explanation for a happening, for most people the inscrutable Will is troubling when it challenges God's assumed benevolence. How can a generous God kill an innocent child?

If one asks such a question or asks 'Why? Why me? Why now?', one has to look for answers elsewhere. These are the most likely options:

Fate (*shans* and *qesmat*) is a basic, all-encompassing choice to explain untimely death, a safe choice like the Will of God because it cannot be disproven. Rarely, though, is it used synonymously with predestination. Rather, although God knows what will happen or wills a happening, 'fate' as a power may be handled as if it was following its own programme, against the purported benevolence of God. Being the supreme deity, God arguably ought to have the power to change a fate but won't – or can't – do so. Even people who are quick to use 'fate' (or God's Will) as an explanation for sad events rarely stop their search for meaning and for how to deal with the situation. 'We'll see what happens' and 'We'll see what our fate really is' sums up the attitude. Often 'fate' is paired with a social or economic judgement. People point out that sick children in poor rural communities have 'no luck' (*shans*) because they are born disadvantaged. This lack of chances is their 'fate' and creates the option to wonder about God's plans that include such obvious inequality and injustice.

Punishment (*muqāfāt*; see also Chapter 2). More specifically, an 'unnatural' death may be ascribed to lack of gratitude (*nashokri*, *nageruni*) towards God but also towards people. A habitually discontented person will attract this negative power. It was said, for example, about the father of a toddler who died of diarrhoea: with this loss the man was punished for his obsessive wish for a second wife that made him mistreat his first wife and angered the whole community. Similarly, an untimely death may be taken as God's punishment for an ancestor's wrongdoing, in the logic of 'it serves the man right to lose his son'.[5] This fits the popular understanding of the logic of retribution that knows no statute of limitations and allows for payback in any form that harms the accused, even the death of his child. This explanation for a death is generally considered to be antagonistic, though, given in anger. In the cases I witnessed it met with criticism based on empathy. Why, one such counterargument went, does the mother have to cry when it was her husband's or his grandfather's misdeeds that God punished her husband for with the boy's death? A local teacher, a champion for learning from mistakes, called this retribution psychologically unsound because to be of use, punishment had to follow the misdeed right away, not three generations later. He dismissed the retribution mode altogether. A mother of six children, talking about an old woman who had lost her mind over the death of all her children (from diphtheria), questioned God's mercy. Even if it had been a retribution for a misdeed of her husband's ancestors, a truly benevolent Almighty easily could have pardoned at least one of the children. No, she said, God had altogether nothing to do with it. Rather, the lack of healthcare in the area killed children. Ten years later, when better food, sanitation, inoculations and the new clinic in town had drastically lowered child mortality, she remembered the times when all these deaths had been called, 'God's Will'. God obviously has changed his mind, she said, as soon as people could take better care of their children.[6]

The opinion of this outspoken woman was less remarkable than that nobody present disagreed. It was a reasonable choice that made sense to the audience. Her argument fit the unspoken conviction that God gives people the ability to think and decide, and that this ability was mostly needed to navigate life. In this notion of an otiose deity, God had done the creation work in the distant past and now let people themselves figure out how to live, using their God-given brains.

When a thirteen-week-old infant died, people's comments pointed to several explanations that combined traditional and 'modern' choices.

> The baby's *grandfather*, a teacher, said, 'The boy was born only twelve months after the mother's first child. He was a *bacce polu* [born soon after another], and such babies always are small and weak because the mother is weak. Some women make *polu* and others don't – this is just the way it is.'
>
> The paternal *grandmother* said, 'The baby was doing well until a fever hit. He got better with my good medicine and slept well but next morning was feverish again and we took him to the clinic, and there he suddenly died.'
>
> The *mother* said, 'The baby was all right, just a bit cranky, had a slight cold. They [her in-laws; it reflects authority] gave him a local medicine (*dava mahalli*) but chills and fever got worse. When they took him to the doctor, he died.'
>
> The *father* said, 'The doctor said it was a bad bronchitis. It was too late. There was nothing he could do or wanted to do.'
>
> A *neighbour woman* said, 'The baby clearly was killed by a child-stone. He had a dark spot above the butt. For sure the pregnant mother had met a woman who had a *mohre bacce*.'
>
> The *neighbour's husband* said, 'He was a beautiful boy with big, round eyes. I know that the family did not take precautions – gossip, the evil eye! All dangerous.'
>
> And the baby's ten-year-old *cousin* said, 'They didn't take him to the doctor in time.'

Seven opinions, in agreement that the death was due to the family's (and maybe the doctor's) neglect. Of course God must have willed it, He wills everything – but the infant's caretakers nevertheless could have done a lot more to try to prevent the death.

Violence. Some explanations for the death of young people are self-evident, such as, for example, that of soldiers who must expect to be wounded or killed in battle.[7] Likewise, most motorbike accidents of young men are 'naturally' fatal. But even in such plain situations there is a grey zone: not all soldiers or motorists die. During the Iran–Iraq war, when the mullahs exhorted young men to go to the front promising them instant paradise if killed, a local fourteen-year-old left with the recruiters, going to his sure death as a mine sweeper. A resolute relative found this so unacceptable that he went after the boy and brought him back from the front, saying that as a mere child and an only son his place was with his family, not in paradise. He called this a matter of reason and common sense, and a pious elderly neighbour saw in it a sign of God's mercy.

Outbursts of violence are frequent, especially among men and against women, but rarely deadly. Local people rarely saw others in town as dangerous. Accidents aside, the violent deaths remembered in the village during the last fifty years were a chief shooting a local man 'over nothing', a manslaughter over water rights that shook people for years, and the accidental death of an outsider in a fight with a local man. However, in 2015 rumours about at least two women's deaths at the hands of male family members in nearby villages that were hushed up as suicides point to a dark side of domestic violence against women that is mostly ignored. The relative peace in town is in contrast to people's distrust of the outside world. Around the year 2000, for about a decade people told stories of children being abducted and killed for their kidneys and of occasional fatal corruption setups they saw on television. Later, a few drug deals turned deadly in the area. The fact that people took such stories to be possible and even likely is more important than establishing their veracity here. In 2015 a story went like this:

> In one of the bigger provincial towns a former khan's relative was known to do 'disgusting, bad things' with boys. People denounced him but the judge was in cahoots with the important man and did nothing. When a persistent claimant, the boys' paternal uncle, did not let go, the judge said he would order the arrest if the uncle paid him a bundle, whereupon the uncle borrowed a revolver from a policeman and shot the pederast.

Qossa is a type of misfortune taken to 'come' like a dangerous enemy to wreak havoc unless it is averted early. Some dreams portend this trouble, such as dreaming about a black bird croak or fly away, an uprooted tree, a black-dressed figure silently passing one's house, teeth falling out of a mouth, a sudden strong wind blowing embers around, a bleeding hand – such sightings in a dream warn of danger and death. Vigilance may not be enough to avoid the impending perils. To ward them off one's family or direct them towards a less valuable aim, such as a chicken, one may make a *rafe qossa*, a sacrifice. It may consist of alms to the poor or a promise of a gift to the shrine of a saint. If one ignored such warnings, one had to blame oneself when the catastrophe hit.[8]

The Evil Eye ('salt-eye', *tië shur; nazar*) is widely considered to be a dangerous power emanating from the eyes of some people. One can anticipate and guard against it by wearing an amulet or a blue bead, a piece of gold, a salt crystal or a wolf's tooth, and by being careful with praise, even silent praise. Praise and admiration are said to cause the power of the evil eye to strike, inadvertently, without the person's intention to cause harm. The first tractor in town was so much gawked at that it turned over, people said. The most attractive and most vulnerable people are, paradoxically, those on the lowest rungs of the social ladder: babies, young children and young women; they are 'weak'. Jealousy, envy or curses that elsewhere link the evil eye to morality are considered dangerous by themselves but rarely connected to the evil eye. People known to have the 'salt-eye' are neither named nor accused. Rather, the emphasis is on prevention: everybody has the power to guard against it by taking precautions.[9] A mother described what led to the death of her son after being 'hit' by the evil eye.

> I was on the migration back from the summer pastures with my four-year old son. On the way a local man who has the 'salt eye' met us and asked me if this was my son – nothing more. Passing through the next hamlet somebody said admiringly how round his little face was, and measured it with her hand without saying *mashallah*. Next day, when I took him to the bathhouse in town, there was a stranger, a woman who asked how old he was. And then she turned to her own boy and belittled him (*nofrinesh dā*): 'You runty midget, you don't grow at all' (*khordelu, hic rosht nikoni*).[10] That same day, my boy fell into a pool and died. He was *nazari*, the salt-eye had hit him three times.

The mother explained the obvious lack of precautionary protection against the evil eye with her lack of resources while she had been in the faraway outposts all summer. For one of the wise women in Sisakht this explanation fit a pattern: knowledge alone does not substitute for action, she said at a similar case of omission. 'The mothers are careless,' she said. 'We all are careless. We think God will help us. God is great, we say!'

Powers in things and people are said to emanate from certain plants, minerals and some people. Occasionally burning wild rue in the house to keep everybody safe from jinn and other invisible dangers was any careful woman's routine domestic ritual. It has lost popularity because people 'have other worries now', as a neighbour woman said, and because 'modern kitchens and bathrooms and the health clinic are better than the wild rue', as her mother said. Women's traditional jewellery was mostly apotropaic. It consisted of iron bangles against jinn and a necklace of beads (of minerals, metals, bone, ceramic, shells, semi-precious stones such as amber and agate), said to protect the wearer and ward off ill effects of other people's powerful stones. The 'child bead' (*mohre bacce*) and gold jewellery were said to be the most dangerous for infants. The pragmatists say that fear of these powers, too, has diminished as people felt better protected by the health clinic.

Furthermore, some features in the town's vicinity are said to carry or exude danger. Rocks falling off a certain cliff may crush a passer-by; water may carry children away when they slip in the wet mud at the river. A nearby precipice was called 'blood-rock' after the second person, a boy, had fallen from it to his death.[11] The southern rim of the plateau on which the town lies has the reputation of being vaguely dangerous and one should not go there alone.[12] It used to take and still needs good thinking, caution and watching one's steps and one's children to avoid and avert dangers. The curse, *marg*! (death, as in 'death on your head', *marg bar serret*, said to a naughty child, for example), is relevant, too, not so much because it actually 'works' but because it is so ubiquitous in Iran. It is used in ejaculations of impatience, vexation and anger about mishaps and in the battle cry of the Islamic Revolution wishing death to America and Israel.[13]

Jinn. The word 'jinn' is said rarely because of the fear that it might summon them. Instead, jinn are referred to as 'those' (*ingelo*) or 'those who are better than we are'. Of all lurking dangers, those posed by jinn, *ghul* and *div* (degraded pre-Islamic divinities mentioned in the Quran) were considered to be the most ubiquitous.[14] Over the years people mentioned them less but they still are in the cultural inventory. Jinn could be expected especially in certain trees, around water places, stored water bags and water faucets; in the bathhouse, around abandoned buildings, barns and outhouses and in the 'wilderness'. They were said to make women ill who had just given birth, and to try to steal, switch or kill infants. Invisible but able to assume many forms, unfriendly, mischievous if not malevolent by nature, jinn could sicken anybody who was careless, and could kill a person who told of encounters with them. People protected themselves when alone outside the village by saying God's name, *bismillah*,[15] by carrying a lantern in the dark and by making noise, especially with metal; women used to wear tinkling iron bangles and hung little jingle-toys on cradles. In a beloved story, a Lur gets the better of 'them':

> A man was walking from here to there, alone, with a backpack (*torba*) that had an iron drop-spindle and a copper pot in it. In a lonely spot he came upon some strangers dancing and singing among the trees. He knew they were jinn but it was too late to avoid them. They invited him to dance with them, singing: 'Mr Salomon,

put your backpack down and hop with us' (*Ka Selemun, torbeta bele verigel, vartelegun*). Quick of wit and tongue, he answered, 'Without the backpack I am afraid, and so I'll dance with the backpack' (*bi torba itarsom, ba torba iraksom*). He started to hop around, the metal stuff in the bag was clanging and banging, and the jinn quickly disappeared. Had they stayed they would have killed him.

A special jinn spirit is the *homzad*, a person's double, born at the same time.[16] It is a pre-Islamic concept locally known but mentioned rarely: good ones are Muslims, bad ones are heathen; all are jealous by nature, quick to anger and to 'hit' the human twin, child and adult alike, resulting in sickness and even death. It is one of God's creations whose purpose and use are declared to be beyond human understanding.

Div, the second major group of malevolent beings, are thought to exist in many shapes, from wind clouds to *ghoul*-monsters in caves, and to cause mishaps from stealing women in high-mountain outposts to sitting on the chest of a sleeper, causing nightmares.[17] Created by God, they have a place in the world order, even if they are a dangerous nuisance for people. Stories of unhappy encounters between *div* (or jinn) and people abound, resulting in accidents such as a deadly fall from a flat roof top; the sudden illness and death of a woman after washing clothes at a brook alone by herself; the perilous fall of a limber boy looking for a lost goat in the rocks; and the befuddled mind of a shepherd after a nap in the shade of an abandoned old mill. In the past a *div* in the shape of an ibex was said to lure hunters astray. Lately, *div* explanations have become rare, though. New, spacious houses, electric light, indoor plumbing, washing machines, the noise of many people, cars, television and radios – the 'modern way of life', as people say, has driven *div*, jinn and fairies far into the wilderness.[18]

Sheitun (satan; devils) are mentioned in the Quran as beings different from jinn and demons, but in everyday speech they have nearly merged with them or even displaced them altogether. '*Sheitunal* are all around us,' said a woman in 2015 who, ten years earlier, had said the same about jinn. Preachers reportedly also talk only about 'devils' now. Jinn-devils are blamed for suicides. They deceive sad people, especially women who are taken to lack stamina anyway, into believing that death would mean peace and comfort for them. One has to be aware of their malevolent intent.

This is an important point: most dangerous powers and beings that may be expected to influence people's health and well-being profoundly are knowable and known and therefore are taken to be manageable with human intelligence and diligence. They cannot be killed but competent people learn how to guard against them.

The dead body

Death itself simply is the end of life, a straightforward, empirically established process with a final point when the life-soul (*jun, nafas*) leaves the body. The closest to a personification of death is the Angel Ezrael, who is said to take or catch the *jun* as it leaves the body and to carry it 'away'. But people also talk about this point as a flying away, visualizing the soul as a bird leaving with no reunion possible. *Raft ke raft*, that is, he or she left for good is a telling expression for death: the person disappeared. Until the 1950s engravings of horses without riders on some gravestones visually expressed the leaving motif.[19] A grieving woman reported:

> My mother was healthy and strong, much better than I am. She visited me often. Nothing was wrong with her, nothing at all. One day she came, sat down, the children were around, we talked a little, and suddenly she got up as if she were in a hurry, and before our eyes she fluttered her arms and flew away, flew like a bird with wings, just took off, flew away. I don't know if it was a misfortune (*qossa*) or her fate (*qesmat*). I was so sad that I got very ill.

There is consensus that a dying person ought not to be left alone – it is 'not good', people say, and I read in their bedside care and mourning behaviour deep emotions about the dying person, an unease with being reminded that nobody will escape dying, and a faint fear of the dead body.[20] Death always is announced by the women in the house with loud wailing as soon as (and sometimes, embarrassingly, sooner than) it happens.[21] This simple, brief ritual is a public notification of death, an expression of grief, and a signal to the dead person to 'go away', as a ten-year-old girl explained, supported by her grandfather. What comes next is both, a well-rehearsed routine performance of burial and mourning rituals with little variation and few choices for their performance, and a jumble of widely differing death traditions.

The lifeless body is removed from the house as quickly as possible, preferably straight to the washhouse for the dead, and from there to the grave.[22] Orthodox believers declare that the questioning angel will not do his job unless the body had a ritual ablution (*ghosl*) and is buried, and that unburied bodies have no hope for an afterlife, that they cease to exist. But the fact that the many fallen soldiers who 'rotted away' on the battlefields were declared to go directly to paradise without burial and washing shaded these assertions with doubt. Another option is to think that these customs will make the dead realize that they no longer belong to their former house. The separation is difficult for them. For the three 'nights of estrangement' (*shou gharibak*) after a death people used to keep a light on the new grave, and some still do so or have a candle engraved on the grave cover. At home, halva or a dinner ought to be cooked and given away to seven houses so that, in the words of an aunt of a just-buried man, 'In the other world where he is a stranger, he will have something to offer to his visitors.' Or else one can assume that while the soul of the dead person stays around for three days, the relatives will provide dinner to people in exchange for *fateha* prayers that will benefit the dead person in some vague way.[23]

There are no further rituals in the house. The dead's place is the graveyard where they will be visited by relatives.[24] The few anecdotes about sightings of dead people focus on the idea of dislocation or confusion on the part of the dead. Their appearance may startle but won't cause fear or panic. Thus, for example, without much ado a recently dead person may be reported as lingering around the building where bodies are washed or as walking with the mourners to the graveyard, signs that it takes the dead a while to get used to being dead. While the body is prepared for burial, brothers or other male relatives are digging the grave, oriented south-west to Mecca. This labour is a memorial duty of love given the hard, rocky soil. The more the dead person was liked, the bigger, deeper, safer from heat, cold and animals and thus more comfortable the grave will be. The shrouded corpse is put into the grave and the space is filled with stones and a layer of dirt or, recently, covered with a slab of cement.[25] New fancy covers and headstones have the dead person's name, images of flowers and Quran verses inscribed on it. Crying and women's loud wailing comment on loss and sorrow; they also may be taken as lightening the mourners' heavy hearts (the *del*, that is, the seat of emotions) and as assuring the dead person of continuing remembrance and care. 'A dead person nobody cries for any more is only a corpse,' said a man walking through the old, abandoned cemetery.

Some graveyard scenes, mortuary customs and occasional remarks and quiet jokes express unease about the dead.[26] They point to the assumption of a continuation of a kind of consciousness or of feelings in the buried body, and of the grave as a *domus aeterna*, the eternal home. Women often brought up their fear of bugs and worms eating the body in the grave, including their own, eventually. Until about a generation ago little girls playfully fed bugs with breadcrumbs, chanting a bargaining-ditty: 'Bugs, I feed you now so that you won't eat my bones later.'[27] People feel the pain and indignity of such disintegration, they say. Trying to banish or at least ameliorate the bad smell of decay that is expected to bother the dead, mourners may sprinkle perfume on the shroud and the grave, put fragrant plants on the grave when visiting and, in the summer, pieces of ice. These residues of embalming rituals are meant to prevent or at least slow down the body's corrupting degradation which one may see as a devilish fight against beauty and goodness. Such acts, too, are said to help the dead – not necessarily to a better position in the afterlife but to a better position right in their 'house'. One of the worst curses was a threat to desecrate somebody's grave-home by defecating on it or by digging up and burning the body, both taken to be grievously harmful for the dead person. A local Mullah Nasreddin story pokes fun at this: the Mullah lets himself be buried alive intent on sticking an iron spit into his moneylender's butt who, enraged by the Mullah's financial escape by death, tries to defecate on the grave in a gesture of utter contempt. (The rest of the joke usually disappears in stifled laughter.) An exposed or burned body may be said to have no afterlife and no resurrection on the Day of Judgement, but preventing such calamity is just one, extreme, option of duties the living have towards the dead.

Ancient images of the hardships of death appear most clearly in some mourning songs where the dead person laments the grave conditions. A depressing picture emerges: the soul has left and is 'somewhere', while the person/body has to be convinced that it is dead and now at home in the grave. This grave-home is described as uncomfortably narrow, dark, cold and lonesome, with the smelly body hungry and feeling abandoned. A mourning song goes, 'I am afraid snow will fall, road after road will close, nobody can see the other' (Mann 1910: 66). A local man, much troubled by his daughter's mistreatment by her husband, found consolation in a dream, seeing the grave of a recently buried, similarly violent man slowly getting smaller, crushing the body. This was a fitting punishment for bad husbands, he said. A mourning song describes it: 'My grave is narrow, for no brother dug it. The mourning for me is cold, for no sister wailed' (Amanolahi 1986: 100). People remember that until the 1950s in this town (and much longer elsewhere in Boir Ahmad), a dead man's sisters, the saddest of all mourners, danced at their brother's grave site. In 1966, on the first day of the Muharram mourning rituals in Sisakht, a group of pre-adolescent girls arranged themselves in a circle, put arms around each other's shoulders and slowly and rhythmically moved sideways and front-back with small steps, bowing after every forward move, to the beat of their own singing. (The choreography was quite different from the only other dances, at weddings.) By the time of the Revolution this dancing had stopped.[28]

Mourners say that they can lighten the dead's pains also by giving alms in their names. Of the four traditional occasions for such offerings (three days after death, Thursday afternoons (*shou jom'e*), the week before the New Year, the first day of the first winter after death), the Thursday offering is the most popular now. Adherents of government Islam see in it a gesture of respect for the dead. Another option to account for the popularity is to think that the dead come back on the afternoon before Friday to see how their families are doing, and will be sad if no visitor is at the grave. Yet another suggests that food offered at graves and alms given to the poor feed the dead or increase the dead's merits. A designated son must give food or alms from his own larder to the poor to benefit his parents. A woman in town and an elderly man respectively told stories that count as proof of the truth of this duty.

> The woman said, 'My aunt got a gift of a chicken from her sister Ana and gave it away as a Friday-offer for her husband's dead mother. That night in a dream my aunt saw her dead mother-in-law complain about not having received anything because Ana's own mother-in-law had taken the offered chicken: Originally it had come from her son, Ana's husband, and therefore it did not belong to Ana's sister but to her, Ana's mother-in-law, and why hadn't her son thought of this?'

This story rests on the tradition (supported by sharia law) that gifts to a woman automatically belong to her husband, and on the patrilineal bias which obliges a son to 'feed' his parents. In practice this means that he will provide the wherewithal and his wife will do the actual work. An old man said:

> My cousin Kerim once travelled with others. Thursday evening they stayed near a graveyard. At night Kerim saw a girl come out of a grave. She went to the next grave and said, 'Give me some bread, my people didn't come today. Tomorrow they will pass by here and then I'll give something back to you.' She got bread and went back into her grave. The next day the caravan moved on but Kerim was curious and stayed. Indeed, another group came, stopped, pitched tents, slaughtered an animal and gave Kerim a chunk of meat as a belated *shou jom'e* offer. Kerim ate it, and at night he saw the girl come out of her grave with just that piece of meat in her hand, which she put inside the other grave.

Doubters and critics have the option of dismissing such 'proofs' for lack of sound reasoning and progressive thinking. However, the mourning rituals themselves are part of the culture people identify with and few will refuse outright to participate in them.

The Islamic Republic's leaders have elevated mourning to the most important religious ritual, people say. Throughout the year, government agencies urge participation in a great variety of mourning rituals for religious and other dignitaries.[29] There is a widespread grumbling that to be a good Muslim now means to 'cry all the time' for dead people one never had heard of.[30]

All these activities are declared to be 'good' for the dead, to make them comfortable, restful (*rāhat*). Every day for many weeks after her favourite sister was buried, a local woman spent hours at the grave despite her workload at home, to ease her own heart and that of the dead sister, she said. And the mother of a young man who had died suddenly in a car crash made it a habit to visit his grave every day for months 'to keep him company and to talk to him'.[31] The salient factor in all this is to remember the dead. As long as people visit graves, talk about the dead relatives, feed them and give alms in their names, the dead are not quite gone, people say. Pious assertions of their paradisiacal future may console some but this choice elicits little enthusiasm. The happy but shaky post-mortem conditions promised by the mullahs cannot quite balance the certain perils of the dead fading out of the livings' memories. While I was walking with a friend past an abandoned small graveyard in town, she paused and murmured a quick prayer, and then said that nobody remembered the people buried there, that 'the poor things got lost' (*fakiral gom ābein*). While nobody described 'being forgotten' explicitly as being lost in the dark, dank, sad existence of shades in the underworld, many mourners' anxious mood fits this ancient notion. Within strictly Islamic teachings people may see an unsettling inconsistency: the mullahs stress the divide between the living and the dead yet encourage a cult of the dead that condones the very mourning rituals that people perform obviously in the belief that they are bridging this divide. Resentment of the official elaboration of the cult of the dead, of having to cry for people one does not know, is an option doubters take who question and dismiss rituals that do not have a demonstrable benefit. A tired woman complained about the growing numbers of long mourning sessions because the local, reality-based doubts about life after death, as well as the Islamic separation of the dead and the living, were negated in the new elaborate mourning customs which she called 'Islamic superstition': 'We are in the cemetery all the time, crying, wailing. It makes us so sad, and it is of no use to the dead. The dead are gone, past, finished. Whatever we do, the dead don't benefit. Visiting graves shows respect for them to their relatives. That is all.'

Summary

Death in old age is taken by everybody as a consequence of time and nature, both God-created and God-willed, with the choice of emphasizing one or the other aspect. Various sacrifice-based, apotropaic rituals may be performed with the stated aim to ward off calamities, but ageing ending in death is unavoidable, part of the natural cycle of all life. Premature death, though, is not natural and needs explanations beyond God's Will. Of these, human agency in the form of taking responsibility for applying one's knowledge of life-preserving options is the single most important factor. People also may choose from several semi-independent dangerous powers to explain perils, and are quick to detect warning signs such as in dreams. Fate and God's Will answer final-cause questions. Despite orthodox theologians' insistence on the firm divide between the living and the dead, mourning and memorial rituals combining prayer, alms, food offerings and grave visitations are meant to keep memories of the dead alive and to help them in their graves and in the other world. All reflect popular opinions about what may happen to a body, a person and/or a soul after death, and fall into the category of 'belief' because nobody can verify them. Elaborate and frequent mourning sessions encouraged and arranged by the Islamic government meet resistance by those who see them as negating the assumption of the strict division between the living and the dead, by those who resent exertions that benefit dead people the mourners do not know or care about, and by those who resent the many interruptions of daily routines for rituals that make them sad.

Figure 7 Sisakht, October 1994. Lights on some graves in the cemetery, as here on a woman's grave, are meant to help the dead in their dark 'house' and to remind visitors to pray for them.

Figure 8 Sisakht, August 1997. Women are crying around the grave of a prominent local woman forty days after her death. The children eat most of the sweets and fruits offered on the grave.

6

Beyond the grave[1]

What happens to the soul

The most widely propagated belief-schema regarding eschatology, and the one closest to Shia doctrine, features the Angel of Death who gets the order – from God – to grab the soul sometime between a person's death and interment. The fact that the Angel has to be everywhere, given that people die all over the world, elicits the standard 'God's Will' comment on the inexplicable. Allotted Time (*ajal*) and this angel always are in synchrony. Clearly, Ezrael is God's specialist for taking souls away. People tell well-worn stories and anecdotes about how this order perplexes him at times:

> When a man learned in a dream that his unexpected death was near, he got on a boat and sailed away to escape. In the middle of the ocean Ezrael appeared, surprised at finding him hale and well so far from home, when suddenly a scorpion fell out of the sail and stung and killed the man.

In a joke the Angel of Death is sent to fetch a certain young, beautiful woman. He bashfully averts his eyes so as not to get impure feelings looking at her and by mistake grabs her old, wrinkled grandmother, whereupon he gets 'a heap of curses' in the 'Other World' (*u dunyā*), including 'Death on your head!'[2]

There are stories of people who claim to see the Angel just before they die. They try to plead with him or shoo him away or even threaten to shoot him but nobody can discourage him. The linking of death with the snatching of one's life-soul appeals even to doubters who see Ezrael as a strong metaphor for a natural process that eliminates people.

Until about a generation ago, what happens after death people saw as a well-ordered, simple unfolding of events rooted in their religion, with a few choices in details and in names of heavenly beings. In 1970 a young teacher, making sure I got the basics of Islamic afterlife right, that is, as he and others understood them, dictated this to me:

Dead people who are not buried will be ignored by Ajal [The narrator merges Allotted Time and the Angel of Death]; they will not get their sins and merits counted, and will not exist in the other world at all. After the burial, Ajal comes to the grave and asks the dead person about religion and about his life [Allotted Time here merges with the Questioning Angel]. The good and bad deeds are all written down. The dead with too many sins will go to a hot desert – like the Sahara in Africa. Suicides go straight to hell. A good person goes to heaven (*asamun*, sky), a very nice place. All stay there until the Day of Judgement.[3]

The stages are clear: a soul leaves or is taken away at a person's death; the body is transferred to its new home, the grave; the soul (or the body) is questioned and judged; merits and sins are weighed, and then the soul goes either to a good or a bad place or hell until the Last Day (*ākherāt*). At that time a final decision will be made (by God or the Mahdi or angels – it is not important who will decide) about the soul's – or resurrected people's – next or eternal fate. The final judgement one can see as an awe-inspiring event one has to plan for while alive, an event every bad person ought to fear, but local people also may choose to be rather unconcerned: no good person will suffer, so why should I worry? And in any case it is so far ahead that one can easily dismiss it. It is not an urgent concern. When a woman came upon a few neighbours talking about the Day of Judgement with me, she joke-scolded us: 'By your souls, do you have nothing better to do?'

With the increase in theological information in the Islamic Republic, what happens after the Angel took the soul became muddled enough to make people form varied opinions. According to Islamic tenets, the next stage in the business of being dead is that two scribe angels (Nakir and Munkar) come to the grave to establish the buried person/body/soul's knowledge of Islam. Locally this may be taken as a purely formal questioning regarding important Islamic names and events. It also may be fused with a judgement on the dead person's morality, a weighing of sins and merits that these angels (or whoever else) had painstakingly recorded throughout the person's adult life to forestall likely denials of bad behaviour and fraudulent claims of good deeds. But things don't end here. Each step is elaborated in sermons, books and stories people hear, complicating possibilities of what might happen after death.

Outsiders or people well versed in the government religion can argue that obviously the tribal rustics do not know the Muslim catechism as well as they should, but this is not the issue here. Rather, in stories and jokes people make it clear that such formalistic procedures don't address people's moral qualities, their standing in the community and the discharging of their duties as parents, neighbours, farmers or in any other capacity – yet these are the important criteria before God.⁴ The disregard for the bureaucratic aspects (the term, *monji* (secretary) for these angels came up several times) might well be a reason for the many contradictory, vague and idiosyncratic options people developed for envisioning the afterlife. A woman uncommonly interested in theological matters expressed the common-sense ethics and morality by which local people readily judge their own and their neighbours' conduct:

> After the breath of a dying person is gone, the *jun* or *ruh* stays around until the body is buried. Then her Excellency Fatemeh – for a dead woman; or the twelfth Imam – for a dead man, enters the grave, lifts up the body's head and asks, 'Why did you say such and such with your mouth?' The dead person says, 'I didn't say this,' and the Excellency says, 'Yes, you did, here it is written. Why did you listen with your ears to what you shouldn't have heard?' The body says, 'I didn't listen,' and the Excellency says, 'Yes, you did, here it is written. Why did you look at such and such with your eyes?' And when the body says, 'I have not seen anything,' the Excellency says, 'Yes, you have, here it is written.' This goes on until the balance between merits and sins is clear. Those who have enough merits next will have to pass a narrow bridge and then become birds and fly to paradise. We are told that it is very pleasant there but nobody knows, really.

People insist that the social sins of gossip, badmouthing others, ogling, envy, competition (committed by ear, mouth and eyes), that is, the sins against people, weigh heavier than sins against God such as sloppy prayer and neglect of fasting. The most important ethical features emerge as those supporting the community and interpersonal relationships. There also is a half-intended joke in the speaker's assumption that a dead Lur – nay, any dead Persian, she said – will lie during such questioning: Who wants to incriminate oneself? 'They absolutely have to have it in writing!' she said.

The questioning in the grave is meant to weed out the ignorant and the deniers (*kāfar*, heathen), sending them to hell or 'somewhere bad, out of the way', as people say. The approved souls (or personalities or bodies) still have to cross the narrow bridge Sira'at, where their good deeds (or an angel or a guardian angel or a beautiful woman-angel – obvious descendants of the Zoroastrian *daena*) will guide them safely, while those with a great burden of sins will disappear or fall into the abyss of *jehenna* (hell), where eventually they will burn and thus possibly cannot even be resurrected on the Day of Judgement.⁵ The Platonic reckoning is quite clear, although when exactly it will happen is not clear and also not really important. More important (and just as unclear) is what happens next to the souls who crossed the bridge: they may enter heaven or re-enter the paradise Adam had lost (*behesht* is used for either in this context) or at least arrive at the door to this eternal garden place, to which those who died defending Islam will have a key, while others might be questioned some more there or may even be turned away, except young children and women who died in childbirth – they will walk straight in; they may have to go back into the grave to wait there for the trumpets of the Last Day while occasionally glimpsing heaven/paradise so as not to get discouraged;[6] or they may wander around somewhere until summoned for the final reckoning, when all the dead will leave their graves and a new world order will be created. Meanwhile, remembrance, prayers and food rituals might – just might – be of help for the dead. People who like to argue theology say that the dead in paradise do not need to be remembered or prayed for, they have arrived; the ones in hell are beyond help; the only needy ones are those who just died and are in the grave or else are milling about in a kind of spiritual no-man's space.[7] The distribution of votive food (*nazr*) for dead relatives is said to add to the dead's merits on the scales of justice or else to still their hunger – a person's last meal before death is called, 'travel-food' (*tusha*). The irony in the fact that good, well-liked, deeply mourned people get a lot more post-mortem attention, unnecessarily so, than people with a bad reputation who would need this help urgently, inspires mild jokes.

These, by and large, are the concepts local people choose from to construct the Islamic afterlife sequence. However, parallel to them run other ideas that inspire options for envisioning what will come next.

One option evokes *denial* of afterlife: life is in a body and ends with the body. A dead person is buried in the earth, the body disappears, and this is the end. All else is talk and hearsay, of use to the mourners, not the body. Arguing about what might come next is arguing about nothing. When challenged, one such realist said that what made him a Muslim was how he lived his life, not how much he repeated what others said about being dead. In the past, women used this 'end is end' argument to underscore how tired they were: 'Life and troubles end – that's all.' This sombre thought is based on common-sense realism based on observations, a de-mythologized attitude towards life, any life. It is an appealing enough choice to come up in discussions, especially in talks among women in times of crises. God wants it that way, they say, and therefore people cannot question it. An elderly woman who often waxed philosophical commented on the unceremonious bulldozing of graves and bones in an old cemetery in town:

> These were our relatives – all gone, forgotten. But they also no longer are in the dark pit, and this is good. I am afraid to walk into a dark room – and a grave is much darker! All other living things stay right where they die. I wish I could

have this, be dead somewhere on the ground, in a field, in the grass, in sunlight. So what, if a hungry wolf eats my body? My body would be good for something and I wouldn't feel it anyway, I don't think.[8]

For people like her, burial and decay are difficult, unpleasant thoughts, as if a dead body still could sense the indignity of slow disintegration. Only bones have lost all human qualities.

Related to outright denial is the idea of death as a *disappearance*. The aforementioned image of death as a going-away or a flying-away of the life-soul (*jun*) does not imply a destination; it implies leaving without expectation of ever meeting again. A mourner may visit the grave – the body, that is, and whatever of its personality is left with it – but these meetings, too, will peter out until even the memory of the dead relative is gone. Mourning rituals reflecting such notions are popular. Metaphors of death in songs and in stories, such as getting lost in the snow, disappearing over the mountain pass, riding away on a wind-colt (an image of death as a demon), flying away as a bird, all point to being unreachable forever. This strong image of leaving for good may be a vestige of the Old Iranian Land of the Dead, the Far Place, the strange country of no return.[9] It is quite different from the notion of the dark, tight, uncomfortable graves as 'houses' (*hune*) where the dead dwell, vaguely conscious and with feelings, and dependent for small comforts on the livings' memorial rituals.

Less radical is an *agnostic* stance: we (humans) do not know; the afterlife is beyond human experience, reasoning and understanding. Nobody has come back from beyond to give us a reliable account. Whatever we hear is just that, hearsay. Only God knows. This notion is widespread in Iran and cannot be reduced to catechetical ignorance in the rural hinterland. People hear differing opinions from religious authorities and know that the theologians are debating these issues. Locally, they adopt a wait-and-see attitude and feel free to envision their own afterlife with ideas based on 'traditions' that reach far back into antiquity. By and large, the images women describe are more varied and pessimistic than those men describe.[10] Men tend to take a shoulder-shrug attitude, saying, 'I lead as good a moral life as I can here, and after I am dead may God do with me what He wants.'

Loneliness, furthermore, is mentioned as a fearsome condition after death. The dead have nobody to talk to. For pre-literate people living in pre-electronic communities that rely on personal contact for social interaction and news, this means bitter isolation. The customary, near-obligatory Thursday-afternoon walks to the cemetery (mostly by women) in Iran are billed as visiting the dead. Relatives will address their relatives there, quietly. The woman who visited her favourite sister's grave daily said she told her everything that happened at home to keep her up to date in her grave, and even asked the dead sister questions which the sister often answered.[11] To think of the dead as still having senses, however faint and impermanent, is a comforting as well as a fearsome option. It is also behind the popular image of the dead attending their own funerals as mourners, walking along to the cemetery until they bump into something without feeling it. This makes them realize the loss of their life-soul and now they will agree to go into their graves. The saints' efficacy at their tombs, too, rests on this belief of the continuation of a personal power that stays around. The theme on which these aspects of the cult of the dead rests is death-as-loneliness, captured in the metaphor of snow as silently, coldly isolating everybody.

An entirely different option to imagine the other world is to expect a *parallel world*. Especially women talk about their fear to find out that the conditions of life will carry over into the other world (*u dunyā*). People there will work as hard as here in this world (*i dunyā*); whoever had a good life here will have it there, too. Bullies will oppress weaklings, beauties will disturb men, and men will watch their wives; a king will be a king, a beggar will beg, and anybody dying in the city will have an entertaining city life there. Injustices of this world will continue in the next. Not once in the hundreds of mourning songs I analysed is social justice mentioned in connection with the afterlife. A literate, well-read and pious elderly man in town said that one should think of death as a door: inside is life and the same life is outside, just a step away. For him and others like him, the horizontal death travel is based on a 'not very disruptive nature of death' (Graf 2004: 33), in contrast to the standard Platonic/Islamic vertical post-mortem travel up to paradise or down to hell, depending on one's moral weight.

In a dream interpretation a woman elaborated the possibilities:

When I was young I thought that talk about the other world was crazy. A body in the grave is eaten by worms, that's all. But then I had a dream. I saw my dead Nana sitting at the fire of her youngest son, my uncle, cooking rice for forty guests. I asked her what it was like where she was living now. She said, 'It is a stony place (*kokolabarde*), and I am a midwife there, and today I was allowed to come here and help out with the rice.' So, how could I have seen this in the dream if it was not so? How could I have known that Nana works there as a midwife, and that the other world is a rocky hill, if Nana had not told me in the dream? Now I know that the other world exists.[12]

In yet another option, *this world* is the model for the other world, but better, without pain, strife and stress. Unlike in this world, everybody there has a job (*shoql*), nobody is idle, nobody is exhausted; people go after their business in peace and everybody is busy but comfortable (*rāhat*).¹³ Mourning songs allude to green pastures, to herds of animals, pleasant hilltops, beautiful vistas. People claim to see this world in dreams. A hard-working woman in a pasture camp, looking down over hills and trees, said that she would not mind dying if she could be sure that the next life would be like this place but with more sleep and less fatigue for her. A local student of psychology explained such delights as wishful thinking. However, it is a pattern, an option, not an idiosyncratic image. In 2002, when a well-to-do local businessman returned from a family vacation in Germany, he joked that now he understood why so many people in Europe did not believe in heaven: right here on earth they enjoy the nature, order, comfort, cleanliness and courtesy that in Iran people have to project onto paradise.

Paradise and the bad place

The terms for paradise, angels, houris, hell and devil(s) are used rarely in everyday speech. *Behesht* (heaven/paradise) is a tumble of possibilities: it is a garden where God has His throne, where the angels are at home and where good Muslims either fly to soon after death or get to eventually to have a good life – forever or else until the Last Day when the *mahdi* (messiah) summons everybody who ever was alive, and when yet another reckoning will determine who stays in, or goes to, paradise, which, however, also could be the promised world to come after the messiah has 'put everything right' but is so far off in the future, and so nebulous, that it is not much help for those alive right now, except that in any case it is a pleasant place because otherwise why should one want to go there? This hodgepodge sentence approximates the matter as people express it. They believe in *behesht*, they say, because they are Muslims and their religion demands it. It is an obligation. In the local version of the 'Greek utopian tradition' (Bremmer 2004: 167), it is presumably a comfortable place, but nobody has been back, and the dead relatives people see in their dreams won't tell much.

In a popular image, paradise merges with the Garden of Eden and is synonymous with carefree, pain-free, leisurely life surrounded by the lush beauty of a *hortus amoenus*, a lovely garden.¹⁴ There is no work envisioned in this paradise, no hunger or thirst, no animosity, no bad words, no violence, no fear. In other words, life's hardships of the tribal people are absent, and this is attractive. As to the lack of work, however, a young local physician said that sitting around in a garden looking at trees is what his grandfather did every day, but it would drive him crazy with boredom and was not an appealing idea for the afterlife. Everybody in paradise furthermore will be young ('fourteen' appears as the ideal age of beauty, health and sexuality) and frisky. For women, this tends to stretch credibility. They declare the apparent absence of their children 'there' to be disturbing and the presence of paradisiacal virgins (*houris*) to be unimportant because in paradise everybody is young and pretty – so what is the deal? But their jokes are rather bitter. The *houris* of the scriptures obviously are made for men, they say, and as earthly women can't compete with *houris*' attractiveness, they will be ignored by men in paradise, no matter what preachers say. When a woman complained about her lazy husband, a neighbour told her, tongue in cheek, to be glad to have him now because in paradise all husbands will be 'busy only with the *houris*'. And to everybody's amusement an overworked mother of several children said that in paradise women have no husbands and thus nothing to do and finally can eat and sleep.[15] People committed to formal government Islam dismiss such thoughts as frivolous and insist that paradise is pleasant for everybody but are careful with descriptions beyond a garden-like, carefree afterlife existence.

Hell (*jehenna*), too, looks different to different people, but all believers declare it to be a 'bad place', with heat, thirst, sadness and torments by the devils. Some women wax poetic about gruesome and eternal punishments of women's misbehaviour such as disobedience, gossip, neglect of duties, laziness. For example, the *jun-ruh* of a 'bad' woman who could not pass the bridge is pushed into the fire but then becomes a body again, goes back into the fire, becomes a body again and so on, or else gets born and dies seven times every day. Such ideas say much about a woman's burden of life. However, these notions are tempered with doubt, as in the words of a middle-aged, well-off, pious woman, in 2015: 'Maybe our religion says all this to make people afraid of doing bad things, and that really there is no fire. We do not know.'

What happens to hell after the Day of Judgement is not settled either and leaves several choices: it may go on forever, which does not make sense if the bad people are burned to non-existence. It also may disappear forever after the Last Day. Furthermore, the inmates of hell and heaven may have the option to come back to life in the new world for a second chance, which the hell people will be glad to take, but why should the people in paradise want it? Over the last generations the concept of hell has lost popularity and is evoked mostly in exceptional anger moments.[16] 'Thinking about paradise is pleasant although we do not know if it exists,' said a young, religiously well-educated and devout local engineer; 'Hell is not pleasant and just as unprovable, so why bother to think about it? Nobody knows what it is except God the merciful Almighty.'[17] Not only doubters and critics of the government religion but also conventionally pious people choose caution when fundamentalist, Party-of-God adherents push ideas that for the local sober realists are fanciful to the point of being unbelievable, beyond their experiences or 'against science'.

Sins and merits, rewards and punishment (see also Chapter 2)

Details of pleasures and pains in the 'Other World' aside, believers are certain that what bodes well for the afterlife are a person's surplus of good deeds and merits at the end of life and a minimum of sins. Innocence (*bi-gonā*, without sin) means not so much an absence of sins against God such as neglecting prayers or fasting – these the generous and merciful God will forgive – than of sins against people. The word 'sin' (*gonā*) is popular in vernacular use and almost exclusively used in this sense. As umbrella it covers all the daily unkind words and actions, the 'thousand lies and swindles' one accumulates over a lifetime, as a middle-aged woman put it; the injustices and violence, and any derelictions of one's duties (*vasife*) as a father, wife, neighbour, trader, craftsman. Included also are some sins one cannot avoid, such as killing animals if one is a hunter or butcher, or not praying as a mother whose hands are 'always soiled',[18] or making a child cry, even if it is 'for his own good'. Sins, furthermore, can be balanced by religious merits (*savāb*). This term is as popular as 'sin' and is used in the same social context: being helpful, generous, reliable beyond the call of duty earns merits. Helping a sick cousin harvest apples, quietly providing a destitute neighbour with food, cleaning a public water channel or digging a grave for a neighbour all carry religious merits.[19] What counts, then, is one's behaviour towards one's relatives, co-workers, the poor, the mighty, towards animals and nature. When people judge others and themselves, they do so using basic ethics that appear in any list of humanist values. 'You don't need to be a Muslim to be a good person,' said a devout neighbour. On this basis people may criticize the heavy emphasis that religious authorities place on merits supposedly gained by participating and financing mosque-organized rituals while reducing traditional humanist (*ensānyat*) values to plain duties that largely go unrewarded.

On the flip side of the coin of rewards and punishment, neglect of the duties of 'a human being (*ensān*) and a Muslim (*musalmun*)', as people say, and doing harm to others in whatever form without remorse and restitution sum up the sins that ought to be punished at the latest after death in the name of justice. A popular argument asserts that on earth justice is so rare that one has to move expectations for it to the next life, and even then it only hangs on a thin thread of hope. Punishment and retribution mostly concern other people's injustices and sins, however. As to one's own behaviour, one easily can insist that God considers circumstances such as poverty, exhaustion, lack of choices or one's good intentions when He is passing judgement. This kind of reckoning lets one bend the Islamic scale of other-worldly rewards and punishments to one's advantage on many occasions. A sarcastic local young man, well versed in the religious conventions of the Islamic Republic, put it this way: 'God's *jemāl*-aspect (beauty and benevolence) pertains to oneself, and the *jelāl* aspect (retribution, judgement) to everybody else.'

All in all, though, retribution and punishment are not favourite topics except for a few people who are committed to a firebrand form of Islam one can hear from some preachers and Party-of-God enthusiasts. Such believers can vividly describe delights and horrors of the afterlife but find it hard to convince local people of their veracity. Over the past two decades, it seems that the most appealing option for most people is to think that hell is no burning issue and paradise is a pleasant mirage. Then and now, the dominant local religious ethos rests on a Sufi bias: not punctual performance of the many proscribed religious rituals will matter in the end, nor wealth or success (as some people claim) but God's love for His humble subjects who tried to do right.

Ethics and the afterlife

The emphasis on social ethics makes public opinion and the regard people have for each other predictive of the afterlife: the higher the esteem of one's peers, the more likely one will have a 'good place' after death, as a young woman summed up her grandfather's excellent chances of such a place in paradise. It needs only five people to speak well of a dead person to assure him or her a good afterlife. The importance of public opinion is one reason for eulogizing dead people in formal speeches, in conversations, in mourning songs and in mortuary architecture. *De mortuis nil nisi bonum* is more than a social convention. It is a vote of approval when the dead are being judged in the other world. It helps the dead. If nobody cares enough for a dead person to remember him or her publicly with praise and prayer, with gestures of mourning such as postponing the pleasures of a wedding or foregoing the New Year's house-cleaning (*hune takuni*), the departed is abandoned and in trouble.[20] Mourning songs tell stories, vent praise and grief, and in so doing honour the dead as well as their relatives.

In the mourning songs I analysed (Friedl 2018a), 'sin' does not appear. Nobody asks to have sins forgiven – one's sins are so small, measured against the merits one has accumulated simply by living as honestly as possible (with the emphasis on possible), that they are unimportant in the eyes of God.[21]

Until the 1950s only a date and salient attributes of the dead body's social persona were given on grave stones. For a woman these were engravings of comb and spindle, for example, and for men, a knife, a rifle or a hunter.[22] There were hints of death but no pointers to the afterlife, unless the signs meant a continuation of the dead person's social standing after death, which was – and is – a lively choice. What counted was the commemoration of the social persona of the dead: important people got bigger graves with bigger headstones than unimportant ones, impressive 'prestige-enhancing memory creations' (Rüpke 2013: 122), and presumably corresponding honours in the afterlife. After the Iran–Iraq war, graves of the martyrs of the war were the most elaborate. Photographs of attractive young men appeared on banners and on headstones, with explanatory texts and Quranic verses engraved on the stone slabs covering their graves, and with ornaments suggesting a bridal chamber.[23] The authorities declared the martyrs to be sitting with the angels in paradise, and grieving relatives said they made efforts to believe them, but a grumbling voice of dissent throughout the country asked why not more mullahs and government officials were fighting on the front if martyrdom really was the direct path to paradise?

The formal Islamic understanding of death as a border between the here and there that cannot be re-crossed in either direction implies an emphasis on one's own responsibilities for one's place in the afterlife because no living person can 'help' a dead one to attain a good place, and the dead cannot get in contact with the living (except in dreams, and this unreliably so). Furthermore, as understood locally, orthodox Islamic eschatology does not support the hope of a reunion with one's dead relatives in the other world. Gravestone texts do not talk of a peaceful rest and of au revoir expectations.[24] Believing in such total separation in the afterlife is an unattractive option for many people. The local woman-philosopher at her loom had this comment: 'It is hard to think that one dies and is not welcomed by one's own people there. Who wants to be among strangers, even if they are angels?' Rather, in contrast to preachers' assertions, in vernacular speech and in traditional mourning rituals death is treated as a porous divide. Relatives can influence their dead's place through acts of remembrance, sacrifices and prayer, and, in the other direction, one expects to meet 'there' the people one liked 'here' and will be spared meeting those one disliked while alive. ('I can name a whole bunch of those!' joked a woman.) Old, frail or discouraged persons complaining about their misery express the wish that their dead mother would 'take' them. It does not matter at all where mother would take them – a bucolic paradise is no issue. What counts is the feeling of comfort, care and security only a mother can bestow, they say; this feeling one can envision to regain in the 'Other World'.

Given such expectations, women say they look forward to seeing their mothers and dead children and grandchildren more eagerly than anybody else in the other world. When I mentioned husbands, a woman chuckled and said, 'Oh well', with an impish face. The idea that souls are 'just souls' without bodies that could mark old and young, pretty and ugly, male and female is an attractive option, especially among women. Souls are not people, they have no bodies. So, what does it really mean to meet or see one's children there? What does all this talk matter?

Summary

As it is spoken of in everyday contexts, the 'Other World' (*u dunyā*, 'that' world, in contrast to *i dunyā*, 'this' world) is a lot more variegated and complex than the seemingly clear dichotomy of heaven and hell suggests. It is beyond empirical understanding, though, cannot be proven or refuted, and inspires a variety of images and beliefs. These range from joyful life in a lush paradisiacal garden to pessimistic expectations reminiscent of the joyless shades in a drab underworld in antiquity; from fear of a cold, dark grave to dependency on mourners' memorial services for easing the loneliness and pains of being dead. In these images morality and orthodox piety are less important than is the visualization of the afterlife as an extension of this life, at best without earthly pains and violence. Dimmer options of eschatology are images of death as final non-existence, or the shape of 'that place' as a continuation of the troubling earthly social order and painful conditions of life. Justice is brittle here and maybe there, too. The Day of Judgement and the promise of a peaceful next world on earth are tagged on to these views, but the prophesied end time is too far away to have much emotional impact. The most comfortable option is to believe that, if anything, grateful acceptance of God's Will and a life lived by doing right by one's dependents and one's community will be noted somehow in the other world.

Figure 9 Sisakht, November 2004. A young woman is helping her sister cook votive soup in memory of a dead brother. The soup will be distributed to neighbours and relatives. The food and the recipients' prayers are said to help the dead person.

Figure 10 Dashtak, Sisakht, May 2006. Orchard in bloom, against the Koh-e Dena. Gardens and bucolic places are among popular images for paradise.

7

Well-being

Being well and at ease is on everybody's mind, as the common Luri thank you phrase, 'May your hand not ache' (*daset dard nakone*) and a host's routine invitation to be comfortable (*rāhat*) indicate.[1] People treat well-being as an existential concern, its fragility as a feature of the shaded side of life. Here I will single out some aspects of well-being that link it to religion.

Feeling well, happy (*khoshhāl*) and comfortable locally is an attractive condition in a popular image of paradise, the place free of work, want and hostilities. In this world well-being is said to be rare, unstable and in constant need of upkeep. Orthodox believers claim that fulfilling God's orders as laid down in the scriptures will make one happy and successful, but knowing that many good, pious people are not well at all is hard to align with this claim. For doubters and critics this is a sign that God either does not care much about humans' comfort or else is unjustly bestowing well-being unevenly for no good reason other than His Will.

The term *hāl* means one's state of being, condition, health.[2] Believers take a person's basic disposition (*maze, tou*) to be God-given just like everything else, but beyond this, every adult has the God-ordered duty to keep body and mind functioning. The aim is to be as calm, well and comfortable as possible. (A standard comment on women's suicide was that the overworked, disheartened women wished to be *rāhat* (removed from overwhelming troubles).) The key word *rāhat* implies a relaxed attitude, congenial surrounds, stress-free work and good health. One has to struggle to limit discomfort and distress by using common sense, tried-and-true wisdom and all available resources. If these lead to morally questionable strategies, one may justify them by claiming 'necessity' (*majburi*). An obligation to obey a demand, fulfil a duty or avoid pain or disgrace will explain, excuse or balance the sin one thereby might commit.

At this point the connection between God and people is fraught. People may choose to argue that God must know that by forcing them to fend for themselves yet making it difficult to stay well, they often will have to disobey Him. A successful professional tribal man described how he got an education as the eldest of several children of a poor farmer who would not or could not pay for his son's middle school in the next town. The twelve-year-old felt *majbur* (forced by necessity) to steal four sheep from another camp, sell them in town and with the money go to school there. He never looked back. His eventual all-round well-being he took to show God's approval of the theft. (Critics use this argument cynically: God prefers rich scoundrels.)

Such thoughts about God's Will allow praise for pious acceptance of one's lot but also for impatience with unhappy, unsuccessful or sick people who don't deal with problems reasonably. One can be a 'good Muslim' by accepting misery as a God-willed condition or as punishment for sins or as a test of one's obedience to God. But one also can be a good – or even better – Muslim by fighting for one's well-being and restricting piety to the belief that one's best effort works only if God wills it to work. Between these extremes are many choices for opinions and behaviour, given people's different inclinations, strengths, weaknesses and requirements that necessitate tailoring actions to fit circumstances.[3] All in all, though, even critics and doubters take religion (*din*) to help people do well in this world, be it by offering the option to visit saints' shrines, perform rituals, use what God provides in nature or else to use it to access opportunities the 'mullah-government' provides for poor and enterprising pious people through welfare projects, loans, government contracts and jobs.

Well-being and knowledge

God's orderly arrangement of nature includes the brain's ability to reason, learn and discern, and to keep body and mind in balance. Discernment and wisdom will prevent uncritical reliance on lies, hearsay and idle talk, including by fundamentalist (*ghaliz*) religious authorities. When a mullah's wife told a local boy to wash his apple in the (muddy, polluted) irrigation channel because the Quran said that all moving water was clean, a bystander loudly accused her of ignorance.

For a healthy equilibrium, people use Galen's principles[4] – reduced to a few binary opposites – to maintain warm–cold (*garm o sard*) and strong–weak (*qouve o zaif*) balances with purported food qualities. Clean and dirty (*tamiz o kassif*) are opposites with moral connotations, whereby a 'clean' body and mind are good and 'dirt' ought to be avoided and voided.[5] This management is based on experience with the culture's know-how options.⁶ Young women use the balance requirement to argue for easing restrictions on their movements because travelling and visiting people 'opens the mind' and prevents depression and ailments. Too much happiness may upset one's equilibrium also, people and some doctors say, and prudently ought to be followed by a sacrifice to prevent it from pulling a balancing, corrective misery.

Local morbidity patterns have changed from those of earlier hunger times with malnutrition and infectious diseases to those in modern lifestyles with 'too much food and sitting' (*khordan o neshastan*) in the words of a diabetic woman; 'too much work and stress' (*kār o feshār*) for a surgeon with heart problems; stories of corruption and cynicism told by just about everybody; 'computer, snacks and television' (*kompu̇tér, shirini o telvizun*) for a mother of two overweight daughters; and with 'artificial living' (*zendegi masnuï*: processed food, medicines) in a discussion of the rise in infertility.⁷ Religion does not figure in these woes except for committed Party-of-God adherents who tend to frame all problems with Islamic morality. For everybody else health and knowledge are matters of personal exertion, God-willed as the outcome might be. Allopathic medicine has added choices for approaching body problems but has not much changed the philosophy of well-being: one has to employ reason to maintain it.⁸ A woman with back pains called a city specialist's advice for exercises 'strange, eccentric' (*ajib*). To lie on the back, moving arms and legs in the air 'like a beetle' was against her assumption that medicines, diet and pleading with a saint silenced bone pains.

Medical tradition includes a substantial pharmacopoeia with over 160 plant- and mineral-based local medicines (*davā mahalli*) known to specialists, mostly older women (Ghafari n.d.). People declared the diligence and hard work behind this knowledge to be religiously meritorious because it benefited ailing people, as did the skills of bonesetters (mostly men) and wound-healers. The know-how was 'true', based on the wisdom of generations, a local healer said – a woman with an encyclopaedic knowledge of medicinal plants and their uses. In this popular view, *shafā*, the quality that makes plants and concoctions beneficial for people and animals is from God, and knowledge, skills and hard work necessary to harness it come from the healer.

Modern health facilities have made knowing about resources more important than knowing about traditions. In 2015 an elderly patient at the health clinic patted his bag of drugs, saying, 'When I was little we had nothing and didn't know anything – now look at this bag!' For him and most others, progress greatly increased choices for managing comfort. A teacher went so far as to call a neighbour's refusal of a treatment 'sinful', and a young woman told of a heated discussion in high school about why the medical science everybody was thanking God for came from the 'bad West' and not from Muslims.[9]

However, not all efforts to increase well-being are successful. Failures can be ascribed to God's punishment of a sin, and given the abundance of sins this is a reasonable argument. The even less refutable moral judgement that an ancestor's 'unlawful seed' (*tokhm harum*, the result of unforgiven, unrepented sins) may have led to a failure links consequences of sins to a wider moral community. No retroactive change is possible. Mothers are pressed to declare their milk lawful (*halāl*) for grown children so that the children may not have to count mother's care and nursing as an unpaid debt.[10] 'Fate' (*qesmat*) is an acceptable explanation for a problem only after all efforts to resolve it failed. Whoever quickly blames one's fate for a failure is said to be too dumb or too lazy to take care of the underlying issues or to follow advice.[11] In 1965 women asked how to prevent being pregnant 'every year, like cows'. They took fertility to be a matter of God's order and will but the control of pregnancies to be a matter of resources.[12] As soon as birth control devices were freely available, the birth rate in town sank dramatically, from 165 to 40 between 1997 and 2000.[13] Relatives of the few couples who leave pregnancy 'up to God' disagree with the stubborn refusal to use the door to a better life that God opened with birth control. Thus, common sense lets one see well-being as a function of knowledge leading to choices for human agency, with all outcomes to be explainable with the Will of God.

These basic principles are accepted as self-evident. Variations in individuals' handling of issues are in details. Thus, one-size-fits-all medical diagnostics and treatments tend to confuse patients because they disregard differences in age, sex, humoral disposition, strength and life circumstances. Patients argue with physicians about medications that agree or disagree with their God-given constitution. The father of a freshly minted physician answered her speech about vitamin deficiencies by declaring that his long life had taught him what food he, personally, needed to 'stand upright and work', and that vitamin pills and fish oil might be good for some but surely not for him. And when a neighbour's face and hands swelled up during wheat harvest, the man called it a heat imbalance (*garmi* in the Galenic sense) but local remedies did not help. The clinic doctor called it *alershi* and cured it with pills. The happy man saw this as God opening a door to dealing with one of His new ailments, and added antihistamines to *garmi* medicines.

Domestic hostilities rank high in causing distress (*narāhat*) but rarely are expected to ease with pills, prayers or help from saints directly. 'God helped us by letting me find a job for affording a little apartment,' said a man about his wife's recovery from depression in his father's house. Indeed, most solutions to mundane social problems depend on money.

Money

Empirically, poverty and pain are a bundled hardship, willed by God but potentially raising people's doubts about God's benevolence, especially concerning children. Children below the age of nine are considered incapable of sinning, and even pious people are hard put to accept that a merciful God makes these innocents suffer. The same argument also holds for animals. The mullah explanation that God might be punishing parents for their or an ancestor's sins by forcing them to watch a child suffer is an unsatisfactory argument, the more so as it is well known that children of wealthy parents are healthier and more successful than poor children. Explaining the woes of innocents with God's inscrutable Will is less problematic because it is irrefutable. Dismissing the God-problem altogether is yet another choice: God probably has nothing to do with the pain beyond having set in motion the natural order that includes poverty, hunger, misery and all injustices. Depending on circumstances, the same person may choose any and all of these options.

In practice, managing pain is cognitively connected to knowledge and wealth. In 1965 women were perplexed when I told them that giving birth was as painful for the presumably rich European women as for them. Locally, Caesarean sections are rising because they minimize pain and fears, women say; because the great expense has the social benefit of showing that the husband is well-off and progressive, and because (for orthodox believers) they are a sign of God's benevolence.[14] When C-sections first became available, poor women who could not afford them said that obviously God loved rich urban women more than poor tribal women. 'The rich are prettier and smell better,' said a retired midwife, causing hilarity.

Even on the most basic level of well-being money is an issue. 'Warm, strong' food such as lamb and butterfat is expensive. A well-off neighbour was caught between bragging about her family's customary breakfast of walnuts, scrambled eggs, cheese and raisins (all expensive and 'good') that showed how well her husband provided and cared, and being embarrassed about it because only few people could afford this. Cheap watered buttermilk, potatoes, cucumbers, cow's milk are 'cold' and one ought to eat them sparingly. 'Cold' goat meat and beef are cheaper than 'warm' mutton, but all meat is expensive. Poor rural people cannot be choosers, though; they have to eat what is available and affordable and thus must expect to be less well than rich people. That even in the humblest food plants are traces of God's goodness, as a woman herbalist said, was 'true but not good enough' for a man recalling how as a little boy he and his sisters often had to sleep hungry because the only good food in the house had fed the elder brothers, the hard workers. 'Well-being depends on money, food and misfortune' (*hāl ve pil o qasa o qossa*), goes a proverb.

In gold, monetary value and potency unite. Gold's power is considered dangerous for the weak, such as for a newborn who may be harmed by a visiting woman's gold jewellery, but a drink of water with a piece of gold in it will settle fright, for brides gold 'binds good fortune', and for adult women gold is a source of strength and security. Indeed, every woman ought to demand gold coins in her marriage contract and ought to wear gold as protection against malevolent powers.[15] When a poor local labourer bought his wife a slim gold bangle, the first piece of gold in her life, she said, her chronic headache disappeared.

While local herbalists, healers and amulet writers don't set a price on their services for fear it would diminish their God-given healing power, doctors expect to be paid well. People suspect that the cheap clinic doctors are less competent than private, expensive doctors or – better and more expensive yet – specialists in cities, and that the best ones are overseas.[16] Rising inequality in access to what is taken to further well-being lets local people feel 'out of place in this world', as a diabetic man said, and 'abandoned by government and God', in the words of a poor widow. The claim of being ignored by authorities, including God, is not new but is gaining popularity. 'How can I thank God if I can't afford an eye-operation?' asked a discouraged grandmother. Wealthy people can earn religious merits by paying doctors' bills for poor relatives with insufficient health insurance. A physician said that by curtailing her pro bono care of indigents she could get rich. Her son, a sardonic young man, said that her compassion (*delsuz*) would zip her up to paradise so fast that not even a questioning angel could stop her.

The ailing economy in Iran makes problems worse.[17] The routine traditional link between governance and people's well-being is heard often, namely, that a good king's subjects are happy, at peace and well-off, and a bad king's subjects are poor, depressed and angry. Thus, the current dissatisfaction and unrest may be seen less as God's doing than as the consequence of bad Islamic leadership of mullahs and functionaries who are ill-trained in economics and administration. People deplore high unemployment, inflation and drug addiction, rampant crime and depression, and the wealth of drug dealers. Doctors report signs of severe stress in patients. While people see choices for guarding against afflictions ascribed to extra-human powers (prayer-based amulets, for example), they know of no protection against current problems. 'There is no *daʾā* (prayer, amulet) against unemployment, votive promises (*nazr*) do not help and we have given up on our saints,' said the father of three under-employed sons. For him and others like him the 'thanks be to God' formula sounded hollow and the customary reliance on reason and human agency powered by knowledge was failing him.

Local saints may be seen as too weak to help but famous shrines have become magnets for pilgrimages (*ziārat*). Stories of miracles create hope. Government agencies subsidize group pilgrimages to places that a generation ago only the rich could visit.[18] The trips boost pilgrims' well-being by the excitement they create more than by the saint, a psychologist said, but it did not matter as long as people felt better. Doctors name domestic discontent, poverty, boredom and lack of diversion as main reasons for depression-related complaints, especially of women,[19] and encourage patients to use 'all that is available' to manage their problems, including pilgrimages and votive sacrifices. A merchant called his business travel to Europe a pilgrimage (*ziārat*) more expensive than the hajj and better for his spirit, and an enthusiastic Kerbela-pilgrim explicitly merged religious ritual and entertaining tourism when she planned to repeat this uplifting 'vacation travel' (*musaferat ta'til*) soon again in these sad times.

Non-human powers

That God's natural order contains beings and powers that influence humans' well-being is generally accepted as fact based on experience, on testimony by authorities and on religious scriptures. Science- and progress-oriented people may doubt specific anecdotes about such powers but few deny the premise of their existence as amoral forces of nature, that is, as doing what God programmed them for. Just as a wolf is amoral when behaving in its (God-given) wolf-way, a gust of wind or an earthquake have no intention to do harm and neither does a disease epidemic that 'hits' a village. People say they feel surrounded by powers whose very existence impinges on that of others and that their own human existence is hurtful and dangerous for other beings as well. This observation entails a deep moral dilemma. A hunter shooting a ram, a butcher slaughtering a goat, a woman killing a chicken are doing so out of (presumably God-willed) necessity for survival or to fulfil the (God-ordained) duties of their profession, yet also commit the sin of hurting and killing an animal with feelings and senses similar to people.[20] To survive, all creatures have to learn the habits and vulnerabilities of other beings and to use them to their own advantage, but only humans thereby commit sins – or do they? The open question leaves a choice for doubters and for those who find a way around the philosophical dilemma by claiming 'necessity'.

Of the more than a dozen potentially dangerous powers in people's repertoire in the 1970s, few were important forty years later, but cautious people keep them in mind. Children, for example, are said to sense jinn, as shown by their fearful reluctance to enter ruins, bathrooms and outhouses (jinn's hang-outs) in the evening; occasional nightmares may be ascribed to a demon, and a tired person may decide not to visit a new mother because exhaustion is known to 'hit' and sicken infants. The most enduring and ubiquitous of these powers is 'wind' (*bād*), blamed for creating aches and pains in the body.[21] A woman healer called it the oldest human malady:

> Adam and Eve had the best figs and honey to eat in paradise. Only wheat was forbidden. But the Devil talked them into disobeying God. Adam roasted some wheat, ate it and liked it. But it bloated his belly with wind for everybody to see and smell, and so he and Eve had to leave paradise. Now all of Adam's offspring have painful wind in the body. It moves around inside, in the head, up and down, everywhere.[22]

Other than having used it as a punishment for Adam in paradise, God has little to do with wind episodes: wind comes 'by itself'. Doctors call *bād*-afflictions *rumatis* or *artrit*; women blame wind for womb ailments and pains when working with ice-cold water, and for diarrhoea in infants. Dietary and work habits can increase or calm wind-aches and doctors' medicines can subdue them but *bād* is a stubborn condition. 'Once wind has you it won't let you go,' said a nurse. In the past, tattoos with pigment mixed with bear-gall were said to drive out wind pains.

The habits of jinn, shape-shifting, partly invisible beings were expected to disturb people more in the past than now, although they are described in the Quran. Like God's Will, jinn, too, are often used as ultimate-cause explanation such as for accidents. When a toddler fell into the water channel, the mother blamed a pushy jinn. In religious teaching and in everyday use, jinn are merging with the devil. Suicide, often ascribed to a malevolent jinn's persuasion in the past, now is said to be the work of the devil deceiving a 'weak' person.[23] And when, in 2006, a young man one morning came home dazed and befuddled after guarding a fish pond all night, his neighbour diagnosed it as 'hit by a jinn, a devil and the evil eye'. People can avoid jinn by skirting places where they may linger, by staying near other people especially at night, by referring to them obliquely rather than by their name, by making metal noises with iron or gold bangles. Afraid of God, anybody can keep them at bay by saying God's name or by wearing an amulet (*daʾa*) consisting of a written Quran verse sewed in a piece of green fabric.[24] These precautions count as reasonable, practical choices, as tried and true.

People occasionally refer to several harmful, intangible powers that may announce themselves in dreams, giving the dreamer time to ward them off with alms to the poor, for example. The most-mentioned powers of this sort are *muqāfāt*, usually taken to be a misery that may be sent by God as a punishment for sins; the largely autonomous (albeit God-willed) *qossa*, a mishap or hurt that may strike any time; and *čeimun*, any epidemic. *Čeimun* is the purported agent in infectious diseases like colds or measles that 'come, go around and go away', leaving sick people in their wake. Progress-oriented people accuse traditionalists of belittling science when they say that inoculations 'repel' a *čeimun* just as an amulet repels a jinn. Infectious diseases of children have become rare, but God's Will as the answer to the bothersome question of theodicy remains a challenge to piety and credibility. In 2015 it was a rhetorical question popular with doubters and believers alike, as was the idea that God first created harmful powers and then showed people how to avoid them. The easiest way to handle this, namely, to expect that these plagues act on their own, unbidden, for no reason, and to let people choose how to handle them, leads to the option of doubting God's singular might: if not God then who controls them?[25]

The mild power of *bu* (smell, odour) may be irritating but also religiously meritorious. Pleasant smells such as from clean clothes, perfume or rose bushes along a walkway are said to carry merits because the nice smell gladdens others. Fragrant grasses are put on graves. For opium smokers smouldering opium was the fragrance of paradise. Odours of cooking, of dung, decay, filth may 'hit' and sicken people, and the 'smell' of a patient can make a visitor sick. By 2006 the stink of sewage and polluted water was largely under control with plumbing and banning herd animals from town. Preachers and their followers pointed to cleanliness as a religious demand, but critics argued that why, then, did it take more than a thousand years until septic tanks and clean water became signs of good governance for a Muslim country? Choosing a progressive or a religious opinion on cleanliness marks one's political identity in the Islamic Republic. The wise choice is to use the argument that fits occasion and audience.

Help may be expected from the power inherent in spoken and written words such as in prayers and amulets, in blessings and formulas of esteem, and in kind words of praise or consolation that lift the spirit. (However, praise without a moral framing such as murmuring 'God willing' or a blessing may allow the evil eye to strike.) Gossip is so dangerous that it is declared sinful. Angry speech, curses and magical spells may cause distress. In 2006 a teacher in the local girls' boarding school was so exasperated by the students' relentless pilfering of 'everything', from soap to food, that she threatened to put a spell on the thieves that blocks urination (a *shashband*).[26] Personal names, too, carry power. Some names 'fit' a child, as shown by the child's good progress, and others don't, as shown by poor health, a whiny disposition, fearfulness. In such cases a name change, especially from a Persian name to an Arabic/Quranic one, is a popular choice that also carries political benefit: Arabic/Islamic names (Hasan, Ali; Maryam, Zeynab) suggest piety and regime loyalty, while old Persian names (Khosrow, Ashkan; Mitra, Homayun) suggest opposition. 'I have so many Hasans and Amins in class that if I call one, half the class jumps up,' a teacher said in 2006. Religion and politics also combine when adults who want to get ahead in the contemporary political climate change their 'old-fashioned' Persian names to Islamic ones.

The toughest force in life people talk about is time, God's essential, reliable ordering device, flowing and cycling outside of human influence. Flowing is seen in the stages of life, in life's linear journey from beginning to end, always moving, like river water. Cycling is in the repetitions of day and night, the four seasons, the movements of the stars, of life in general.[27] God does not alter this order, ever. Expressions such as the 'wheel of time' and 'wheel of the world' highlight inescapable, juggernaut-like change. 'The world's revolving time makes one old-sick' (*zamun-e dunyā pir ikone*) is a proverb. The seasons are known to influence how people feel: blood 'boils' in the spring, making lust surge and people accident-prone; summer brings heat-related ailments (*garmi*); windy fall brings aches (*bād, rumatis*), and winter brings colds (*sarmākhordegi*). The lifecycle also has predictable health challenges. Infants and toddlers die easily and quickly from diarrhoea; young children are prone to accidents and childhood diseases; adolescence brings foolishness, mood swings, sexual urges and menarche.[28] Back- and joint pains afflict the middle aged. Old age (*piri*) counts as a disease that makes one ugly, cross, impatient and suffering from stiff limbs, weak senses, prostate troubles, loss of zeal and joy of life (*zouq*). There is a gender difference, though: while old age weakens retired old men and mellows them, it won't let women retire from housework and will increase wrinkles and bad temper fast, making it difficult for others to like them.[29] There is no cure for old age. No matter how much care one gets one ends in a small hole in the ground. Nobody and nothing can outlive one's God-given Allotted Time (*ajal*).

Time is stressful for farmers who have to discharge their God-ordered duties squeezed by bad weather, long winters and pests. Worried about getting their animals through the winter in the pastoral past, men said, 'We hope every morning to make it to evening, and thereby we strike the days off our own lives.'[30] For a few years before the Revolution of 1978 and again around the year 2000, 'progress' (*pishraft*, literally, 'going forward') was a vehicle to a better life, people remember, but then 'God averted his eyes', a bad government derailed progress, and time now heeds only itself. Committed Party-of-God members and adherents of the government religion call such laments misguided and tend to blame 'The West' rather than the government or God's Will for the bad socio-economic situation.

Pessimism regarding time and well-being is an easy choice for realists who know that one is born with sure death ahead and that decay is part of all existence. 'Rocks and walls crumble, too,' said a mason. According to the scriptures the world itself has only an allotted time span. Some generations ago people mentioned women's literacy as a sign for the near end and now see signs for it in widespread drug use, stress and discontent, decline in fertility, malaise, insubordinate children and in wars among Muslims. Scriptures predict the start of another world cycle. 'Hopefully God will make the next world-time less painful,' said a man waiting for his weekly kidney dialysis.

Rituals

Many small, everyday rituals are meant to help people get through the day. Although they lost importance over the years, they are known still. When dumping hot ashes or hot water, a quick *bismillah* ('in the name of God') will warn jinn, expected to linger near houses at dusk and to retaliate if accidentally burned. With modern kitchens this danger has diminished, but the exclamation still accompanies pouring out boiling rice water. In 2015 a neighbour refused to hand a pot with yoghurt to her cousin in the evening because, she said (and all bystanders knew), that the colour white attracts jinn at dusk. When her cousin made doubtful noises, the milk woman scolded her, saying that the young cousin's sick cow and the theft of a bag of wheat happened because she did not heed the dangers from 'those' (the jinn). Prophylactic rituals to manage extra-human powers may have decreased but the powers continue to provide choices to explain mishaps ahead of fate or God's Will.

Alms giving, promises of votive offerings and asking saints for help have increased in popularity over the past generation, and pilgrimages to the big shrines have become extraordinarily popular, expected to further one's well-being, success, health and children's progress. In 2004 an elderly woman praised a local saint[31] for help with sudden paralysis of her back and legs. She gave alms to honour the saint, slept in the saint's shrine and in a dream there grabbed the saint's skirt and demanded healing. Next morning the woman woke up well and limber. Stories of such miracles may be taken as proof of the healing powers of saints and the beneficial effects of pilgrimages and temple-sleep,[32] while doubters may accuse orthodox leaders of 'using religion to make people stupid'. Only misanthropes, though, deny that such rituals increase participants' joie de vivre. Psychologists and local people alike credit intention (*niat*), a fervent wish and strong will, for success at shrines, elevating human agency to a prime element in miracles.

Some rituals offered choices to boost weather-related expectations for farmers and herders who have to deal with steep hills, stony soils, cold, snowy winters and hot, dry summers.[33] For example, on the first day of Esfand, the last month in the Persian solar calendar, the weather is expected to 'turn away' from winter, and people may say, 'We'll see if the Old Woman threw her burning log into the water or into the fire today,' which would bring good rain or else a drought.[34] Old people remember a rain-ritual: when rain was needed, a group of children walked from house to house, chanting a ditty about rain. The serenaded 'house' had to give them a handful flour (and was mocked if nothing was offered), and when they had enough, they made a fire, mixed dough, put a pebble in it, formed a thick patty, baked it in hot ashes, divided it among themselves and ate it. Whoever got the pebble was beaten until he – the sacrifice to the power withholding rain – reported that rain would fall. Sometimes it did and sometimes not, but the ritual was fun and thus enduring, said a man who remembered that to avoid the beating he once swallowed the pebble and nearly choked.

Just about everybody finds social and psychological benefits in rituals: they bring people together, especially women who do not often see relatives ('I see her only at funerals,' said a mother about her daughter, married in another village); they support peace, help the poor, facilitate matchmaking. 'Chic' new birthday parties entertain children, henna-painting brings health for a bride and groom, music and dancing at weddings are 'a feast for eyes and ears'. Women's cooperative house cleaning in the spring, hiking parties, outings to gather greens mark the seasons. Any visiting (*āmad o raft* (coming and going)) is said to 'open the heart' (*del*) by breaking humdrum routines in a joyful way or else 'lighten the heart' by crying at mourning visits. Mourning and bringing joy are said to bestow religious merits.

Small, casual, everyday rituals such as burning wild rue or making a sacrifice when moving into a new house are done to protect people; a circle drawn around a new mother's room and gifts of food or baby clothes are counted on to keep mother and baby safe. Well-wishing formulas and blessings calling on God and the saints are uttered and exchanged in greetings routinely throughout the day, from polite thanks for questions after one's well-being to expressions of benevolence, gratitude and submission in the mode of *ta'rof*, the elaborate politeness that people are ready to perform at any social occasion. While orthodox mullahs and their followers disparage most joyful rituals, calling them 'superstition', and promote rituals that are mostly about mourning,[35] local people suggest that their useful traditional rituals show that they are members of a reasonable, beneficial, God-pleasing culture.

Feeling well

The greatest challenges to well-being people talked about were lack of hope (*omid*) and lack of gratefulness (*nashukri*), the bad economy and difficult interpersonal relationships. This list has not changed much over time.

Hope and trust – in God among religious and traditionally pious people, in social and political development generally – are deemed necessary for well-being. They have become rare, as traditional institutions can no longer be relied upon, not even the family, and as 'God has eyes but won't look,' in the opinion of a pious political dissident. Sayings like 'God has eyes only for the rich' and 'God doesn't care about this world any more' show that to feel dejected has become a realistic choice.[36] Begged by her ill brother to implore God to either make him well or let him die, a woman in 2006 said God didn't listen and if He did, He turned everything she asked for into the opposite. This feeling of defeat pervades the whole country. In the 2018 Gallup Global Emotions Report, Iran ranks third in 'Anger', fourth in 'Worry' and fifth in 'Stress', globally (Ray 2019).[37] Even pious people committed to their religion complain that the religious establishment puts great pressure on people by its demands, controls of behaviour and by putting 'everything' into a moral frame that makes people sad. Although nobody I asked wanted the old days back, a longing for the purportedly close, uncomplicated, reliable relationships in the earlier, simple life emerged at many occasions despite the fact that the stories people tell about the past mostly are about pain and poverty. A poor economy makes people nostalgic.

Economic woes may be blamed on the government and on outside enemies but also on a relentless pursuit of the good life. Lifestyle creep exceeds the income of most people, and money issues cause 'more misery than war and cholera did in the past', said a father who was 'paralyzed with unhappiness' over money-related hostilities among his adult children. The sins of *nageruni* (dissatisfaction with one's lot) and *hamčeshmi* (a jealous, competitive look at others) are a main reason given for depression and anxiety.[38] Laments and bitter jokes about debts, pyramid schemes, frauds and loan-swindles abound. Unlike woes brought about by extra-human powers, these calamities are declared man-made, propelled by progress aims, competition and lack of leadership. 'God has nothing to do with it,' said an angry trader, 'it is our own fault.' Hezbollah-leaning people blame disobedience to God and disregard for the scriptures for the misery. A pious government employee said that praying more would reduce stress and make people feel better.[39] Another option for staying calm is to cultivate the habits of a dervish who renounces the seductions of modern society and lives a quiet life of pious contemplation. This, though, may invite the verdict of failure because such a man likely is unable to keep a family fed and content.

Problems caused by discontent within the family hierarchy and by the attitude that marriage is a woman's immutable fate continue despite a decline in arranged marriages and increase in neolocal residence and wife-initiated divorce.[40] When bolstered by scriptural pronouncements on husband–wife relations, the tight traditional structure of men's authority and responsibility from top down and women's obedience and service upwards make well-being for couples precarious. There is little choice. Men continue to say they suffer under their obligations, and many also under 'unsupportive, demanding' wives. Workloads in the family economy have eased for women but demands and unfriendly treatment by husband and in-laws continue for many. Wife-beating was so common in the past as to hardly merit comment. It is common still, although now can be criticized as 'oppression and violence' (*zolm o zur*) under the banner of 'Islamic human rights'. People who support wife punishment see it as men's God-given duty to keep order in the house by any means and insist that a 'good' wife will accept whatever her husband provides, bread and blows, and will forgive him 'everything'.[41] In the past, this was not an option but *normál*, a grandmother said. Authoritarian relationships change only slowly. Most local men assume full responsibility for their wives and children as a (God-ordained) duty with no alternative, while increase of (God-allowed) polygyny, of divorce and of extravagant alimony demands by young women have added troublesome choices for everybody.[42] In 2015 the town council (*shora*) was overwhelmed with cases about land disputes and intra-family problems in Sisakht, and about polygyny, family fights and men's violence against family members in surrounding villages. It is 'very difficult to be quiet and at ease (*ārum* and *rāhat*)', a retired craftsman summed up the situation in 2015. A worried mother said, 'Well-being? What's that?'; a male student was convinced that 'nobody' in Iran was well, 'not even mullahs', while a young hezbollah man saw it as a benefit reserved for 'true Muslims' – only people who did not obey God were miserable, he said. Like others, he was angry, though, mostly about people who only pretend to be pious, and about Iran's foreign enemies who he declared to ruin the country's culture and economy.

Well-being creates good memories. Talking about them in 2006, a retired teacher remembered the happiness (*khoshhāli*) she felt when, in 1971, she and some other hungry students were invited to the shah's 2,500-year celebration of the Persian Empire. The many beautiful, nice people there and the lavish spread of good food 'opened my heart (*del*) wide for three days', she said. Travels and pilgrimages create good memories, too, as do memories of sunny, 'wide-open' days in green spring pastures. But well-being is fleeting and, all in all, has become 'rarer than gold', said a bureaucrat discussing bleak political and economic realities. People reported feeling well in congenial get-togethers; in a quiet, well-behaved 'house'; when meeting a person they liked; when watching a beautiful groom and bride or eating good food; when they can laugh, hold a baby, receive good news, travel, learn of a child's success, hear music, watch movies and roam the internet (young people say); and when they are outside in the orchards and pastures. Visiting God's nature is a choice that lifts the spirit. Hiking in the mountains, gathering acorns and wild greens, having a picnic at a waterfall or a river, listening to the rain, watching birds, all provide spiritual experiences similar to those at a pilgrimage, people say.[43] An elderly woman bothered by cars, noise and unhappiness 'inside and outside' said she would like to live alone in a faraway cave with a bear and a boar as companions, never mind that both are religiously unlawful, polluting animals. This and similar statements are a comment on women's experiences of life: they wish to be away from crowds and people, in 'God's pure creation', a peaceful wilderness. A discouraged mother of two unemployed sons opted for a long shot when she said, 'I hope we will be more at ease in the gardens of the other world.'

Summary

Pious people say that God likes people and that following His orders leads to being well. This irrefutable link between God and well-being is a near-mantra of supporters of organized religion in the Islamic Republic, but local people's experiences prompt severe caveats that lead to various choices in the doubt-and-criticism category. Well-being emerges as an issue of social ethics and human agency rather than morality and piety. Given humans' bodily, social and moral frailty as (inexplicably) willed by God, well-being is described as a longing whose fulfilment is dependent on economic means, on knowledge about resources and how to access them, and on a great deal of personal effort, with final outcomes – good and bad – ascribed to the Will of God. The greatest challenges to well-being emerging in discussions were interferences by extra-human powers (weakening over time); pain and poverty, the gap between rich and poor, lack of hope, lack of grateful acceptance of one's lot, the bad economy and difficult interpersonal relationships – all increasing at present. Socially and economically disadvantaged tribal people complain about the lack of access to the many attractive opportunities for a good life available to the well connected, the ruthless, the hypocrites and the wealthy. Experiences of well-being are linked to good health, to good company, peace and feelings of safety; to funny events, travels, shrine visitations, and to beauty such as in flowers, nature, gardens, attractive young people. These provide spiritually uplifting, if fleeting, thoughts and feelings that let one experience God's goodness, people say who otherwise claim that not God but inept political leadership and the waning of humanist-Persian ethics in modern society are responsible for people's existential challenges.

Figure 11 Sisakht, 1994. Doing one's daily duties well pleases God and people. The old woman, baking bread for her daughter-in-law, said she thanked God when she felt at peace, working quietly by herself, at her own pace.

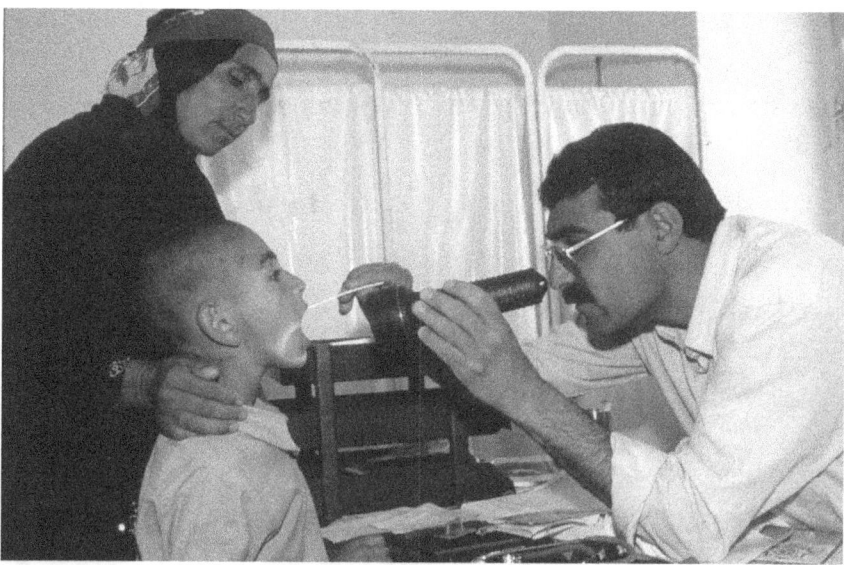

Figure 12 Chin, Central Boir Ahmad, 2006. Instituted by the Pahlavi government and expanded in the Islamic Republic, the nationwide public healthcare programme considerably improved the physical well-being in tribal/rural areas. Ramin Azizi, MD, a native of Sisakht and much appreciated by his patients, worked at clinics in the tribal area until his death in a car crash in 2018. He did so, he said, because he liked his God-given ability to take care of his people.

Notes

The setting

1. The area's archaeology lacks systematic documentation. Ghasidian (2018) reports on a Palaeolithic site in the southeast of the province, for example, and Potts (2016) discusses the reach of Elam into the Zagros area. Friedl and R. Loeffler (2013) describe various archaeological sites encountered while traveling in the area. On aspects of tribal life and history, see Baver (1945), R. Loeffler (1989, 2002), Safinejād (1989: 133–5).
2. The name of the province has no standard transliteration. Local people pronounce it 'bearamad' or 'beiramad'. For local amateur folklorists this means, *be rāh-e Med*, that is, the way along (the southern border of) the Median Empire, between the ninth and seventh centuries BC. Kohgiluye, the southwestern part of the province, is locally pronounced *Kukhgiluye*, which in local etymology may refer to a wood-and-stone hut (*kokh, kukh*) plus the name of a giant demon (*gelu, gilu*), or else a half-underground dwelling.
3. In Sisakht literacy is nearly 90 per cent; formal, secular education (beyond Quran lessons) is considered a gateway to progress since the 1920s and was driven by local people and some heroic teachers who faced often violent opposition from the tribal elite until the 1960s.
4. R. Loeffler and Friedl (1967), R. Loeffler, Friedl and Janata (1974) cover the complete material culture in the settlement of Sisakht in the 1960s in a catalogue of their collection of artefacts, now at the World Museum in Vienna, Austria. Digard (1981) describes the similar, traditional material culture of the neighbouring Bakhtiari. See also the ethno-archaeological studies of Kramer (1982) and Watson (1979) of Kurds in the central Zagros. For prehistoric artefacts, see Hole (2004) and Abdi (2003, 2012).
5. Water-driven mills had been in use by a previous population in the area and continued there until being replaced by motor-driven mills in the mid-twentieth century.
6. Mostly lentils, known in West Asia for some 9,000 years; see Arranz-Ortaegui et al. (2018).
7. The oldest known, similar flatbread, made of ground barley, is documented from about 12,400 BC in a hunter-gatherer site in Jordan (Arranz-Otaegui et al. 2018). The local acorn-meal bread (*kalg*) was vilified as poor back-country people's food, but rather than disappearing from the list of food choices it has become a nostalgic status food item.

8   Ghafari (n.d). In the mid-twentieth century, poppy cultivation (for opium, outlawed in the 1960s), tobacco and sugar beets provided too little income to sustain people. Profitable fruit cultivation started in the 1970s.
9   For examples of such elements in Islam, see Fakhry (1999); Bdaiwi (forthcoming).
10 Around 1950 local chiefs demanded labour, a third of their tribesmen's harvests and 'gifts' such as lambs or honey. Their demands increased steadily.
11 Abdullah Khan Zarghami (c. 1904–63) was assassinated by a bribed servant on behest of the government for his violent opposition to the White Revolution, especially the land reform.
12 Locally, fertility dropped so fast that the Islamic Republic's government became alarmed (see A. Loeffler and Friedl 2014). With the decrease, childrearing practices changed, too; see Friedl (2017).
13 The chiefs protested but the 'peasants' won; see R. Loeffler (1971).
14 The environmental deterioration in the high Zagros happened within twenty years. In the early 1940s Koelz (1983) and Garrod (1946) saw lush pastures and abundant wildlife throughout the Zagros range, but also an 'inordinate rate' of destruction and deforestation by the 'nomadic hunters' (Garrod 1946: 33). By 1965 all natural resources were severely stressed if not depleted. By 1970 hunting no longer was a realistic choice for getting meat because edible wildlife was gone and only few men were licensed to have a gun. For a history and discussion of the khans' rule, see R. Loeffler (1971, 2002, 2011) and Ganzer (2008). Safinejad (1989) on page 739 describes sociopolitical issues in the wider area of central Iran.
15 Personal communication by the head of the research committee, 1985 and 1995. By 1995 conditions had 'improved', she said. Ill health among tribal women, though, is still an issue that public health officials and local physicians discuss for tribes in Iran generally.
16 A general pattern in Iran, it is worse in Boir Ahmad. Iran has the lowest labour participation of women in the Middle East according to the Global Gender Gap Report (2018: 127). This is a neglected topic in social science research on Iran.
17 Ganzer (2008) saw this as an expression of genuine Shia religious fervour, while local people explain that poor people expect economic assistance when they support government authorities. Sisakhti people describe such tribal Party-of-God adherents as wild and uneducated beneficiaries of the Islamic Welfare State.
18 Ivanov (1961) summarized what was known about the area at that time, including from Persian sources.
19 How we got permission to go there is, I understand, a matter of speculation among some colleagues. The fact is mundane: we travelled on Austrian passports, and during long, frustrating weeks in Tehran trying to get permission to visit Boir Ahmad, we had the good fortune of establishing contacts among Austrian and German expatriates that led to help from a high-ranking police officer who recommended us

to the police in Shiraz. The relationship with these officers established a track record for our subsequent applications for visas and research permits.
20 In 2018 it was a city of nearly 100,000 people with a university and a medical school. It keeps growing by attracting people mostly from central Boir Ahmad and from other provinces.
21 The successful tribal mobile school programme, directed by Mr Mohammad Bahmanbegi (1920–2010) from the Qashqa'i tribe, was initiated by the United States Point Four Program in 1951 and provided basic education for migrating tribal groups. For a discussion, see Shahbazi (1998).
22 This then-and-now litany is meant to highlight what people see as the difference that development made to their lifestyle options over fifty years.
23 Such support ranged from vouching for us and using influence with officials, several times without our knowledge, to demonstrative support of our presence. When an itinerant preacher refused to pray in the presence of the 'foreign unbeliever', my husband, the 'unbeliever', left. But a prominent local leader, stomping his cane, loudly declared that with this refusal the preacher's prayer now would be invalid before God. The incident made history in town.

Introduction

1 Given my linguistic limits and the local gender-indexed lifeways, I cannot distinguish language differences between men and women much beyond noticing that men more likely than women address me in Farsi. However, I understand most of what men, women and children say and I ask for clarification when in doubt.
2 Several publications were translated into Farsi but as Iran is not signatory to copyright agreements, I am not notified about publications. To foster accessibility I try to write as plainly as the topics allow, to let the many local people who know some English appreciate the texts in a general way. Opinion leaders among them spread the verdict that what R. Loeffler and I write is 'true' and 'respectful' of Sisakht even if it is critical of many issues.
3 Key functionalist social elements in organized religion such as supporting ethics and fostering identity and a sense of community are evident here but they are not the book's focus.
4 Most local people acknowledge the great variety in their values and behaviours between 'good, right' and 'bad, sinful'. They may explain 'bad' acts with 'necessity' (*majburi*) such as 'to save my reputation I was forced to lie', or with the need to satisfy customs or Islam or progress or responsibilities for dependents, such as 'If I don't show up at the government-organised demonstration my son won't get accepted at university.' A psychiatrist from Boir Ahmad saw people's versatility

in manipulating ethics and choices as rooted in their history and in their difficult socio-economic and psychological circumstances.

5 Conditions are declining, though, and poverty is increasing. It is anybody's guess how long the debt- and sanctions-burdened economy of Iran will keep people from hunger, a local retired government employee told me in 2019. In 2020 conditions worsened yet, and many additional people fell well below poverty. In addition, Covid-19 muted New Year's celebrations (21 March); 'God is punishing the whole world,' said an old friend.

6 See Friedl (2020); the articles in Afary (2020) speak to this and to related themes in Iran.

7 People credit the foresight and progress-oriented energy of their famous chief, Qobad Nikeqbal (c. 1860–1937) for the village's development, for vineyards and orchards, schools and a resident cleric. 'Mulla Qobād' was known throughout the area (Christian 1919: 65/6). Preceding a name, 'Mulla' means a learned, literate person, male or female. A religious specialist is called *ākhond*, translated as 'mullah' or 'cleric' in English.

8 For the history, forms and importance of progress in town, see R. Loeffler (2011), Friedl (1991, 2017a).

9 Recent research documents the psychological and neurological basis of what we call religious beliefs as pan-human, in evidence already for early humans. For discussions of various aspects of the development of religion see, for example, Boyer and Bergstrom (2008), Dennett (2007); Peoples, Duda and Marlowe (2016).

10 A common question about the sponsors of students' tuition in state colleges in my hometown was about the reaction of the sponsors' heirs to losing their inheritance. In 2015, according to a story from Shiraz, the sons of a wealthy man who planned to build a school in a poor village with what they saw as their future inheritance successfully took him to court to block the deal. By contrast, religious taxes, endowments (*vaqf*) and support of religious rituals are expected to bring benefits in the form of religious merits and are not routinely linked to inheritance. Locally and among poor people neither form of generosity is important, though.

11 See Jeldtoft (2011) for the splintering of the meaning of 'Islam' and 'Muslim identity' if looked at closely within the frame of 'lived religion'. For the difficult theoretical issue of representation see, for example, Fadil and Fernando (2015) and the discussion following their essay.

12 Ernst (2005: 224) describes it within the historical formation of the concept 'Islam'. The Islamization of local pieties is greatly aided by modern media-technology that disseminates televised sermons and lectures by mullahs even to tent camps and small villages in Iran, and by travel opportunities to shrines that unite Muslims globally.

13 It is also potentially dangerous. In August 2019 the sociologist Kameel Ahmady, who reports on controversial cultural and legal matters regarding women and children in Iran (Ahmady 2017), was detained by police there for several weeks.

14 Such sleight-of-hand arguments are the backbone of magical thinking and popular in all religions-as-lived.
15 Grand Ayatollah Khomeini officially was the thirteenth Imam in Iran. For a comprehensive introduction to Shiism in Iran see, for example, Richard (1995). The largest non-Muslim minorities in Iran are Christians, Zoroastrians, Jews and Bahai. All are dwindling under governmental pressure; see Annual Report (2018.) The only non-Shiites in Boir Ahmad are some Baha'i families living in their own small villages. Persecuted since soon after the Revolution, most have converted or left.
16 This effect is known from participants in any organized religious group. For the epistemic value of the logic of belief, see Townsend (2019).
17 On a recent global misery index ('Misery Index Scores' 2018), Iran is the third most miserable country in the world (see also Ray 2019). In March 2019 the government increased the minimum wage in the private sector to $480 per month for a family of four with one earner, which is half of the official consumer costs; unemployment and inflation are in double digits, and after pay rises the bazar quickly increases prices (Jalili 2019).
18 As used locally, 'hezbollah' implies political and religious commitment rather than a direct political connection to the Hezbollah Party in Lebanon. For defining and naming Islamic formations such as 'fundamentalism' see, for example, Lewis (1988: 117). Occasionally, I use 'traditional Islam' for local, pre-hegemonic features of Islam.
19 This concept (Ammerman 2006; McGuire 2008) shifted official religious norms to religious ideas in a community and to individual differences in religiosity. The articles in Gasparini et al. (2020) make one think that we know more about lived religion in antiquity than in modern Islam.
20 Demant Mortensen (1993: 121), claiming to speak for 'all writers except one' who discuss the Lurs, came to the conclusion that Lur people 'have only a faint idea of orthodox religion and to a large degree have been ignorant of and indifferent to the Islamic doctrines, while at the same time they indulge in superstitious rites and have deep veneration for local pirs and saints'. Melotti (2019: 243) calls this statement a 'primitivistic view' that allows scholars to ignore 'otherness'.
21 The two archaeologists' twenty photographs of shrines they saw during archaeological surveys in the Pusht-i-Kuh part of Luristan (another Lur province in the Zagros mountains) document the great variety of shrine structures there. They suggest a saint-cult similar to that in Boir Ahmad.
22 Jeldtoft (2011: 1134), talking about Muslims in Germany and Denmark, warns: 'By focusing on institutionalized forms of Islam we run the risk of reifying Muslims as being "all about Islam".
23 Black-Michaud (1986: 131–2) describes the link between organized religion and political power in Luristan that we also saw in Boir Ahmad: members of the elite can afford time for religious activities and generosity towards religious institutions, and 'generally use their godliness to compel respect'.

24 For people who see the past as prologue to the present, most of these powers are identifiable as descendants of ancient deities, and many rituals as reminiscent of ancient practices. For discussion and examples see Henkelman and Redard (2017); Kreyenbroek (2002, 2011).
25 See Moaddel (2009). Three panels at the Thirteenth Meeting of the Association for Iranian Studies in 2020 address these topics.
26 We seem to know more about Muslims' complex everyday practices in Europe than in Iran; see Dessing et al. (2016). Kolb and Yildiz (2019), describing Islamic diversity in Austria, discuss the heuristic problem in essentializing approaches to Muslims' religious lives.

Chapter 1

1 Pre-Socratic disbelievers rejected the myths of the day as unprovable assertions, starting a tradition of empirical inquiry as the legitimate path to knowledge. A local elderly woman with a similar mindset said, 'I *know* (*dunom*) that above the Dena-mountain is no more air to breathe; so, I just have to *believe* (*bāver konom*) that the Prophet survived going up to heaven.' In logic, Justified True Knowledge and the links among experience, authority-based, binding beliefs and what one knows remain an epistemological problem (Gerken 2017).
2 See Shayegan (1996).
3 See Mt. 7:12. In Farsi it is *qānun-e talā-ii* (Golden Law): people ought to treat everybody as they want to be treated themselves; or judge your own behaviour as you judge that of others.
4 See the Introduction about this misconception. R. Loeffler (1988) was the first to describe the great diversity in religious thinking in a tribal place, contradicting Barth's (1961) and Planck's hasty suggestion of a 'religious indifference of nearly all villagers' (1962: 62) that they had studied briefly in places near Boir Ahmad.
5 For the evolution from an imagistic to a doctrinal mode of religiosity as societies grow, see Whitehouse (2019).
6 I thank my librarian friend and historian, Beatrice Beech, for the discussions leading to this term.
7 Farsi, *ādat-e ruzmarih*. They come close to the Roman *mos maiorum* (ancestors' habits), seven pillars of ethics that guided private and public life, which, in turn, are similar to Persian *ensānyat* (humanity, good human qualities).
8 In local words, 'everything goes bad; all things fall and tumble; it is hard to keep order, to keep a straight line', and such. The ancient notion of divine logos pitted against chaos is visible here. A local woman summed up the end of the exploitative, ruthless rule of the last chiefs in Boir Ahmad with, 'Slowly the world returned to its own orderly place' (*yāvash dunyā ve jā khosh umā*).

9 In 2006 a literate, outspoken man described it: 'In this world the wolf eats the sheep, the big fish the little fish, the fox the chicken, and strong humans "eat" the weak. God can interfere if He wishes, can make a weak man strong and fell a strong one. The Quran and our poet Sa'adi say that eventually human beings will figure out everything except God.'

10 God's whereabouts are of little interest. He may be resting on a throne in heaven (*behesht*), as traditional believers say, or 'somewhere in paradise' or even 'everywhere' in the nature He created. Contemporary Islamic theologies regarding God's residence that reach local people are said to be vague and contradictory.

11 Recently, the link between social structure and people's ideas about deities emerged in a multidisciplinary research project. It suggests a teleological function of religion: 'Belief in morally concerned supernatural agents culturally evolved to facilitate cooperation among strangers in large-scale societies' (Whitehouse et al. 2019).

12 'Mullah' and 'cleric' are the terms used in English for what in Iran is *ākhond*. A mullah is not only a preacher but also a judge; Iran's sharia law, although administered with independent judicial power, is heavily influenced by religious laws. People call the present time the 'period of the mullahs' (*doureh ākhondal*).

13 Pedagogies of piety (Szanto 2012) in schools have produced several champion Quran reciters in Sisakht. School tests contain questions on Islam. Many jokes play on the theme of oppression, such as 'After the Revolution, an American, an African and an Iranian are asked their opinion about meat-vouchers. The African says, "What is meat?" The American says, "What is a voucher?" The Iranian says, "What is opinion?"'

14 For the government's persecution of minorities like Bahaï and Christians, see Ensor (2018). Most local people see this persecution as unworthy of 'true Muslims'. In Iran, conversions to Christianity happen despite the danger of apostasy accusations. The Hebrew Immigrant Aid Society in Vienna reports having assisted some 25,000 religious refugees from Iran since 2001 ('Caring for Iranian Religious Minorities', n.d.).

15 Several young men were executed, others fled abroad. Most remain lost; a few established contact years later but, afraid of reprisals against relatives, only let them know they were alive.

16 A sad joke from the Iran–Iraq war (1980–8), when fallen soldiers were said to go straight to paradise, has a dead soldier look for it. He sees Husein (the Prophet's martyred grandson) sitting at a door and asks him the way. Husein says, 'I have been waiting here to be let in for more than thousand years. Just sit down and wait with me.'

17 Boir Ahmad is a mountainous hinterland, but this has not prevented new ideas from moving there. It has a long cultural history. See Friedl and R. Loeffler (2013).

18 I have heard this in Iran as well as in the expatriate Iranian community in the United States. This optimism is based on elitist–paternalistic condescension towards

rural/tribal people and is resented locally. A local medical student at a northern university pretended to be from Shiraz, a big city, to avoid the stigma of 'Lur' or 'tribal villager'. This is a common practice.

19 In Sisakht the first organizers of the Shia passion play (*tazië*) were from outside the tribal area, in the early 1960s. It was a mostly male affair, with four times as many male as female spectators in 1965. Although widely popular, people also called the dramatic ritual 'child's play, un-Islamic, undignified commotion'. 'I don't need to watch a dressed-up horse to know that I am a Muslim,' said a young man in 1981, before watching anyway. In 2006 women said they felt obligated to make the weekly graveyard visits.

20 The old mosque was a one-room mudbrick house like any other, only bigger, a prayer hall where occasionally men got together socially or to pray, and where votive meals were cooked. The new, domed mosque was built in 2002 by an urban man living in town who elicited funds from a rich Iranian woman expatriate in Kuwait. 'We got a good mosque and she gets merits from our prayers inside it,' joked a worker.

21 'People's hearts have turned' (*del mardom veri vābi*) and 'Money rides, people walk' (*pil suvār vābi, ādam va pā*) are popular sayings. People point to the flexibility of Islamic ethics as shown in Islamic scholars' different interpretations of scriptures, in the different Islamic legal schools and in various personal pieties. Ourghi (2019) sees a need for reform of Islamic ethics.

22 Mullahs are said to be rather uneducated in matters outside religion. In 2015 people wondered about the differences in the messages between sermons and science-oriented programmes on the internet. Several government-religion adherents declared science broadcasts to be illegal propaganda by Western enemies, whereupon most everybody else called the critics 'illiterate'.

23 In 2015 critics of the government routinely called the mullahs' promise of paradise and hell 'a lie' and the promoted cult of saints, 'superstition'. In jokes, 'Hajj Agha' represents government leaders: 'Hajj Agha was wearing two different shoes. A neighbour remarked on it. Hajj Agha said, "Yes, indeed. Strangely, I have another such mismatched pair at home."' In a joke about mullahs' purported avarice, a mullah is asked to divide an inheritance and says, 'From the ground to the roof of the house is only six meters – this be my small fee; from there upwards it is endless – this is for the heirs.' People take dreaming of a bearded man (*merdak pashmelu*), that is, a Party-of-God member or a Revolutionary Guard, to be a bad omen. Such 'weapons of the weak' (Scott 1985) do not change the political landscape, though, and are dangerous for jokers and critics.

24 The Hebrew root of *din*, implying law, legal power and judgement is visible in the emphasis on rules and obligations in Islamic scriptures and sermons. The Arabic term for religion, *mazhab*, is replacing *din* in many sermons, people say, purging 'religion' even more rigorously of 'old superstitions'. Avestan *daena* (revelation, understanding) may also be included in *din* but is not in evidence in local usage.

25 This pertains not only to remote Boir Ahmad but to varying degrees to Shia Iran generally, no matter how hard the guardians of the faith try to eliminate non-Islamic elements such as the rituals around the Zoroastrian New Year (*nowruz*) or non-authenticated saints' shrines. In Boir Ahmad, however, the confluence of beliefs and rituals typical of small-scale societies and those surrounding a moralizing 'Big God' of a complex society is visible to this day under the umbrella of a syncretized Islam. See Kreyenbroek (2002) for historical aspects of the 'powers-to-deities' development.

26 Locally, the proselytizing, that is, the 'Islamization of Islam', started already in the 1960s. Earlier yet, khans and village chiefs tended to be patrons of imported clerics and their formal and scripture-bound practices. The first resident mullah, in the 1940s, reportedly was a poor young *Mirza* (son of a Seyed's daughter) from a village in Fars Province known for its fundamentalist piety. In 2015 an old man remembered that the local chief hosted the 'beggar-mullah' in exchange for permission to take many temporary wives, the girls and women 'the chief had stolen from other villages'. As the mullah prospered he called himself Seyed, a patrilineal descendant of the Prophet. His son married a daughter of the chief (R. Loeffler 1989: 17–29).

27 Seyed is every male in the patrilineal line of the Prophet Muhammad. Ayatollah is a Shia religious leader, an expert in Shia theology and jurisprudence. Imam is a particularly exalted spiritual and religious leader. Shia doctrine accepts twelve Imams who led the faithful in the early years of Islam. The old farmer objects to the inclusion of Seyed Khomeini in this special, revered group. Imamzadeh are patrilineal descendants of the twelve Imams; many are revered as 'saints' in shrines erected above their burials; see Chapter 4.

28 A nosebleed was taken to indicate the saint's rejection of a 'bad' pilgrim. People said that in the past the fear of such public humiliation kept 'many' people from visiting the big shrines. Upon return, a pilgrim to Kerbela is addressed with the honorific 'Kerbelai' in front of the name.

29 In fundamentalist Hezbollah circles, this civilizing function counts as 'culture' (*farhang*), shown in modest dress and gender relations, regime loyalty and knowledge of Islam.

30 'Muslims are troublemakers,' said a retired local teacher who regularly listened to the news.

31 Soon after the Revolution, people said that the biggest goat and sheep herder in the province now was an absentee owner, a wealthy urban mullah who somehow had been able to get grazing rights over tribal pastures.

32 For 'progress' in Boir Ahmad, see Friedl (2017a). Local people participate in the country's brain drain, escaping ideological and economic pressures as they do elsewhere (Hegland, personal communication, June 2018). Admirers of the Iranian-born late Field Medal recipient Maryam Mirzakhani of Stanford University point

out that she had to go abroad to earn fame and success. After widespread unrest, in January 2018 President Rouhani demanded that the government 'increase domestic capacities' as the Iranian people demanded (Darian and Falcone 2018) but people say conditions are not improving.
33   I did not learn of a young woman dervish but theoretically this choice is open to all. Local unmarried women joke that they hide in their father's or a brother's house.
34   People mocked idle men for 'sitting around and keeping their hands on the penis so that the cat won't take it'.
35   A similarly 'crazy' student stunned his relatives when he came from the city for a visit clean shaven, dressed in white, his hair dyed blond. He and his likeminded friends were honouring Ali, the Prophet Muhammad's paternal cousin and son-in-law, who is described as light-skinned and light-haired, by copying his appearance.
36   During Muharram, the first month in the lunar Islamic calendar, Shiites mourn the Prophet's grandson, Husein, who died in the battle over leadership of the faithful, in AD 680. See, for example, Chelkowski (1979).
37   The village Khour (Khafr) has a shrine that is popular with Sisakhti pilgrims. The pass, over 3,000 metre high, has snow until mid-summer. The road is dangerous to this day.
38   During this war, 1980–8, young recruits who were used as minesweepers and frontline fighters reportedly received such keys to paradise.
39   Religion, government and swindle also came together when a local man complained about a large utility bill for an empty house. His monthly statements supported his complaint, whereupon the utilities clerk turned the table and accused him of agitating against the Revolution and Islam.
40   'Traditionalists' here include old-timers with old ideas about gender as well as proponents of gender separation within the state religion. Iran has one of the lowest rates of women in the labour force in the Middle East ('Iran Labor Force Participation' 2018).
41   Demands for more freedom (*āzādi*) are getting louder, but in 2019 the government nevertheless tightened rules by telling people to report on neighbours' 'moral crimes' and on infractions of 'public chastity' (Daragahi 2019) in order to curb the ordinance-defiant behaviours of young urban women and men.
42   The so-called Five Pillars of Islam (*arkān al-din*, based on the hadith of Gabriel) in formal Shia use contain basic choices for handling morality issues that define Muslims.
43   'We must pray because our *din* demands it: girls start at nine years of age, boys at fourteen. God does not need our prayers; they are for our own benefit,' said a teacher, and a physician was even more specific: 'Prayers heal.' Publications such as Qummi (1999) contain hundreds of prayers and detailed proscriptions for their performance that are claimed to heal, protect and bestow other this-worldly benefits.

44 Ramadan, the ninth month in the Islamic moon calendar, falls on different dates each year in the solar calendar. It commemorates the revelation of the Quran to the Prophet Muhammad.
45 Endangering one's health in the name of religion may be declared meritorious although it neglects the duty to care well for one's body. A missed fast has to be made up later.
46 Neither the pretence of the empty kettle nor the sheep rustling drew comment. The pardoning of the thief showed that feeding the hungry morally outweighed the (necessary) theft. In the past, when there was no food in a house, a woman could pretend to cook to avoid drawing embarrassing attention to her and her husband's inability to feed the family.
47 These are the choices for pilgrims' reasons: the hajj is a duty for those who can afford it; it bestows honour on the pilgrim; it is a pleasure; it is a visit to the esteemed and beloved saints, that is, to the places where they had lived or were buried. With the visit comes the hope that they will help in some way. (However, visits to saints at home are more important for 'help' issues and easier to do.) For the hajj see Wheeler (2019).
48 The government subsidizes such pilgrimages. In 2002 a bank clerk explained the expenses for a pilgrimage to Kerbela, Iraq (to the shrine of the Prophet's grandson Husein, slain there by his political enemies in AD 680): for each Iranian pilgrim the Iraqi government demanded 400,000 toman. For the 3,000 Iranian weekly pilgrims the fee was some $7.8 million. There is no point in asking if this sum is factual – it was what he and others believed. Despite the subsidies, most pilgrims in Sisakht take loans for such trips.

Chapter 2

1 Such incongruities appear in any religious behaviour. Kaźmierczak (2017) elaborates this theme in discussing the writings and sermons of Meister Eckhart, a famous medieval mystic.
2 The terms have political overtones. Critics of the 'Arabic mullahs' assert that Lurs knew *khodā* long before the Arabs knew Allah. Reportedly, some Malaysian Muslim preachers object to Christians using 'Allah' in prayers because Allah is the true God of Islam.
3 A joke has a hurried cleric inadvertently touch a dog, which makes him ritually impure and in need of changing his clothes. Instead, he mumbles, 'God willing, it was a cat,' and hurries on. *Bismillah* ('in the name of Allah') is said to repel jinn and fairies; *mashallah* ('may Allah will it') to prevent the evil eye from striking; and *alhamdulillah* ('Allah be praised') to express relief and heartfelt gratitude. Young people tend to call such ejaculations quaint and old-fashioned.

4 Pious Muslims point to the ongoing expansion of Islam: whoever studies Islam will embrace it, convinced of its intellectual and moral superiority.

5 God has no grammatical gender, but as a powerful creator, ruler and judge is perceived as male. Atheists' arguments that endlessness and eternity preclude the universe's creation by any universal mind or God (Empedocles, 495–430 BC; see Jayne 2018: 28) is unconvincing for believers: God is eternal precisely because He is not bound by humans' limited reasoning. Boyer (2010) discusses atheists' arguments relevant for our theme.

6 See R. Loeffler (1988), Friedl (2001: 125–33). For a rare, illuminating discussion of disbelief in antiquity see Jayne (2018).

7 Quran verses are the prime example although their beauty and meanings have to be taken on faith because few people read Arabic. The earthly garden is more than a metaphor for the heavenly garden: to design or tend a garden is said to accrue religious merits.

8 For example, *makhlut* (mixed up), *harj-o-marj*, *khert o pert* (topsy-turvy, helter-skelter, chaos), *sholugh* (tumult, uproar), *picide* (crooked, convoluted), *kelu* (crazy, out of turn, incoherent), *houj* (noise, unrest, agitation).

9 In 2015 a troubled local student listed his doubts: 'Why did God make me? I had no choice, He just did it, like a dictator. What does God need the creation for? I see no point in it at all. What for does an almighty God need people's prayers and fasting? I think they belittle God. What is His reason for the suffering in the world? What did He create criminals for? Character is in the genes – so, the genes are God?' He ended with a joke: 'I guess I have to believe in the afterlife so that I can ask God directly.'

10 This verse also implies that people who do well in this world show by their success that they can match and resist God's harmful powers.

11 The poor health of weaned children in the past was said to show that relying on father's food made toddlers weak, that unlike mothers, fathers did not provide well for their children.

12 For a discussion of the complex Sufi gratitude theology, see, for example, Khalil (2016).

13 For this and other forms of 'fate', see Chapter 3.

14 Local healers, herbalists and bonesetters used traditional skills, refined and expanded by experience, to help people, without requesting payment. Their knowledge was a gift from God, not a business, they said. Modern medicine, by contrast, is a business based on science (not on God directly or knowledge available to everybody), is expensive and produces better results, people joke.

15 In 2010 the local fiancée of an expatriate Iranian asked him to send documents not on Saturday but on Monday. He called this 'superstition' but complied.

16 Until around 2006 local people excused urban holiday tourists who stole from their orchards: 'poor city-folk' had no choice, they lacked fresh fruits at home, they said.

17 On the effects of quiet and often maligned Sufi principles in Islam, see Ernst (2005). For a concise history of Sufism in Iran, see Van den Bos (2007).
18 Farsi *durugh* (lie, deceit, confusion) is based on Avestan *druj*, a spirit-principle in opposition to truth and order, *asha*. See Boyce (2001), Foltz (2013).
19 The hadith is a compilation of legends about and purported sayings of the Prophet Muhammad that provide guidance beyond the Quran.
20 There is no sin in assuring an anxious mother that her dying child will get well. Physicians in Iran insist that such lies are a small price for the benefit of preventing shock and depression even though they create distrust in diagnoses. See A. Loeffler (2015).
21 In the past, local morality based on Islamic principles and enforced by political powers demanded the death of a woman who engaged in illegal sex. The local chief allegedly burned one to death in the 1950s. Given that catastrophe the above story makes good sense. Until recently, flirtations were either nipped in the bud or turned into conventional courtship to prevent gossip. Sexual mores are changing fast in Iran and are taken out of the discourse of morality especially by young people. See Afary (2009), Hegland (2020), Mahdavi (2009).
22 Portentous dreams heralded a local mullah's death. While he was on the hajj, his nephew at home was troubled by a dream about the uncle coming home on a truck under a green blanket. Next a relative in a dream saw him fall off a pulpit, and then a Mecca pilgrim phoned that he had dreamt that the Mullah had delivered a strange, shaky sermon. Two weeks later he died, in 2002.
23 Legal justice (Farsi *edālat*) locally is *haqq* (law) in the sense of what is one's due.
24 For children see Friedl (1997); for political conditions see R. Loeffler (1971, 2002), Hegland (2014).
25 A functionalist explanation is that such rituals keep chaos away by protecting one's tolerance for inconsistencies that challenge the order of one's world (Peterson 1999).
26 A sacrificial 'blood-spilling' (*khinrizi*) is done for causes ranging from preventing an evil eye injury to helping a sick child and protecting a house. Poor recipients of the meat will bless the donor. The benefit is placed in a social ethic, coming (from God) via the poor's blessing.
27 See also Chapters 1 and 3. Here I discuss the 'good person' as it relates directly to God-attributes.
28 *Marg bar komunisi si ce igon khodā nise.* They had learnt it in school, children said.
29 They commented that it was 'good' because it emitted blessings and because it demonstrated to visitors their own religious (and thus political) allegiance.
30 The argument that the Prophet had four main wives is not convincing. This was *then*, people argue, but now it won't work, and therefore it is a sin. Believers attuned to the government religion simply argue that co-wives 'must get along' because the Quran demands it. Polygyny has become a great worry for women in the Islamic

Republic but also, for some, an opportunity to become the second wife of a wealthy man, a 'love-wife' with an easy life.
31 God will not punish a 'good' thief who is kind, helpful and takes care of his family.
32 The sin is in troubling the dead child. A distraught mother dreamt that her tears were stirring up mud in her thirsty dead child's water bowl. While adults ought to cry in gratitude for dead parents who raised them, a parent whose young child dies has no such obligation: the child has not done anything (yet) for the parent. Parent-centred ethics inform traditional intra-family relations.
33 The Boir Ahmad historian, Mr Ata Taheri, had this example: 'The Lur ethic is about survival. If a praying man learns that his cow got lost, he will stop the prayer and go after the cow' (Personal communication, June 2015).
34 *Zan ve gashtan, mard ve neshastan.* Educated people see this as a major obstacle for women's work outside the home, and people steeped in government religion see it as part of God's order.
35 Yet, even theft has a twist in a pauper's morality schema: a rich person refusing a beggar's request commits a sin, while the beggar commits no sin if he then steals what he needs.
36 It was part of the pillage-and-plunder life before the tribal chiefs' power was broken in the 1960s. Since then, one manslaughter happened locally in a fight over water rights, another in a drug-dispute in a neighbouring village, and a third in 2014, when a baker's altercation with a stranger who demanded service ahead of waiting women and children ended in the man's fatal fall into a ditch. Largely forgotten are the deaths of at least two young women at the hands of male relatives within the past twenty years that were rephrased as suicides. Violence against women weighs less than violence against men.
37 Party-of God adherents credit this development to good Islamic leadership, but it had started before the Revolution. People credit 'progress' for women's falling suicide rates and blame the men's rising suicide rate on economic and domestic hardships due to incompetent leadership.
38 For Shiites, Amir al-Mu'minin, 'Commander of the Faithful', is Ali, the Prophet's highly regarded son-in-law. The Imams are the twelve early Muslim leaders, descendants of the Prophet. By calling on them here the speaker expresses her impatience with the question.

Chapter 3

1 Multiple universes are an option when thinking about God. In 1966 an illiterate woman argued herself into this multiplicity, saying that according to the scriptures, God will create another world after ours, and this means that probably He had

made others before ours, maybe wanting to make each better. Nobody around her had heard of philosopher-theologians like al-Ghazali who mulled these questions. For al-Ghazali's theology see Ormsby (1984).
2 For these terms see also Segal (2004: 651). The Arabic *nafs* usually is translated as soul, the self.
3 The argument goes: if you are shot in the head, you will die; if you are shot in the foot, you will not die. Ergo there is more life-*jun* in the head than in the foot.
4 Devout Muslims and Muslim theologians give such doubters unfriendly names like misguided ignoramuses, heathens or blasphemers because their arguments are 'unscientific', as they say: doubters believe in microbes which they cannot see either. Even women have become cautious when stating their opinions.
5 In Luri this condition has a different term, without 'soul': *harasa*, as in *harasa tang* (a tight, heavy, disquiet, depressed mind).
6 According to the Twelver Doctrine in Iranian Shiism, the Twelfth Imam, Muhammad al-Mahdi (AD 869–941), the 'Hidden Imam', is alive, in occultation until the Last Day, when he will lead the faithful in a new, just and peaceful world.
7 This proverb (*mish ve pei khosh iarkeshen, boz ve pei khosh*) implies relativism: personal and general differences (such as male and female, rich and poor) will be taken into consideration by the other-worldly judges of morality. Here it is used to express in a roundabout way the widespread doubt about the desirability of husbands and wives to be reunited in paradise. 'What would my husband want me for with all the houris around?' is a standard joke of women.
8 Before roads were built in the province in the 1960s, such pilgrimages took 'weeks' on foot and were dangerous. The speaker counts easy travel as part of the better life she now enjoys.
9 *Muqāfāt* may be a punishment from God or else a misfortune coming by itself. A man in the former chief's family with two impaired children ascribed this misfortune to his 'bad luck' (*shans bad*) and to 'God's Will' (*meile khodā*). A neighbour called it a punishment of the man's aggressive ancestors' misdeeds (*kār harum*) and unlawful 'seed' (*tokhm harum*).
10 The urban version of this ritual (*estekhāre kardan*) does not involve Fatemeh. Questions are, for example, 'Should I accept the marriage proposal? Is this girl a good wife for my son? Will I find my lost cow again?'
11 She prays, 'Oh *qeble*, your final pilgrimage; Oh speechless tree, Oh flowing water, Oh crossroad of Morteza Ali, tonight the new year starts – God willing, you bless all Muslims and especially my children.' Pilgrimage, tree, water and crossroads refer to the legendary life of Ali, the cousin and son-in law of the Prophet, whose shrine is in Nejaf, Iraq.
12 *Ruzegār* may also be conceived of as a kind of wind that brings with it whatever happens.

13 These powers can be seen as survivors of pre-Islamic deities acting as the creator-God's managers. One such power is 'Old Woman' (*pirezan*), likely a descendant of a weather-deity, providing a background to several traditional, quaint idioms, such as 'We'll see where Old Woman will throw her burning log' (*tā binim pirezan koloftsha kuco verr ide*). During the last night of the second winter month, a pot with *dengu* (a dish of lentils, beans, peas, mung beans, wheat and barley) likely will be cooking to keep Old Woman from throwing her log into the fire, causing a dry year. (If there is no food, she also might pee into the fire; 'I'll pee on you' is a curse.) In 2006 Mr S. Ceraqi, a local amateur folklorist, told the nearly forgotten story. 'One cold, snowy day two boys were looking after their goats and disappeared in the snow. Their mother, Old Woman, took a log from the fireplace and went after them, crying, "Dear Ahmedi, dear Mahmani, a burning pistachio log is my light. I'll trawl the world with fire." At the river she threw her log into the water, a big cloud rose and it rained.' 'Now we say that if the log falls into the river, rain will come; if it falls in a bush, wind will come; if it falls on dry ground, a drought will come.'
14 The amulet usually consists of words of the Quran written on a piece of paper and wrapped into a piece of fabric; its power comes straight from the power of the holy words.
15 A poor Seyed in town got a second wife as a *nazr* (offering) without paying a bride price. He had to accept her but did not have to be subservient to her father like an ordinary son-in-law. The big problems this troublesome arrangement caused were 'written on the foreheads' of the two wives, people said.
16 Eid-e Qorban commemorates God's permission for obedient Abraham to substitute a sacrificial animal for his son.
17 For relevant observations on magic see Lewis (1986).
18 A corpse is buried on its back with straightened legs, the head towards Mecca. 'Incorrect' means buried with feet crossed or pointing towards Mecca, thus 'upsetting God's order'. Doubters call these ideas superstition but honour the burial practices as an established custom.
19 For the Zar cult see Segal (2004: 347), Beeman (2018).

Chapter 4

1 Since antiquity little has changed in the making of saints, in the etiquette for approaching them and in their uses for people. For historical aspects see Bowersock (2017), Dignas and Winter (2007), Meri (1999), North (2011), Rüpke (2013), Winkelmann (2007).
2 For examples see Eickelmann (1976), Fartacek (2003), Ghavashelishvili (2018), Malikov (2010), Segal (2004). Cults of saints also flourish in Sunni groups that

officially decry them as polytheism or suppress them for ideological reasons (Bonora, Pianciola and Sartori 2010; Kikuta 2017). For a recent eyewitness account of healing rituals at shrines in Sunni Kazakhstan, see Kambar (2019). For a subversive interpretation of the hajj obligation in Maliki jurisprudence, see Hendrickson (2016).

3 Unlike in other Shiite areas, 'living saints' are rare in Boir Ahmad. See Fremdgen (1998) for a description of the transition of a living saint to one venerated at a shrine in a Sufi context.

4 Fenton's essay (2019) on the mystical tradition in saint veneration in Islam (and Judaism) is most illuminating for the saint–client relationship in Sufism and as envisioned by local pilgrims, especially before pilgrimage tourism to the big Islamic shrines became popular.

5 In Boir Ahmad, the Shah Qāsom shrine is an example. The biggest shrine complex in Shiraz is Shah Ceragh, the Great Light (Honarpisheh 2013).

6 Christian saints are different. Their power rests on exemplary virtue or martyrdom that, together with God's grace, allows them to intercede with God on behalf of ordinary people.

7 Descent is counted through males: a brother and sister belong to the same patrilineage (their father's) but in the next generation only the brother's sons and daughters belong.

8 The most famous shrine in Iran is that of Imam Reza, the eighth Imam for Shia Muslims (AD 765–818) in Mashhad. Pilgrimages there, some 1,500 kilometres away from Sisakht, are said to have helped several local people. One was a violent, 'totally deranged' man in the khan's family who rode there on horseback and came back calm and reasonable, in the 1930s.

9 Imam Reza's sister Bibi Hakimeh is said to have died or disappeared while hiding from her enemies in the cave at the site. Her shrine is famous among Shiites around the Persian Gulf. (See photographs at various internet sites under 'Bibi Hakimeh Tomb'.) Except for pilgrimages to Mashhad, pilgrim-tourism inside Iran is underdeveloped (see Poulaki (2015) for Greece; Ebadi (2016)). Despite Turner's much-cited classic idea-based study of pilgrimages (Turner 1978), recent scholarship in the social sciences have a functionalist bias. See, for example, Sunith (2018), dealing with sociological aspects of pilgrimage in South Asia.

10 Conepa (2019) discusses ancient relationships between nature and shrines and their meaning for Persian identity. Kreyenbroek (2011) connects water and caves in pre-Islamic contexts.

11 The site is near the ruins of a Sasanian town. 'Khingah' means 'place of blood' and contains a memory of bloodshed when Zoroastrians in the area resisted conversion to Islam. Although 'Qāsom' is the Arabic/Muslim name 'Qasim', the absence of a grave made a local friend wonder if the power of the place might be that of a Zoroastrian 'saint' who was killed there by Muslims (Friedl and R. Loeffler 2013: 212).

12 In 1970 we visited a similar open-air site near the graveyard of the village of Bādengun. It had the layout of a Zoroastrian temple with remnants of four columns surrounded by a low wall with niches where people lit candles and put food offerings. In the space between this wall and a parallel one a few steps further out people stored firewood and tools – nobody would steal from an Imamzadeh. The area was littered with shards, signs of an earlier, sedentary population. A high rock in the background had the small man-made caves of Sasanian rock burials. Local people knew about the site's archaeological, pre-Islamic significance. They called it 'Emamzada Shahzadeh Abdullah' after somebody had dreamt that it was a saint's burial place. When we visited again soon after the Revolution, in 1981, government agents had razed everything. (R. Loeffler's photographs of the place disappeared when a thief stole the camera. It was the only time we were robbed in this 'country of robbers'.)

13 See Friedl and R. Loeffler (2013: 219). In Iranian mythology, Bānu Gošasb is not a 'kind lady'. A short epic from the twelfth century, the *Bānu Gošasb-nāma*, describes her as a fierce fighter, the daughter of the hero-king Rostam whom she battles by mistake, and the wife of Gēv, whom she does not treat kindly, either (Khaleghi-Motlagh 2012). By what quirk of history this formidable woman warrior became a 'kind lady' in Boir Ahmad is a mystery. In the opinion of a local amateur folklorist, people probably merged her with Zoroastrian *daenas*, the kind 'ladies of the good deeds' who, representing all that is good in people, were said to greet and accompany the dead in the afterlife (Sundermann 1992).

14 The largest and most important Emamzada in Iran, that of Imam Reza in Mashhad, is built over a Zoroastrian temple. The shrine of Darbe Ahanin, in Mamasani, a Lur tribal area adjacent to Boir Ahmad, is near a Sasanian fort. The archaeology of shrines in the area merits investigation. See Friedl and R. Loeffler (2013).

15 For example, Layard (2013: 110) mentions the 'conical tombs' in Kurdistan.

16 The Iranian archaeologist Adel Alehassan kindly sent me a photograph of such a grave in an email, 2 November 2017, identified as 'child's grave, gender unknown. No head stone, no inscripts'. A layer of stones also covers every interred body. A heap of little stones, called *kelkele*, marks the point along a road wherefrom an Emamzada is first visible, to 'honour the saint'.

17 The World Heritage Tomb of Cyrus II (600–530 BC), a Zoroastrian, is in Pasargadae, Fars Province, about 120 kilometres southeast of Boir Ahmad. For the tumult there, see Esfandiari (2017).

18 In a version of the foundation story of the settlement of Sisakht, a famously pious man living in Karyak, a village in the area with a well-known shrine, dreamt of a lion circling a certain tree near a spring in what then was an unpopulated pasture on the plain of Sisakht. This meant, the lion was doing *ziārat*, walking around the grave of an Imamzadeh, and people built a shrine there. The dreamer

planted walnut trees – traditionally the first step in establishing a settlement – and then people built houses. Thus the story links the founding of the shrine, of the settlement and one of the nine original families of Sisakht, in the late nineteenth century.

19 Ten years later, the Ayatollah's mausoleum complex covered acres in the largest graveyard in Iran and now attracts thousands of pilgrims annually.
20 Two Emamzada have the same Mongolian name ('Bibi Khatenun'); a few more have old Persian, Zoroastrian names.
21 Throughout the Near East, some people's breath ('efficacy of breath') and saliva count as potent healing agents. Saglam (2018: 15) describes this for contemporary Turkey.
22 This saint was said to be so powerful (*mojeze*, miraculous) that she once thwarted a thief by making pilgrims invisible to him long enough that they could catch him.
23 The vow (from Latin, *votum*, vote) is like a vote: a saint without vows is not popular, loses power, won't accept the visit or the offering (*nejādesh nemide*), and is forgotten just like a politician nobody votes for. See Honarpisheh (2013: 401) for an example of an abandoned shrine.
24 Petitions do not vary or change much. El-Missiri (1965: 64–8) listed the most prevalent ones in a village in Egypt at that time: to conceive a child, recover from illness, make a safe journey, succeed in school, find a job, take revenge on enemies (reported in Smith and Haddad 1981: 243). For women's 'controversial vows' in Iran, see Betteridge (2001: 134–43).
25 A local infertile woman had twins after a pilgrimage. Ghavashelishvili (2018) describes pilgrimages for this purpose in a Christian context in contemporary Georgia.
26 I thank Mary E. Hegland for this example (Personal communication, 12 November 2017).
27 I saw such a plea for examination help from a Muslim student in the biggest Marian pilgrimage place in Austria, written in Farsi, in 1998.
28 Reportedly, smugglers ask for protection of their high-risk journeys at a rich, new shrine near Shiraz people in Sisakht call 'Smuggler-Shrine' (Emamzada *Qāčākhči*).
29 This is sewn into a piece of velvet and hung around the neck of a baby or a sick person in expectation of protection against harm from jinn.
30 In this context, a dervish is a mendicant ascetic who seeks closeness to God through humility, poverty and meditative practices. The footloose lifestyle, reliance on begging and purported magical powers of dervishes make many people suspicious or afraid of them.
31 'The Saint granted the request' (*hājat ravā midād*; *hājatom barāvorde vābi*) is the 'Islamic' formulation, a neutral statement of fact. But 'The Saint did not listen to me' (*Sey gush vam nadā*) and 'The Saint looked at me' (*Sey seilom kerd*) are

loaded statements about the relationship between saint and petitioner, while 'May the Imamzadeh consent to your visit' (*Imamzādeh ziāratet qābul kone*) puts the interaction into a commercial frame: the saint has to approve the offering before helping the petitioner.

32 Abulfasl is Abbas ibn Abd al-Muttalib (AD 568–853), a paternal uncle and supporter of the Prophet Muhammad, buried in Medina.

33 The commercial side of such transactions is an issue among local critics of religious rituals but 'true believers' see the point, too. An experienced, avid pilgrim with regular votive obligations explained that 'like everybody else, the Imamzadeh want to get something before they help a supplicant'. For her, a realist, this was reasonable.

34 Betteridge's account of shrine veneration in the city of Shiraz covers not only dozens of shrines but also written requests and pleas for help that pilgrims dropped in shrines and shrine custodians then collected (Betteridge 1985, 1993: 239–47, 2001: 134–43). See also Khosronejad (2012). In Boir Ahmad most people were illiterate until a few generations ago, and written petitions were not customary. A local school girl said that saints could not possibly read petitions in the dark tombs, that it was better to talk to them, 'inside oneself, not with the mouth'.

35 For Iran, see volume 1 of Kriss and Kriss-Heinrich (1960). Honarpisheh (2013) describes pilgrimage places and pilgrimages in Shiraz, frequented also by pilgrims from Boir Ahmad. Flaskerud (2010) describes aesthetics of Shia piety in the images and performances of rituals around big urban shrines in Iran.

36 Votive meals may consist of other foods, too, especially when prepared for mosque gatherings and big religious rituals. In cities, cauldrons with votive rice dishes line streets where processions move at certain significant Islamic high-ritual occasions.

37 In 2015 women said a mullah on television had advised to freeze rice from votive meals and to eat a kernel every day because each kernel provided religious merit. This provoked astonishment and anticlerical jokes for doubters, and satisfaction in Party-of-God adherents.

38 Here is one of many recipes: 'Cook five kilogram each of meat and rice in water until tender; add three kilogram of a mix of lentils, peas, beans, mung beans, more water and cook all until everything is mushy; pound it with a pestle; add onions roasted in butterfat, dried wild green onions, parsley, coriander, mint, salt, and cook for two more hours.' 'It will feed quite a few neighbours and your dead grandfather,' the cook said.

Chapter 5

1 A mourning song is specific: 'The wheel of time broke me and killed me' (Friedl 2018a: Nr. 494). The 'Seven Mills' of Islamic eschatology grinding down everything

is another such image. For insights into refined Islamic notions on such topics, see Schimmel (1994).
2. Argued the other way, the existence of the complex natural order is taken as proof of God's creatorship (see Chapter 1).
3. In moments of vexation or impatience with old people, this may be said like a scolding, in the sense of, 'You finished your life, now die already!'
4. People talked about such epidemics as if they were tangible entities: measles 'came' to town, 'hitting' the children, an idea reminiscent of the disease demons of pre-Islamic cosmologies. See Cohn (1993: 91); Nünlist (2015). See also Chapter 7.
5. I heard such arguments mostly regarding men and the patrilineal line.
6. Behind this stands the often-voiced opinion that the people of the province were victims of oppression by their leaders who deprived them of the means to stay healthy (R. Loeffler 1971).
7. A line in a poem from the time of incessant violence in the area has the image that 'under every oak tree a fallen fighter is buried'.
8. 'May your misfortune fall on my head' (*qossata men serrom*) is an expression of endearment of a mother to a child, for example, or of giving weight to a plea.
9. Elsewhere in Iran, even anthropologists may be identified as having the evil eye (Nadjmabadi 2004: 603–12). Plutarch (1969) (AD 46–120), by describing it as invisible rays of potentially dangerous energy emitting especially from light-coloured human eyes, advanced the first explanation of this purported quality of the human gaze. The phenomenon, however, is much older. Spreading from Egypt and Mesopotamia, the apotropaic blue colour and eye motif are documented for the third millennium BC in the area. For a scientific hypothesis behind the belief, see Ross (2010).
10. The stranger protected her own child by making him out to be unattractive.
11. For this drama, see Friedl (1997: 181–4).
12. It is the place of an eighteenth- or early nineteenth-century bloodshed where a group of invading tribal people killed and dispersed inhabitants of a local settlement (Friedl and R. Loeffler 2013: 183–231).
13. Such death curses were heard again in 2018, this time from black-clad women-emojis on the internet.
14. About jinn in Islam see El-Zain (2009); about them in Abrahamic tradition generally, see Jung (2007).
15. When a man in Sisakht became convinced that his cat was a jinn, he dispatched it for good by addressing it with an Arabic/Islamic name in a magical formula: 'Mr Jafar, go away and don't come again' (*Agha Jafar borro da neio*).
16. The Persian *homzād* may be the Quranic *qarin* of Sura 43:36, translated as 'devil' in Ali (1990).
17. 'May Yal hit you!' (*Yāl bezanet!*) is vexed mothers' traditional curse on a child. Likely it summons Ialdabaoth, son of the goddess Sophia, who morphed from

an ancient powerful creator-deity into a dangerous div in the Zagros mountains (Athanassiadi and Frede 1999: 13).
18 The fairies (*peri*), descendants of the Zoroastrian *fravashi*, were seen as dangerous only for hunters and men who fall hopelessly in love with them; they, too, often merge with jinn and *div* now. See R. Loeffler (1983). For *div* and other demons in Islam see Nünlist (2015).
19 For images from similar gravestones in Luristan, see Demant Mortensen (2010).
20 There are jokes about this stage, as in this Mullah Nasreddin story: the Mullah had died, the women brought sweet halva to pass around and wailed and cried, and the men left to dig the grave. When they returned, the halva was gone and the dead Mullah had sugar around his mouth.
21 It is said that if the life-soul has not yet left completely when wailing starts, it may be stalled and the dying person will linger between life and death: this wailing 'turned his/her soul around' (*juneposhtesh kerden*), which is sinful.
22 If this is not possible, the body is taken to the mosque; leaving it in the house overnight is no option. The person who performs the disagreeable ritual of rinsing, anointing and shrouding of the body is said to accrue religious merits (*sabāb, savāb*) for the afterlife.
23 Before re-entering their own house, mourners ought to wash their faces to avoid a calamity in the house from the *fateha* prayer that is still clinging to the face in full power-mode.
24 There are three traditional mourning gatherings: after the funeral, forty days later and a year later, with visits to the dead person's former home, prayers, mourning songs and sharing of food. The hostess ought to put her hands over the food and say, 'For the souls of . . .' followed by the names of the dead to be honoured (and helped). Guests then pray the first surah of the Quran and listen to Quran recitations, thus rooting this ritual firmly in Islamic conventions. The dead also are remembered with sacrifices at other times such as at *eid morde* (the Celebration of the Dead) a few days before the New Year. By 2015 the *celle*, the forty-day commemorative party, had been abandoned because so many local people and noteworthy men nationwide were dying that the mourning rituals seriously impeded work, people said.
25 Until the 1950s headstones with engravings of gender-emblems (gun for men, spindle for women, for example) marked the graves of notables. Everybody else's dirt and stone graves with three big stones (for women) or two (for men) on top returned to 'just soil' quickly. By contrast, recent graves are 'covered by tons of crumbling cement', a visitor said. Many young dead soldiers got a bridal chamber (*hajle*) arranged on the grave, with objects pointing to the (missed) pleasures of a wedding night, such as, in 1989: a photograph of the young man, plastic flowers, garlands, a mirror, a bottle with perfume, a Quran, rose petals in a bowl, a small curtain. Pairing death and sex was noteworthy for a local psychologist.

26 Off-hand remarks such as, for example, 'The dirt will suffocate him well' and 'With that much cement on top he surely can't come back!' speak to interpersonal relations as well as to a faint fear of the dead.
27 A mourning song lauds the skilled hands of a woman weaver: 'Your hands are weaver-skilled, ants will eat them' (*daselet kinugare, dasel bekhare mur*).
28 In the Islamic Republic dancing in a cemetery would be taken as an abomination. Ethnographically, funeral dances are known from Australia to Africa, and historically from ancient Egypt (van Lepp 1987) to modern Ghana ('Ghana's Funeral Dancers' 2017).
29 For example, the elaborate cult of remembrance for the Prophet Muhammad's death (28th Safar) locally started in 1970. Some people choose to boycott and criticize the commotion with remarks like, 'I know that I am a Muslim without such a show. If those who provide the meals spent the money for repairing our streets, everybody alive in town would benefit.'
30 There are jokes, though, such as this: 'A mullah is doing his best to get the mourners to cry at his grief performance but only an old woman sobs. He praises her and she says, "I am crying because when you talked your beard was hopping up and down just like the beard of my goat that died yesterday."' The mood of drab doom also strikes foreigners living in Iran as a feature of contemporary lived religion there, as Zahedi (2018) describes.
31 Parallels to antiquity are striking for all these sentiments and customs, and some local people comment on one or another either in admiration or as a challenge to claims of Islamic superiority. See Erasmo (2012: 120–4), discussing ancient Greek and Roman ideas relating to death, such as graves as extensions of 'home', the dead's reliance on being fed, food shared at grave sites, and the importance of visitations to prevent being forgotten.

Chapter 6

1 This chapter includes information discussed in an earlier article on eschatology (Friedl and R. Loeffler 2018c).
2 Neither the joker nor the audience commented on the fusion of person and soul that the Angel's order to fetch a young woman implies. The soul seems to bestow a body with personality and to retain the personality after death.
3 The speaker here confounds Ajal, the lifespan, with Death and the Questioning Angel, and merges heaven (*behesht*) with sky, simplifying Islamic death theology. He also draws attention to the importance of burial and differentiates between an impermanent, uncomfortable space for ordinary dead sinners and a terminally very bad place, hell, for suicides. To compare this with standard Islamic ideas, see Lange (2015), Smith and Haddad (1981), Waldman (1987).

4   A joke in the popular self-deprecatory style of Lur humour is about a dead man who answers the angel's question about a holy personage of the scriptures by ranting against and cursing his relative, a scoundrel by the same name. He passes the test nevertheless because he is a 'good person' who cares for his family (Friedl 2018b: 75–7).

5   The idea that fire precludes resurrection is known locally and is one way of illustrating the danger of hell. It does, however, contradict the resurrection story on the Last Day. The locally popular Farsi curse and expletive for a despised person, *pedar sukht* (burnt father), plays on this idea, as does the Lur folktale motif of a grave-robber intent on burning the corpse of his buried enemy. For historical roots of these notions see, for example, Segal (2004: 185–6).

6   The Last Day is the Day of Judgement (*ruz-e qeiyāmat*). The term is used routinely as an ejaculation of bewilderment, and also to tell somebody off by implying, 'never'. Answering a physician's suggestion to take a rest from heavy work, an elderly patient said, 'Sure, after the Day of Judgement.'

7   This limbo has no name locally but obviously is based on notions in Abrahamic traditions of *barzakh*, the period and place after death and before acceptance in paradise or the Day of Judgement. For the history of *barzakh* in Islam see Segal (2004: 650–3).

8   Such vaguely Zoroastrian notions are known locally but the image of towers of silence where bodies are food for raptors is universally declared repulsive. The practice of heaping stones in or on a grave people explained with the mourners' duty to deter scavengers.

9   It appears not only in words of grief-stricken mourners but also in mourning poetry, Vahman and Asatrian (1995: 19–20, 30).

10 All ideas about the afterlife are known to both, men and women, although not everybody agrees to their validity or likelihood. Women seem to be more ready to talk about such issues, especially about less-fundamentalist notions. I thank Reinhold Loeffler for augmenting my own observations. See also R. Loeffler (1988).

11 See Luhrmann (2012) for a discussion of evangelical Christians in the United States who 'talk' with Jesus in quite the same way. Such silent conversations are psychologically sensible wherever a mourner is intimately familiar with the speech patterns, opinions and habits of the dead relative (or of 'friend Jesus' as portrayed in scriptures and sermons).

12 The speaker is a great believer in the veracity of dreams. According to the inheritance rule of ultimogeniture, grandmother had lived with her youngest son. Even after her death she feels needed in his house. A rock-strewn slope does not appear habitable, but piles of rocks marked gravesites in the past – rocks and death go together. *Kokolabarde* is the name of a traditional boys' game but its two parts both refer to rocks and stones, and the speaker used it to describe a landscape. (I thank Mr Alehassan for this clarification. email, 30 January 2019.)

13 Regarding work in paradise, see Johnston (2004: 85–100).
14 The 'lovely garden' is a beloved image with a 2,000-year history of varying specifics that reflect changing sociocultural contexts. Relevant examples of the copious literature on the garden motif are Bockmuehl and Stroumsa (2010), Bremmer (2004), Goodman (2010), Marzolph (2003), Subtelny (2008).
15 For a feminist assessment of the Islamic afterlife in the scriptures, see Smith and Haddad (1981), Friedl (2001). Ruffle (2011) shows how differently text-based Islam can be handled by women in another culture. Afkhami (1998) suggests that a new, women-oriented reading of scriptures and traditions can educate Muslim women to claim their human rights.
16 The comment of an outraged local man on a banking scandal that cost many Iranians their life-savings and fuelled protests throughout the country in 2017 was that 'surely for these swindlers and liars there is a hell' (telephone conversation, 30 December 2017). Hell also lost popularity in Catholic Christianity. See Reese (2018) for the pope's difficulty in talking about hell as a place of torture.
17 All contemporary religions exist in the shadow of naturalism. This and a growing Unitarian relativist understanding of an all-loving God have lowered the public's interest in afterlife locations in other Abrahamic traditions, too (see Talbott 2017). For relevant and illuminating discussions of the history of the concepts of paradise and hell, see Cohn (1993) and Segal (2004); for the devil, Roskoff's (1869) history of the devil stays relevant to this day.
18 To achieve a valid prayer one has to be (ritually) clean.
19 When I mentioned that in my hometown some wealthy people anonymously established a fund to cover college tuition for all qualified high school graduates in town, the reaction was that the donors amassed a lot of merits, and that it shows how easily rich people can get to paradise (see www.kalamazoopromise.com).
20 A feared former chief of Sisakht and his executed son were mourned by only a few relatives, which people in town saw as just punishment of their earlier oppression. Although the 'shaking out' (the spring cleaning) is tiring for the women who do it, it is done in high spirits, with jokes and banter about all the bad stuff swept out with the dust.
21 For individual elaborations of such ideas among men, see R. Loeffler (1988).
22 The use of grave stones has increased over time. See Demant Mortensen (2010) for graves of the culturally similar, neighbouring Bakhtiari.
23 This sex-death link is a reminder that the soldiers never had the pleasure of a first night. The texts of several mourning songs can also be sung at weddings.
24 By contrast, such sentiments can be found on many grave stones in Catholic Austria, for example, clearly expressing quite different expectations of the afterlife despite eschatological similarities. (Author's fieldwork notes, Neuberg, Austria, 2017.)

Chapter 7

1 This is in contrast to several Arabic/Farsi *shukr*-formulas of gratitude and the urban French-derived *mersi*, both pan-Iranian now.

2 The Indo-European root relates *hāl* to 'hale' and 'health'. It is used in greetings such as *hālet cetoure?* (How is your health, how are you?) and in expressions like *khoshhāl*, happy, *hāl na'ārom, bihālom*, I am unwell; *hālom bāham khard*, I broke down.

3 For example, women's purported trend to cold imbalances and related ailments has to be balanced with 'warm' food. A weak child needs 'strong' food, an old person 'light, warm' food. It is pointless to advise a poor mother of six children to 'take a rest and eat lamb-roast'. She has neither time nor money for either.

4 Galen of Pergamon (AD 129–210) emphasized the body's equilibrium of what locally are called 'temperaments' (*tou*). In vernacular local medicine, a 'cold/moist' imbalance is more common and harder to treat than a 'warm/dry' one. For a discussion of Galenic medicine, see Gill, Whitmarsh and Wilkins (2010). For medicine in Iran, see A. Loeffler (2008a, b).

5 An immoral person is called 'dirty'. Menstruation and birth are taken to expel accumulated dirt in the womb. For 'womb' infections, physicians and midwives used to suggest a pregnancy to clean out the womb.

6 For a relevant discussion of knowledge and action, see Pavese (2016).

7 A study of health complaints in five Boir Ahmad villages by Dr M. Yazdonpena at Yasuj Medical School identified problems fitting these categories and added cardiovascular diseases and drug abuse 'everywhere' (personal communication, Yasuj, 15 March 2015).

8 A. Loeffler (2008a) discusses the reception of so-called Western medicine in Iran.

9 Such rhetorical-critical remarks are popular. A local young man joked that Thomas Edison, admired and blessed in Iran for 'bringing light to everybody', ought to be declared a saint in Iran.

10 Usually, a mother will do this at a son's or daughter's marriage. Soldiers requested such pardon routinely. In mourning songs mothers regret their own failure to pardon it, thus burdening the dead sons with the sin of debt.

11 Dr Jacob Polak, the Austrian physician of Shah Naser al-Din (1831–96), wrote that instead of the placid intrepidity that the Islamic 'fatum' belief supposedly encourages, Persians fled an epidemic much faster and sooner than did Europeans (Gaechter 2019).

12 Abstinence was no realistic choice. It is considered unhealthy for men to hold back semen fluid, which makes sex on demand from a wife a health-necessity. Hard work and exhaustion are said to lower the sex drive, while men in easy jobs with 'white, soft hands' are said to have a vigorous 'dragon' (sex drive).

13 See A. Loeffler and Friedl (2014). Other villages in Boir Ahmad retained a relatively high birth rate longer. Faced with an aging population, the government started to curb access to birth control in 2013.
14 In 2015 they cost at least two months of a teacher's salary. With 48 per cent C-sections per 100 live births, Iran has one of the highest rates in the world. In 2015 the government started to limit the practice, whereupon a gynaecologist joked that doctors just got richer because now women had to buy a second opinion to attest to a medical reason for the surgery.
15 Pious Muslim men may only wear silver. Their power is in the ability to buy gold for their wives, a mullah's wife joked.
16 Local healers accepted tokens of appreciation, and some clinic doctors accepted gifts the villagers offered in expectation of preferential treatment.
17 See Bozorgmehr (2018) about effects of the United States' economic sanctions on Iran.
18 In 2015 a young man joked that 'Sisakht' ought to be changed to 'Hajjitown' in honour of the many local people travelling to Mecca.
19 For insights into such topics with emphasis on young people in present-day Iran's urban culture, see Behrouzan (2016).
20 This is a popular thought. A woman whose hens died because she had not moved them out of the hot sun called her neglect 'a big sin'. See also R. Loeffler (1988: 143, 147).
21 Its ancestor, a storm deity, was said to invade/inhabit humans and make them sick or mad. In local folktales this notion appears in a dangerous wind with a name, riding on a cloud. A survivor of this deity is the *bād* in the Zar-Cult, a possession- and healing cult in the Gulf area (see Moghaddam 2009). In Boir Ahmad possession-cults are not a common choice for healing.
22 For another version of the story, see Chapter 3.
23 A hospital physician in my presence scolded a local woman after her suicide attempt for having believed the devil's false promises of rest and comfort after death. Mullahs and their hezbollah-minded followers ascribe suicide to lack of piety, saying that truly devout Muslims have no reason to kill themselves, and that therefore religious education should be intensified. This also wrote a local sociology student in his thesis on local beliefs about death (Khalili 2010).
24 Green is the colour of the Prophet. Infants and young children had such amulets pinned on their shirts.
25 Such thoughts and questions are confined to local 'deep thinkers' but they are well within the local philosophy.
26 Black magic (*da'ā se, sahar, jādui*) is rare locally; people say its use is sinful. A neighbouring village is famous for its shrine, its resident Seyeds and specialists for spells. These specialists put sin, if there is one at all, on the user of the magic, not the maker, and even claim religious merits such as for a spell to prevent a husband taking a second wife.

27 'Dawn follows dusk and dusk follows dawn, so it rolls on' (*pasin-ghorub o ghorub-pasin, ei mičarkhe*) captures this feeling. About a successful co-worker, a man said, 'He is dumb but time is rolling along well for him.'

28 The category 'teenager' (*bolugh*) cognitively did not exist until a generation ago. Around menarche girls were married. Boys and girls were treated as adults-in-training, and hard work prevented many teenage problems. With leisure and the internet, pornography has become an ubiquitous pastime especially of young men. Parents likely call it unhealthy, the pious call it sinful, and some elderly call it funny.

29 Although there are many beloved grannies in town, for people socialized to devalue women and to value beauty and imbue it with success and goodness, old, tired women rank low on the scale of likeable humans. (Old woman is 'bad' in folktales, old man is neutral.)

30 R. Loeffler, personal communication. Time phrases used for a missed chance, a dashed hope, a missed opportunity suggest to accept that a time-spot is gone forever.

31 This is *Bibi Zahra Khātun*. The shrine of her brother, Imam Reza, in Mashhad, is the biggest in Iran. Several of the Imam's relatives are said to be buried in Boir Ahmad.

32 In the big shrines pilgrims may use temple-sleep as an oracle. They lock themselves into a chain, formulate a wish or a question, sleep and next morning take the unlocked (or still-locked) chain as a positive (or negative) answer.

33 The town's origin myth has thirty (*si*) heroes having a hard (*sakht*) time in deadly snow on the pass above the village. Snow is a metaphor for death and isolation in mourning songs. 'Hot, dry desert' is an image of hell. As a sign, Iran's catastrophic rains in 2019 reportedly pointed to two main choices: to God's punishment of the 'cauldrons of sins' in Iran or else to God's disgust with everything, including the religious leaders, that made God avert His eyes from the country.

34 The saying comes from a fertility-sacrifice story: a woman whose sons got lost in the snow grabbed a burning log and went after them. Not finding them, she threw her log into the river, a cloud rose up and the new year was wet and green.

35 Festivities around the Persian New Year were abolished as un-Islamic after the Revolution and only after loud discontent and open disobedience (and, people say, because many mullahs themselves are Persians after all) were tolerated again.

36 This I heard frequently, modified occasionally by anti-Arab, anti-clerical sentiments such as 'We will get hope and God back once the Arabs are gone.'

37 Dehghanpisheh (2018) describes such anger. In 2006 a hospital physician in Yasuj said that more than a third of all inpatients had mental disorders such as depression, conversion and obsessive compulsive disorders, and drug-related problems. In 2015 a young man explained that his debilitating back pain started after his university entrance test (*konkur*) was disqualified for poor answers on the compulsory religion questions. This disappointment (i.e. the ruined future) 'broke' his back.

38 'Everybody' says this in Iran. In 2015 a television series about mansions of the world's glitterati captivated households. Without a story line it was an advertisement for the gilded life.
39 That prayer prohibits immorality and wrongdoing and therefore keeps one well is based on Quran surah 29:45 (al' Ankabut, The Spider). Prayer books recommend prayer rituals in great detail, such as, for example: 'This Namaaz is highly effective to disperse calamities, and to remove hardships and difficulties.' And 'When you come to IYYAAKA' recite it 100 times and continue to recite the Soorah in full' (both in Qummi 1999: 795).
40 Locally, monogamy is considered 'good' and 'normal.' Other marital arrangements allowed by sharia law and encouraged by clergy are unpopular, as are child marriages. There is a growing literature on sexual and marital arrangements in urban Iran. Three panels on 'Sexualities and Intimate Relations' are on the programme of the Thirteenth Iranian Studies Conference, 2020. Ahmady (2017) writes about child marriage in Iran.
41 In 2006, while collecting wild artichokes (*kangar*), a woman remembered this rhyme: 'I brought artichokes with prickly leaves; I killed my wife about nothing' (*kangar ārdom per pič, zanma koshtom ser hic*). Wife-beating is said to be justified by Quran surah 4:34 (An-Nisa, The Women). The *Iran Times* (2019) discussed wife-beating and pious wife-complicity after an urban man in a popular television programme had said he was proud of beating his wife and that good wives ought to agree to being beaten. The audience's loud criticism suggests that many people now discuss what they see as a mullah-sanctioned injustice.
42 Polygyny is mostly based on Quran surah 4:3 (An-Nisa) and asserted in sharia law in Iran.
43 This kind of spirituality is part of old Persian and Sufi religiosity but also appears in secular modern societies. See, for example, Heelas and Woodhead (2005).

References

Abdi, Kamran (2003), 'The early development of pastoralism in the central Zagros mountains', *Journal of World Prehistory*, 17 (4): 395–448.

Abdi, Kamran (2012), 'The Iranian plateau from Paleolithic period to the rise of the Achaemenid Empire', in Touraj Daryaee (ed.), *Oxford Handbook of Iranian History*, 13–36, Oxford: Oxford University Press.

Afary, Janet (2009), *Sexual Politics in Modern Iran*, Cambridge: Cambridge University Press.

Afary, Janet, ed. (2020), *The Changing Nature of Family and Marriage in Contemporary Iran*, London: I. B. Tauris.

Afkhami, Mahnaz (1998), *Claiming Our Rights: A Manual for Women's Human Rights Education in Muslim Societies*, n.p.: Sisterhood is Global Institute.

Aghaie, Kamran Scot (2004), *The Martyrs of Karbala: Shi'i Symbols and Rituals in Modern Iran*, Seattle: University of Washington Press.

Ahmady, Kameel (2017), *An Echo of Silence: A Comprehensive Study on Early Child Marriage ECM in Iran*, Hauppauge, NY: Nova Science.

Alehassan, Adel (2017), *Pir Ahmad Graveyard of Nomads around Gotvand, Khuzestan* (unpub. ms).

Ali, Ahmad, trans. (1990), *Al-Qurān, A Contemporary Translation*, 3rd edn, Princeton, NJ: Princeton University Press.

Amanolahi, Sekandar and W. M. Thackson (1986), *Tales from Luristan: Tales, Fables and Folk Poetry from the Lur of Bala Gariva*, Cambridge: Cambridge University Press.

Amanolahi-Baharvand, Sekandar (1975), *The Baharvand: Former Pastoralists of Iran*, Houston, TX: Rice University Press.

Ammerman, Nancy T. (2006), *Everyday Religion: Observing Modern Religious Lives*, Oxford: Oxford University Press.

Annual Report of the United States Commission on International Religious Freedom 2018, Washington, D.C. Available online: www.USCIRF.gov (accessed 15 July 2020).

Ansari, Sarah F. and Vanessa Martin, eds (2002), *Women, Religion and Culture in Iran*, Richmond, VA and Surrey: Curzon.

Arjomand, Said Amir (2016), *Sociology of Shi'ite Islam*, Leiden: E. J. Brill.

Arranz-Otaegui, Amaia, Lara Gonzalez Carretero, Monica M. Ramsey, Dorian Q. Fuller and Tobias Richter (2018), 'Archaeobotanical evidence reveals the origins of bread 14,400 years ago in northeastern Jordan', *Proceedings of the National Academy of Sciences*, 115. Available online: https://doi.org/10.1073/pnas.1891071115 (accessed 15 August 2019).

Athanassiadi, Polymnia and Michael Frede, eds (1999), *Pagan Monotheism in Late Antiquity*, Oxford: Oxford University Press.

Ayaz, Morvarid (2012), 'Between history and memory: A case study of a martyr mausoleum in north of Iran', in Pedram Khosronejad (ed.), *Saints and their Pilgrims in Iran and Neighbouring Countries*, 83–104, Wantage: Sean Kingston.

Barth, Fredrik (1961), *Nomads of South Persia: The Basseri Tribe of the Khamseh Confederacy*, Oslo: Oslo University Press.

Bauman, Richard (2008), 'The philology of the vernacular', *Journal of Folklore Research*, 45 (1): 29–36.

Bausani, Alessandro (2000), *Religion in Iran: From Zoroaster to Baha'ullah*, trans. J. M. Marchesi, New York: Bibliotheca Persica.

Baver, Mahmud (1945), *Kohgiluye va ilāt-e-ān* (Kohgiluye and its Tribes), 1324, Gacsaran: n.p.

Bdaiwi, Ahab (forthcoming), 'Early Shi'ism as a late antique religiosity: Some preliminary remarks', in Manolis Ulbricht and Adam Walker (eds), *From Oriens Christianus to the Islamic Near East: Theological, Historical and Cultural Cross-Pollination in Late Antiquity*, Piscataway, NJ: Gorgias.

Beck, Lois (1986), *The Qashqa'i of Iran*, New Haven, CT: Yale University Press.

Beck, Lois (1991), *Nomad. A Year in the Life of a Qashqa'i Tribesman in Iran*, Berkeley, CA: California University Press.

Beeman, William O. (2018), 'Understanding the Zar', *Anthropology of the Middle East*, 13 (12): 69–81.

Behrouzan, Orkideh (2016), *Prozak Diaries. Psychiatry and Generational Memory in Iran*, Stanford, CA: Stanford University Press.

Betteridge, Anne (1985), 'Ziarat: Pilgrimage to the Shrines of Shiraz', PhD diss., Chicago: University of Chicago.

Betteridge, Anne (1993), 'Women and shrines in Shiraz', in Donna Lee Bowen and Evelyn Early (eds), *Everyday Life in the Middle East*, 239–47, Bloomington, IN: Indiana University Press.

Betteridge, Anne (2001), 'The controversial vows of urban Muslim women in Iran', in Nancy Auer Falk and Rita M. Gross (eds), *Unspoken Worlds: Women's Religious Lives*, 3rd edn, 134–43, Belmont, CA: Wadsworth.

Black-Michaud, Jacob (1986), *Sheep and Land: The Economics of Power in a Tribal Society*, Cambridge: Cambridge University Press.

Bockmuehl, Markus and Guy G. Stroumsa, eds (2010), *Paradise in Antiquity: Jewish and Christian Views*, Cambridge: Cambridge University Press.

Bonora, Gian Luca, Niccolo Pianciola and Paolo Sartori, eds (2010), *Kazakhstan: Religions and Society in the History of Central Eurasia*, Turin and New York: Umberto Allemandi.

Bowersock, Glen W. (2017), *The Crucible of Islam*, Cambridge, MA: Harvard University Press.

Boyce, Mary (2001), *Zoroastrians: Their Beliefs and Practices*, London: Kegan Paul.

Boyer, Pascal (2010), *The Fracture of an Illusion: Science and the Dissolution of Religion*, Göttingen: Vandenhoeck and Ruprecht.
Boyer, Pascal and Brian Bergstrom (2008), 'Evolutionary perspectives on religion', *Annual Review of Anthropology*, 37: 111–30.
Bozorgmehr, Sharafedin (2018), 'Iran jobs go as U.S. sanctions start to bite'. Available online: https://www.reuters.com/article/us-usa-iran-sanctions-jobs/iranian-jobs-go-as-u-s-sanctions-start-to-bite-idUSKCN1NO14C (accessed 19 November 2018).
Bradburd, Daniel (1998), *Being There*, Washington, DC: Smithsonian Institution Press.
Bremmer, Jan N. (2004), 'Contextualizing heaven in third-century North Africa', in Ra'anan S. Boustan and Annette Yoshiko Reed (eds), *Heavenly Realms and Earthly Realities in Late Antique Religions*, 159–73, Cambridge: Cambridge University Press.
Bromberger, Christian (2018), 'On anthropology and ethnography of and on Iran', *American Anthropologist*, 120 (1): 147–50.
Brooks, David (2002), 'Sacred spaces and potent places in the Bakhtiari mountains', in Richard Tapper and Jon Thompson (eds), *The Nomadic Peoples of Iran*, 90–111, London: Azimuth Edition.
'Caring for Iranian religious minorities' (n.d.), *Hebrew Immigrant Aid Society*. Available online: https://www.hias.org/hias-vienna-caring-iranian-religious-minorities (accessed 10 October 2019).
Chelkowski, Peter J., ed. (1979), *Tazieh. Ritual and Drama in Iran*, New York: New York University Press.
Christian, Albert J. (1919), *A Report on the Tribes of Fars*, Simla: Government Monotype Press.
Cohn, Norman (1993), *Cosmos, Chaos, and the World to Come: The Ancient Roots of Apocalyptic Faith*, New Haven, CT: Yale University Press.
Conepa, Matthew (2019), 'Transmillenial ecologies of Iranian religion and identity', [Lecture] Pourdavoud Lecture Series, University of California, Los Angeles, 9 January.
Cronin, Stephanie (2006), *Tribal Politics in Iran: Rural Conflict and the New State, 1921–1944*, London: Routledge.
Daragahi, Borzou (2019), 'Iran regime invites people to turn in neighbours for "moral crimes" via text message', *Independent*, 11 June. Available online: https://www.independent.co.uk/news/world/middle-east/iran-text-message-moral-police-code-violation-tehran-crimes-a8952361.html (accessed 23 September 2019).
Darian, Shiva and Bryan Falcone (2018), 'Rouhani doubles down on conservatives with "Digital Economy" plan', *Iran Digest*, 12–19 January. Available online: www.us-iran.org/news/2018/1/20/iran-digest-week-of-January-12-19 (accessed 25 January 2019).
Davis, Dick (2015), 'Religion in the Shahnameh', *Iranian Studies*, 48 (3): 337–48.
Dehghanpisheh, Babak (2018), 'Facing new sanctions, Iranians vent anger at rich and powerful', *Reuters*, 7 November. Available online: www.reuters.com/article/us-usa-iran-sanctions-anger/facing-new-sanctions-iranians-vent-anger-at-rich-and-powerful-idUSKCN1NC0J5 (accessed 7 November 2018).

Demant Mortensen, Inge (1993), *Nomads of Luristan: History, Material Culture and Pastoralism in Western Iran*, London: Thames and Hudson.

Demant Mortensen, Inge (2010), *Luristani Pictorial Tombstones: Studies in Nomadic Cemeteries from Northern Luristan, Iran*, Leuven: Peeters.

Dennett, Daniel C. (2007), *Breaking the Spell: Religion as a Natural Phenomenon*, New York: Penguin.

Dessing, Nathal M., Nadia Jeldtoft, Jørgen S. Nielsen and Linda Woodhead, eds (2016), *Everyday Lived Islam in Europe*, New York: Routledge.

Digard, Jean-Pierre (1981), *Techniques des nomades Baxtyari d'Iran* (Technology of the Bakhtiari Nomads in Iran), Cambridge: Cambridge University Press.

Dignas, Beate and Engelbert Winter, eds (2007), *Rome and Persia in Late Antiquity*, Cambridge: Cambridge University Press.

Donaldson, Bess Allen (1938), *The Wild Rue: A Study of Muhammadan Magic and Folklore in Iran*, London: Luzak and Co.

Ebadi, Mehdi (2016), 'Shrine veneration (ziyārat) in Turco-Iranian cultural Regions', *International Journal of Religious Tourism and Pilgrimage*, 4 (1): 70–7.

Eickelmann, Dale F. (1976), *Moroccan Islam: Tradition and Society in a Pilgrimage Center*, Austin, TX: University of Texas Press.

El-Messiri, Nawal (1965), 'Sheikh Cult in Dahmīt', MA thesis, American University of Cairo.

El-Zain, Amira (2009), *Islam, Arabs and the Intelligent World of the Jinn*, Syracuse, NY: State University of New York Press.

Ensor, Josie (2018), 'Iran arrests more than 100 Christians in growing crackdown on minority', *The Telegraph*, 10 December. Available online: www.http://telgraph.co.uk/news/2018/12/10/Iran-arrests-100-christians -growing-crackdown-minority/ (accessed 9 October 2019).

Erasmo, Mario (2012), *Death: Antiquity and Its Legacy*, Oxford: Oxford University Press.

Ernst, Carl W. (2005), 'Ideological and technological transformation of contemporary Sufism', in Miriam Cooke and Bruce B. Lawrence (eds), *Muslim Networks: Medium, Metaphor and Method*, 224–46, Chapel Hill, NC: University of North Carolina Press.

Esfandiari, Golnaz (2017), 'Who's afraid of Cyrus the great?' *Radio Free Europe*, 28 October. Available online: https://www.rferl.org/a/iran-fears-persian-king-cyrus-day-gathering-nationalist-chants/28821191.html (accessed 28 October 2017).

Fadil, Nadia and Mayanthi Fernando (2015), 'Rediscovering the "Everyday" Muslim: Notes on an anthropological divide', *HAU Journal of Ethnographic Theory*, 5 (2): 59–88.

Fakhry, Majid (1999), 'From the eighth century to the present: Philosophy and theology in Islam', in John Esposito (ed.), *The Oxford History of Islam*, 269–304, Oxford: Oxford University Press.

Fartacek, Gebhard (2003), *Pilgerstätten in der Syrischen Peripherie* (Pilgrimage Places in the Syrian Periphery), Vienna: Academy of Sciences Press.

Fenton, Paul B. (2019), 'The ritual visualization of the Saint in Jewish and Muslim mysticism', in Alexandra Cuffel and Nikolas Jaspert (eds), *Entangled Hagiographies of the Religious Other*, 193–231, Newcastle upon Tyne: Cambridge Scholars.

Fischer, Michael, M. J. (1990), *Debating Muslims: Cultural Dialogues in Postmodernity and Tradition*, Madison, WI: University of Wisconsin Press.

Flaskerud, Ingvild (2010), *Visualizing Belief and Piety in Iranian Shiism*, London: Continuum.

Foltz, Richard (2013), *Religions of Iran: From Prehistory to the Present*, London: Oneworld.

Foroutan, Yaghoob (2017), 'The construction of religious identity in contemporary Iran: A sociological perspective', *Journal of Persianate Studies*, 10 (1): 107–27.

Fremdgen, Jürgen Wasim (1998), 'The Majzub Mama Ji Sarkar: A friend of God moves from one house to another', in Pnina Werbner and Helene Basu (eds), *Embodying Charisma: Modernity, Locality and the Performance of Emotion in Sufi Cults*, 140–59, London: Routledge.

Friedl, Erika (1991), *Women of Deh Koh*, New York: Penguin.

Friedl, Erika (1997), *Children of Deh Koh: Young Life in an Iranian Village*, Syracuse, NY: Syracuse University Press.

Friedl, Erika (2001), 'Islam and tribal women in a village in Iran', in Nancy A. Falk and Rita M. Gross (eds), *Unspoken Worlds: Women's Lives in Non-Western Cultures*, 3rd edn, 157–67, Belmont, CA: Wadsworth.

Friedl, Erika (2006), 'Old plants and new woman in the Zagros mountains of Iran', in Z. Füsun Ertug (ed.), *Ethnobotany: On the Junction of the Continents and the Disciplines: Proceedings of the Fourth International Congress of Ethnobotany*, 475–81, Istanbul: Ege Yayinlari.

Friedl, Erika (2014), *Folktales and Storytellers of Iran: Culture, Ethos and Identity*, London: I. B. Tauris.

Friedl, Erika (2017a), 'Heirs of modernity in rural Iran', in Amir Sheikhzadegan and Astrid Meier (eds), *Beyond the Islamic Revolution: Perceptions of Modernity and Tradition in Iran before and after 1979*, 112–28, Berlin: De Gruyter.

Friedl, Erika (2017b), 'A brief history of childhood in Boir Ahmad, Iran', *Anthropology of the Middle East*, 12 (1): 6–19.

Friedl, Erika (2018a), *Folksongs from the Mountains of Iran: Culture, Poetics and Philosophies of Everyday Life*, London: I. B. Tauris.

Friedl, Erika (2018b), 'Deep jokes from Boir Ahmad, Iran', in Regina Bendrix and Dorothy Noyes (eds), *Terra Ridens – Terra Narans. Festschrift zum 65. Geburtstag von Ulrich Marzolph*, 67–86, Dortmund: Verlag für Orientkunde.

Friedl, Erika (2020), 'A short history of marriage in Boir Ahmad, Iran', in Janet Afary (ed.), *The Changing Nature of Family and Marriage in Contemporary Iran*, London: I. B. Tauris.

Friedl, Erika and Reinhold Loeffler (2013), 'Archaeology and cultural memory in Boir Ahmad, Southern Zagros, Iran', *Archiv Weltmuseum Wien*, 61–2: 183–231.

Friedl, Erika and Reinhold Loeffler (2018), 'Eschatology in Boir Ahmad, Iran', *Anthropology of the Middle East*, 13 (1): 53–68.

Gaechter, Afsaneh (2019), *Der Leibarzt des Shah* (The Shah's Personal Physician), Vienna: New Academic Press.

Ganzer, Burkhard, and Ata Taheri (2008), *Deutsche Agenten bei Iranischen Stämmen* (German Agents among Iranian Tribes), Berlin: Klaus Schwarz.

Garrod, Oliver (1946), 'The nomadic tribes of Persia to-day', *Journal of the Royal Central Asian Society*, 33 (1): 32–46.

Gasparini, Valentino, Maik Patzelt, Rubina Raja, Anna-Katharina Rieger, Jörg Rüpke and Emiliano R. Urciuoli, eds (2020), *Lived Religion in the Ancient Mediterranean World: Approaching Religious Transformations from Archaeology, History and Classics*, Berlin: De Gruyter.

Gerken, Mikkel (2017), *On Folk Epistemology: How We Think and Talk about Knowledge*, Oxford: Oxford University Press.

Ghafari, Yaqub (n.d.), *Maqadame darbāre pushesh giāhi Kohgiluye va Boir Ahmad* (Introduction to the Plants of Kohgiluye and Boir Ahmad), Yasuj: Dariush.

'Ghana's Funeral Dancers' (2017), *BBC News*, 26 July. Available online: https://www.facebook.com/BBCnewsafrica/videos/10155659187950229/ (accessed 20 September 2019.)

Ghasidian, Elham and Saman Heydari-Guran (2018), 'Upper Paleolithic raw material economy in the southern Zagros mountains of Iran', in Y. Nishiaki and T. Akazawa (eds), *The Middle and Upper Palaeolithic Archaeology of the Levant and Beyond*, 157–175, Singapore: Springer.

Ghavashelishvili, Elene (2018), 'Childless women in Georgia: Between religious restrictions and medical opportunities', *Anthropology of the Middle East*, 13 (1): 24–42.

Gill, Christopher, Tim Whitmarsh and John Wilkins, eds (2010), *Galen and the World of Knowledge*, Cambridge: Cambridge University Press.

Goodman, Martin (2010), 'Paradise, gardens, and the afterlife in the first century CE', in Markus Bockmuehl and Guy G. Stroumsa (eds), *Paradise in Antiquity. Jewish and Christian Views*, 57–63, Cambridge: Cambridge University Press.

Graf, Fritz (2004), 'The bridge and the ladder', in Ra'anan S. Boustan and Annette Yoshiko Reed (eds), *Heavenly Realms and Earthly Realities in Late Antique Religions*, 19–33, Cambridge: Cambridge University Press.

Haerinck, Ernie and Bruno Overlaet (2008), 'Holy places in Pusht-i Kuh, Luristan. Rural Islamic shrines in the Central Zagros, W-Iran', in Kristof D'hulster and Jo Van Steenbergen (eds), *Continuity and Change in the Realms of Islam*, 287–310, Leuven: Peeters Publisher.

Harris, Kevan (2017), *A Social Revolution. Politics and the Welfare State in Iran*, Oakland, CA: University of California Press.

Heelas, Paul and Linda Woodhead (2005), *The Spiritual Revolution: Why Religion Is Giving Way to Spirituality*, Malden, MA: Blackwell.

Hegland, Mary Elaine (1983), 'Aliabad women: Revolution as religious activity', in Guity Nashat (ed.), *Women and Revolution in Iran*, 171–94, Boulder, CO: Westview.
Hegland, Mary Elaine (2014), *Days of Revolution: Political Unrest in an Iranian Village*, Stanford, CA: Stanford University Press.
Hegland, Mary Elaine (2018), [Paper], 'Social mobility in the Shiraz suburb of Aliabad: Living standards, marriage, and desires for diaspora', Presented at the 15th Biennial Conference of the European Association of Social Anthropologists, Stockholm, 11–14 August.
Hegland, Mary Elaine (2020), 'Marriage and sexuality in a revolutionary context 1978–1979: Iranian perceptions and practices, content and meanings', in Janet Afary (ed.), *The Changing Nature of Family and Marriage in Contemporary Iran*, London: I. B. Tauris.
Hendrickson, Jocelyn (2016), 'Prohibiting the pilgrimage: Politics and fiction in Mālikī Fatwās', *Islamic Law and Society* 23 (3): 161–238.
Henkelman, Wouter F. M. and Celine Redard, eds (2017), *Persian Religion in the Achaemenid Period*, Wiesbaden: Harrassowitz, 2017.
Hole, Frank (2004), 'Neolithic age in Iran', *Encyclopaedia Iranica*. Available online: www.iranicaonline.org/articles/neolithic_age_in_Iran (accessed 22 July 2019).
Honarpisheh, Donna (2013), 'Women in pilgrimage: Senses, places, embodiment, and agency. Experiencing *ziyarat* in Shiraz', *Journal of Shi'a Islamic Studies* 4 (4): 383–410.
'Iran Labor Force Participation'. *The Global Gender Gap Report* (2018), World Economic Forum: 127. Available online: weforum.org/reports/the-global-render-gap-report-2018 (accessed 7 October 2019).
Ivanov, Mikhail C. (1961), *Plemena Farsa. Kashkaickiye, Khamse, Kukhgiluiye, Mamasani* (The Tribes of Fars. Qashqa'i, Khamse, Kohgiluye, Mamasani), Moscow: Academy of Sciences Press.
Jalili, Saeed (2019), 'Iran continues to struggle to keep workers content', *Al-Monitor*, 29 March. Available online: https://al-monitor.com/pulse/originals/2019/03/iran-worker-rights-wage-salary-increase-government-inflation.html#ix225ky0ya.JgN (accessed 4 April 2019).
Jayne, Edward (2018), *An Archaeology of Disbelief: The Origin of Secular Philosophy*, Lanham, MD: Hamilton Books.
Jeldtoft, Nadia (2011), 'Lived Islam: Religious identity with "non-organized" Muslim minorities', *Ethnic and Racial Studies* 34/7: 1134–51.
Johnston, Sarah Iles (2004), 'Working overtime in the afterlife; or, No rest for the virtuous', in Ra'anan S. Boustan and Annette Yoshiko Reed (eds), *Heavenly Realms and Earthly Realities in Late Antique Religions*, 85–102, Cambridge: Cambridge University Press.
Jung, Leo (2007), *Fallen Angels in Jewish, Christian and Mohammedan Literature*, Eugene, OR: Wipf and Stock.
Kalinock, Sabine (2004), 'Supernatural intercession to earthly problems: Sofre rituals among Shiite Muslims and Zoroastrian women in Iran', in Michael Stausberg (ed.), *Zoroastrian Rituals in Context*, 173–87, Leiden: E. J. Brill.

Kamalkhani, Zarah (1998), *Women's Islam: Religious Practice among Women in Today's Iran*, London: Kegan Paul.

Kambar, Kaldarhan A. (2019), 'Ordinary miracle of nomads'. Available online: www.academia.edu/39864281/Ordinary_miracle_of_nomads (accessed 22 July 2019.)

'Kameel Ahmady: British American Academic "arrested in Iran"' (2019), *BBC News*, 14 August. Available online: https://www.bbc.com/news/world-middle-east-49341885 (accessed 14 August 2019).

Kaźmierczak, Zbigniew (2017), 'A trial of interpretation of Meister Eckhart's thought on God and Man, through the analysis of its paradoxes', *Artykuły. Roczniki Filozoficze*, 65 (1): 5–22. Available online: http://dy.doi.org/10.18290/rf.2017.65.1-1 (accessed 2 April 2019).

Keddie, Nikki, ed. (1972), *Scholars, Saints, and Sufis: Muslim Religious Institutions since 1500*, Berkeley, CA: University of California Press.

Khaleghi-Motlagh, Djalal (2012), 'Gošasb Bānu', *Encyclopaedia Iranica*, 11 (2): 170–1.

Khalil, Atif (2016), 'The embodiment of gratitude (*shukr*) in Sufi ethics', *Studia Islamica*, 111: 159–78.

Khalili, Reza (2010), '*Bazras jame'e shenākht nagaresh mardom be vāqe'e marg dar zendegi ensān dar shahrestān Denā 1388-1389*' (Inquiry into people's knowledge about death in human existence in Dena county, 2009-10), MA thesis, Free Islamic University Arak, Iran.

Khosronejad, Pedram, ed. (2012), *Saints and their Pilgrims in Iran and Neighbouring Countries*, Milton Keynes: Lightning Source.

Khosronejad, Pedram (2014), 'Reflections on the diversity and religious function of holy places and sacred stones among Bakhtiari Nomads', *Anthropology of the Contemporary Middle East and Central Eurasia*, 1 (2): 143–69.

Kikuta, Haruka (2017), 'Venerating the *pir*: Patron saints of Muslim ceramists in Uzbekistan,' *Central Asian Survey*, 36 (2): 195–211. Available online: https://doi.org/10.1080/02634937.2016.1261801 (accessed 4 January 2018).

Koelz, Walter N. (1983), *Persian Diary*, Ann Arbor: University of Michigan Press.

Kolb, Jonas and Erol Yildiz (2019), 'Muslim everyday religious practices in Austria. From defensive to open religiosity', *Religions*, 10 (3): 1–15. Available online: https://www.academia.edu/38924651/Muslim_Everyday_Religious_Practices_in_Austria._From_Defensive_to_Open_Religiosity (accessed 4 July 2019).

Kramer, Carol (1982), *Village Ethnoarchaeology: Rural Iran in Archaeological Perspective*, New York: Academic Press.

Kreyenbroek, Philip Gerrit (2002), 'Millenarianism and eschatology in the Zoroastrian tradition', in Abbas Amanat and Magnus Bernhardsson (eds), *Imagining the End: Apocalypse from the Ancient Middle East to Modern America*, 33–55, London: I. B. Tauris.

Kreyenbroek, Philip Gerrit (2011), 'Some remarks on water and caves in pre-Islamic Iranian religions', *Archaeologische Mitteilungen aus Iran und Turan*, 43: 157–63.

Kriss, Rudolf and Hubert Kriss-Heinrich (1960, 1962), *Volksglaube im Bereich des Islam* (Popular Belief in the Realm of Islam), 2 vols, Wiesbaden: O. Harrassowitz.

Lange, Christian (2015), *Paradise and Hell in Islamic Traditions*, Cambridge: Cambridge University Press.

Lankarani, Mohammad Fazel (1999), *Resalah of Tawdhih-al-Masael: The Islamic Laws to be Followed by Muslims while Performing Islamic Obligations*, Tehran: Islamic Cultural Publication Center, 1378.

Layard, Austen Henry (2013), *Niniveh and Its Remains*, reprint of 2 vols. edition 1848, 1849, New York: Skyhorse.

Lewis, Bernard (1988), *The Political Language of Islam*, Chicago: University of Chicago Press.

Lewis, Gilbert (1986), 'The look of magic', *MAN* new series, 21 (3): 414–37.

Loeffler, Agnes G. (2008a), 'The indigenisation of allopathic medicine in Iran', *Anthropology of the Middle East*, 3 (1): 75–92.

Loeffler, Agnes G. ([2008b] 2015), *Health and Medical Practice in Iran* (2nd edn of *Allopathy Goes Native*), London: I. B. Tauris.

Loeffler, Agnes G. and Erika Friedl (2014), 'The birthrate drop in Iran,' *Homo: The Journal of Comparative Human Biology*, 65 (3): 240–55.

Loeffler, Reinhold (1971), 'The representative mediator and the New Peasant', *American Anthropologist*, 73 (5): 1077–91.

Loeffler, Reinhold (1983), 'Lur hunting lore and the culture-history of the Shin', in Peter Snoy (ed.), *Ethnologie und Geschichte. Festschrift für Karl Jettmar*, 399–409, Wiesbaden: Steiner.

Loeffler, Reinhold (1988), *Islam in Practice: Religious Beliefs in a Persian Village*, Albany: State University of New York Press.

Loeffler, Reinhold (1989), 'Boir Ahmadī I: The tribe', *Encyclopaedia Iranica*, 4 (3): 320–4.

Loeffler, Reinhold (2002), 'The world of the people of Deh Koh', in Richard Tapper and Jon Johnson (eds), *The Nomadic Peoples of Iran*, 134–43, London: Azimuth Editions.

Loeffler, Reinhold (2011), 'The ethos of progress in a village in Iran', *Anthropology of the Middle East*, 6 (2): 1–13.

Loeffler, Reinhold and Erika Friedl (1967), 'Eine ethnographische Sammlung von den Boir Ahmad, Südiran' (An ethnographic collection from Boir Ahmad, South Iran), *Archiv für Völkerkunde*, 21: 95–207.

Loeffler, Reinhold, Erika Friedl and Alfred Janata (1974), 'Die materielle Kultur von Boir Ahmad, Südiran' (Material Culture in Boir Ahmad, South Iran), *Archiv für Völkerkunde*, 28: 61–142.

Luhrmann, Tanya Marie (2012), *When God Talks Back*, New York: Alfred Knopf.

Mahdavi, Pardis (2009), *Passionate Uprisings: Iran's Sexual Revolution*, Stanford, CA: Stanford University Press.

Malikov, Azim (2010), 'The cult of saints and shrines in Samarqand Province, Uzbekistan', *International Journal of Modern Anthropology*, 3: 116–24.

Maner, Çigdem (2018), 'Weaving revolution in Anatolia. Historical and material value of wool from the Neolithic to the Iron Age', in Filiz Yenisehirlioglu and Gözde Ç. Yücel (eds), *Weaving the History: Mystery of a City, Sof*, 43–63, Ankara: Ankara Studies Research Center.

Mann, Oskar (1910), *Die Mundarten der Lur-Stämme im Südwestlichen Persien*, Berlin: Georg Reimer.

Marzolph, Ulrich (2003), 'The martyr's way to paradise: Shiite mural art in the urban context', *Ethnologia Europaea*, 33 (2): 87–98.

Massé, Henri (1954), *Persian Beliefs and Customs*, trans. C. A. Messner, New Haven, CT: Human Relations Area Files.

McGuire, Meredith B. (2008), *Lived Religion. Faith and Practice in Everyday Life*, Oxford: Oxford University Press.

Melotti, Marxiano (2019), 'The goddess and the town: Memory, feast and identity between Demeter and Saint Lucia', in Jussi Rantala (ed.), *Gender, Memory and Identity in the Roman World*, 230–81, Amsterdam: Amsterdam University Press.

Meri, Josef (1999), 'The etiquette of devotion in the Islamic cult of saints', in James Howard-Johnston and Paul Antony Hayward (eds), *The Cult of Saints in Late Antiquity and the Early Middle Ages: Essays on the Contributions of Peter Brown*, 263–86, Oxford: Oxford University Press.

'Misery index scores for the most miserable countries in the world 2018', *Statista*. Available online: https//:www.statista.com/statistics/227162/most-miserable-countries-in-the-world/ (accessed 9 July 2019).

Moaddel, Mansoor (1998), 'Religion and women: Islamic modernism vs. fundamentalism', *Journal for the Scientific Study of Religion*, 37 (1): 108–30.

Moaddel, Mansoor (2005), *Islamic Modernism, Nationalism, and Fundamentalism*, Chicago: University of Chicago Press.

Moaddel, Mansoor (2009), 'The Iranian revolution and its nemesis: The rise of liberal values among Iranians', *Comparative Studies of South Asia, Africa and the Middle East*, 29 (1): 126–36.

Moghaddam, Maria Sabaye (2009), 'Zār', *Encyclopaedia Iranica*. Available online: www.iranicaonline.org/articles/zar (accessed 20 June 2018).

Nachman, Alexander (2018), [Paper] 'The messianic republic: Khomeini and the question of esoteric politics', *12th Biennial Iranian Studies Conference*, University of California at Irvine, 14–17 August.

Nadjmabadi, Shahnaz (2004), 'From "alien" to "one of us" and back: Field experiences in Iran', *Iranian Studies*, 37 (4): 603–12.

North, John A. (2011), 'Pagans, polytheists and the pendulum', in John A. North and Simon R. F. Price (eds), *The Religious History of the Roman Empire*, 479–502, New York: Oxford University Press.

Nünlist, Tobias (2015), *Dämonenglaube im Islam*, Berlin: Walter de Gruyter.

Ormsby, Eric L. (1984), *Theodicy in Islamic Thought*, Princeton, NJ: Princeton University Press.

Ourghi, Abdel-Hakim (2019), *Reform of Islam: Forty Theses for an Islamic Ethics in the 21st Century*, Berlin: Gerlach.

Pavese, Carlotta (2016), 'Skill in epistemology I: Skill and knowledge', *Philosophy Compass*, 11 (11): 642–9. Available online: Wiley Online Library, https://doi.org/10.1111/phc3.12359 (accessed 31 May 2019).

Peoples, Hervey C., Pavel Duda and Frank E. Marlowe (2016), 'Hunter-gatherers and the origins of religion', *Human Nature*, 27: 261–82.

Peterson, Jordan (1999), *Maps of Meaning: The Architecture of Belief*, New York: Routledge.

Planck, Ulrich (1962), *Die sozialen und ökonomischen Verhältnisse in einem Iranischen Dorf* (The social and economic conditions in an Iranian village), Köln und Opladen: Westdeutscher Verlag.

Plutarch (1969), *Moralia*, vol. VIII, Loeb Classical Library 424, trans. P. A. Clement and H. B. Hoffleit, Cambridge: Cambridge University Press.

'Population and housing census 2016', Tehran: Statistical Center of Iran. Available online: amar.org.ir/english/Population-and-Housing-Censuses (accessed 12 September 2019).

Potts, Daniel T. (2016), *The Archaeology of Elam*, 2nd edn, Cambridge: Cambridge University Press.

Poulaki, Panoraia, Chrysanthi Balomenou and Dimitrios Lagos (2015), [Paper] 'Religious tourism in Greece and regional development: The case of Samos island', *Presented at the 55th Annual Meeting of the European Regions Science Association*, Lisbon, Portugal. Available online: www.academia.edu/31056351/Religious_Tourism_in_Greece_and_regional_development_The_case_of_Samos_Island (accessed 12 December 2018).

Qummi, Sheykh Abbas (1999), *Supplications, Prayers and Ziarats: Call on Me I Answer You*, Qum: Ansariyan.

Ray, Julie (2019), 'Americans' stress, worry and anger intensified in 2018', *Gallup Global Emotions Report*, 4 (25), 2019. Available online: www.gallup.com/poll/249098 (accessed 28 April 2019).

Reese, Thomas (2018), 'Pope Francis and hell', *The National Catholic Reporter*, 3 April. Available online: https://www.ncronline.org/news/opinion/signs-times/pope-francis-and-hell (accessed 20 January 2019).

Richard, Yann (1995), *Shi'ite Islam: Polity, Ideology and Creed*, trans. Antonia Nevill, Oxford: Blackwell.

Roskoff, Gustav ([1869] 2012), *Geschichte des Teufels* (History of the Devil), Charleston, SC: Ulan.

Ross, Colin A. (2010), 'Hypothesis: The electrophysiological basis of the evil eye belief', *Anthropology of Consciousness*, 21 (1): 47–57.

Ruffle, Karen G. (2011), *Gender, Sainthood, and Everyday Practice in South Asian Shi'ism*, Chapel Hill, NC: The University of North Carolina Press.

Rüpke, Jörg (2013), *Religion: Antiquity and Its Legacy*, Oxford: Oxford University Press.

Safinejād, Javad (1989), *Ashāyer-e Markazi-e Iran* (The Tribes of Central Iran), Tehran: Amir Kabir, 1368.

Saglam, Erol (2018), 'Aestheticised rituals and (non-)engagement with norms in contemporary Turkey: A contribution to discussions on piety and ethics', *Anthropology of the Middle East*, 13 (1): 8–23.

Sakurai, Kaiko (2012), 'Shi'ite women's seminaries (*howzeh-ye 'elmiyyeh-ye khahran*) in Iran: Possibilities and limitations', *Iranian Studies*, 45 (6): 727–44.

Schimmel, Annemarie (1994), *Deciphering the Signs of God*, Albany, NY: State University of New York Press.

Scott, James C. (1985), *Weapons of the Weak*, New Haven, CT: Yale University Press.

Segal, Alan F. (2004), *Life after Death: A History of the Afterlife in the Religions of the West*, New York: Doubleday.

Shahbazi, Mohammad (1998), *Formal Education, Schoolteachers, and Ethnic Identity among the Qashqa'i of Iran*, PhD diss., Seattle, WA: University of Washington.

Shahshahani, Soheila (1982), *The Four Seasons of the Sun*, Ann Arbor, MI: University Microfilms International.

Shayegan, Yegane (1996), 'The transmission of Greek philosophy to the Islamic world', in Seyed H. Nasr and Oliver Leaman (eds), *History of Islamic Philosophy*, 89–104, New York: Routledge.

Shirazi, Faegheh (2005), 'The *sofreh*: Comfort and community among women in Iran', *Iranian Studies*, 38 (2): 293–309.

Shirazi, Faegheh (2009), *Velvet Jihad: Muslim Women's Quiet Resistance to Islamic Fundamentalism*, Gainesville, FL: University Press of Florida.

Skjarvo, Prods Oktor (2010), 'Middle West Iranian', in Gernot Windfuhr (ed.), *The Iranian Languages*, 196–278, New York: Routledge.

Smith, Jane Idleman and Yvonne Yazbeck Haddad (1981), *The Islamic Understanding of Death and Resurrection*, Albany, NY: State University of New York Press.

'State TV in crosshairs for program that shows husband boasting of beating wife', (2019), *Iran Times*, 49 (1), 15 March.

Subtelny, Maria (2008), 'The traces of the traces: Reflections of the garden in the Persian mystical imagination', in Michel Conan (ed.), *Gardens and Imagination: Cultural History and Agency*, 19–39, Washington, DC: Dumbarton Oaks.

Sundermann, Werner (1992), 'Die Jungfrau der guten Taten', (The virgin of good deeds), in Philippe Gignoux (ed.), *Recurrent Patterns in Iranian Religions von Mazdaism to Sufism*, 169–73, Paris: Association pour l'avancement des études iraniennes.

Sunith, C. K. (2018), 'Sociological significance of festivals and pilgrimages', *International Research Journal of Human Resources and Social Sciences*, 5 (11): 13–23. Available online: www.aarf.asia (accessed 14 June 2019).

Suzuki, Yuko (2011), 'Evolution structurelle d'une société tribal du sud-ouest de l'Iran en consequence de la modernisation politique: une étude anthropologique de la communauté des Owrizi de la tribu Došmanziyāri dans le département de Kohgiluye va Boirahmad', (The Structural Evolution of a Tribal Society in Southwest

Iran as a Consequence of Political Modernisation: An Anthropological Study in the Community of the Owrizi of the Doshmanziari Tribe in the Province of Kohgiluye and Boirahmad), PhD diss., École des Hautes Études en Sciences Sociales, Paris.

Szanto, Edith (2012), 'Illustrating an Islamic childhood in Syria: Pious subjects and religious authorities in Twelver Shi'i children's books', *Comparative Studies in South Asia, Africa, and the Middle East*, 32 (2): 361–73.

Talbott, Thomas, 'Heaven and hell in Christian thought', in Edward N. Zalta (ed.), *Stanford Encyclopedia of Philosophy*, Palo Alto, CA: Stanford University Press. Available online: https://plato.stanford.edu/archives/fall17/entries/heaven-hell/ (accessed 2 December 2017).

Torab, Azam (2005), 'Vows, mediumship and gender: Women's votive meals in Iran', in Inger Marie Okkenhaug and Ingvild Flaskerud (eds), *Gender, Religion and Change in the Middle East: 200 Years of History*, 207–22, Oxford: Berg.

Torab, Azam (2007), *Performing Islam: Gender and Ritual in Iran*, Leiden: E. J. Brill.

Townsend, Leo (2019), 'Staying true with the help of others: Doxastic self-control through interpersonal commitment', *Philosophical Explorations*, 22 (3): 243–58.

Turner, Victor and Edith Turner (1978), *Image and Pilgrimage in Christian Culture*, New York: Columbia University Press.

Vahman, Fereydun and Garnik Asatrian, eds (1995), *Poetry of the Baxtiaris*, Copenhagen: Royal Danish Academy of Sciences and Letters.

Van den Bos, Mathijs (2007), 'Elements of neo-traditional Sufism in Iran', in Martin Van Bruinessen and Julia D. Howell (eds), *Sufism and the Modern in Islam*, 61–75, London: I. B. Tauris.

Van Lepp, Jonathan (1987), 'The Dance Scene of Watetkhethor: An Art Historical Approach to the Role of Dance in Old Kingdom Funerary Ritual', MA thesis, University of California at Los Angeles. Available online: https://Encyclopedia.jrank.org/articles/pages/51/Funeral-Dances.html (accessed 10 December 2017).

Varjavand, Parviz (2011), 'Emāmzāda III: Numbers, distribution and important examples', in Ehsan Yarshater (ed.), *Encyclopaedia Iranica*, 8 (4): 400–12.

Vivier-Muresan, Anne-Sophie (2006), *Afzād, Ethnologie d'un village d'Iran*. Teheran: Institute Français de Recherche en Iran (IFRI).

Waldman, Marilyn R. (1987), 'Eschatology in Islam,' in Mircea Eliade (ed.), *The Encyclopedia of Religion* 5, 152–6, New York: MacMillan Reference.

Watson, Peggy J. (1979), *Archaeological Ethnography in Western Iran*, Tucson, TX: University of Arizona Press.

Wellman, Rose (2018), 'Almost mahram', *Anthropology of the Middle East*, 13 (1): 117–20.

Wheeler, Brannon (2019), 'Sacrifice and pilgrimage', in Babak Rahimi and Peyman Eshaghi (eds), *Muslim Pilgrimage in the Modern World*, 49–64, Chapel Hill, NC: University of North Carolina Press.

Whitehouse, Harvey, Pieter Francois, Patrick Savage, Thomas E. Currie, Kevin C. Feeney, Enrico Cioni, Rosalind Purcell, Robert M. Ross, Jennifer Larson, John

Baines, Barend ter Haar, Alan Covey and Peter Turchin (2019), 'Complex societies precede moralizing gods throughout world history', [Letter] *Nature*, 567: 226–29.
Widengren, George (1965), *Die Religionen Irans*, Stuttgart: W. Kohlhammer.
Winkelmann, Friedhelm (2007), *Geschichte des Frühen Christentums*, 4th edn, München: C. H. Beck.
Zahedi, Ashraf (2018), 'Negotiating between Shi'a and Catholic rituals in Iran: A case study of Filipina converts and their adult children', *Anthropology of the Middle East*, 13 (1): 82–96.

Index

accident   33, 34, 80, 82, 83, 86, 116
   fatal   30, 56, 71, 91, 125
Achaemenid   x, 66, 68
   Sasanian   x, 66, 69, 76
adaptation   2, 10
   Big God   13
   Big Government   13, 15
afterlife   22, 36, 40, 49, 51, 60, 97, 102, 105
   bridge Sira'at   97
   doubts about   91, 98, 99, 102
   eulogy   104
   kinds of   98, 100, 106
   kin reunion   106
agriculture   x, xi, xiv–xvi, 119, *see also* herding
   college   xviii
   farming   xi, xix, 119, 120
   orchard   xvi, 4, 31, 51, 53, 54
alms   36, 39, 59, 117
   purpose   60, 83, 89, 120
America   57, 63, 95
amulet   10, 59, 71, 84, 114, 117
ancestors
   feared   41, 76
   sins of   41, 81, 112, 113, 116
angel   31, 36, 45, 51, 54, 97, 105
   of death (Ezrael)   86, 95
   Gabriel   55
   questioning   86, 96, 114
animals   xv, 113, 116, 117, 123, *see also* herding
   bear   32, 116, 123
   bee   33
   beetle   111
   bird   80, 86, 99, 123
   boar   123
   cat   4, 5, 33
   chicken   41, 90, 115
   cow   33
   donkey   xix
   fish   117
   Gazelle   32
   goats   xi, xii, 115
   horse   86
   ibex   86
   lamb   41, 53, 80
   lion   68
   locust   10
   mouse   33
   scorpion   95
   sheep   xi, xii, 59
   snake   32
   wolf   10, 17, 84, 99, 115
   worm   32
antiquity   x, xi, 57, 64, 81, 99
apotropaic   59
   God's name   5, 117, 118
   light   85
   jewellery   85, 114
   metal   85, 91
Arab   17
   Arabic   7, 42
archaeology   x, xi
atheist   30, 76
Ayatollah Khomeini   19, 68

belief   2
   knowledge and   15, 50, 106, 108 (*see also* knowledge)
blood money   57, 80
Boir Ahmad   ix, x, xiv, xvi
   culture   2–4
   God   29
   remote   xvii, xviii
   shrines   64, 69
   social conditions   7, 8, 10, 11
   tourism   70
   villages   x, xiii, xvii

calamities   36, 41, 55, 86
   averted   39, 41, 83, 92
charity   5, 60
child   1, 3, 30, 32, 36, 38, 52

abducted   83, 85
  birth   38, 82, 85, 98, 113
  death   30, 43, 80–3, 98
  infant   5, 75, 80, 85, 118
  parents and   21, 23, 38, 49, 53, 81, 83, 120
  sick   59, 65, 82, 113, 116, 117
  sin   44, 113
  stress   39
city   xv, 11, 16, 113, 114
colour   xv, 25, 117, 119
corruption   31, 40, 49, 111, 122
cosmic order   14, 31, 79
culture   5, 111
  contradictions   3
  identity   121, 123
  provides choices   3, 4, 6, 111
Cyrus the Great   68

dance   xi, 89, 120
Day of Judgement   21, 25, 49, 50, 74, 89, 96
  doubts about   102
  next world   98, 102
  resurrection   50, 97, 98
dead
  care of   10, 22, 67, 88, 89, 93, 117
  fear of   86
  fire   50, 89, 102
  decay   88, 99
  disappear   99
  feelings   88, 89, 91, 99
  linger   88, 100
  lost   91
  memorial rituals   22, 59, 88, 91, 99
  needs of   89, 98, 99, 104
  talk to   91, 100
death   5, 9, 30, 49, 86, 95, 98, 125
  as agent   61
  as border   75, 91, 92, 105
  child   43, 80–3, 98
  as curse   85, 95
  duties   10, 23, 49, 87, 88
  metaphors   99
  natural process   79, 80, 86
  prayers   19, 87, 88, 107
  rituals   87–9, 91
  theology   9, 79, 86, 91, 106, 119
  violent   83
  of women   83, 98 (*see also* suicide)
deity   2, 19
  care of   64
  otiose   31, 40, 82
  pre-Islamic   75, 85, 86
  tutelary   14, 37, 76
Dena
  county   xv, xviii
  mountain   xvi, xix, 108
dervish   21, 71, 122
devil   51, 61, 86, *see also* jinn
  paradise   47, 54, 55, 116
din   16, 18
  theology   19, 47
doubt   13, 19, 27, 38, 42, 48, 52, 60, 62, 80
  afterlife   91, 98, 99, 102
  authorities   110, 124
  death   86, 90, 91, 95
  God's benevolence   113
  shrines   69, 75
  theology   98, 109, 117, 124
dream   36, 39, 41, 59, 61, 83, 117
  other world   100
  shrines   64, 68
dwellings   xi
  branch hut   xvii, 22
  houses   xi, xiv, 42, 52, 59
  grave as   73, 88, 89, 96
  of jinn   116
  tent   xi, xii

economy   xi, xiii, xiv, xvi, 3, 56
  access to resources   3, 114
  aspirations   xvi, 3, 11, 121
  bad   114, 121
  cash   xv
  health and   113, 114
  inequality   xv, 3, 14, 34, 114, 121, 124
  jobs   3, 21, 24, 26, 33, 43, 56, 75, 82, 113, 114, 117, 119
  possibilities   xvi
  subsistence   2
  success   42, 110
  trader   xv, 43
  unemployment   xv, 114, 123
  wealth   26, 31, 114, 115
  welfare   110, 122
education   3

Bahmanbegi xvii
  tent school program xvii
  and economic success 110
  literacy xiii, xiv, xvi
  Lurs xvii
  schools xiii, xiv, xviii, 63, 112, 118
  student xvi, 36, 42, 50, 56, 57, 110, 112, 118, 123
  teacher xiv, xv, xix, 81, 95, 112, 118, 123
    and science 4, 81, 82, 111
    theology 56, 95
Emamzada, *see* shrine
emotions xvii, 21, 81, *see also* health
  good xvi, 109, 111, 121–4
eschatology 95, 105
ethics xvi, 5, 39
  common sense 7, 97
  Golden Rule 13
  humanism 7, 10, 17
  paupers' 22
  and religion 2, 17, 21, 43, 124
  social ethics 2, 10, 11, 21, 22, 43, 53, 103–4
ethnography 6, 9, 11
  aims 2
  fieldwork xviii, 1, 4, 6, 8
  of Islam 6
  methodology 4, 6
  themes in 2, 9
  writing xix
evil eye 37, 40, 59, 82, 83
  prevention 83, 117, 118

family xiii, xiv, xv, xvi, 82, 90
  authoritarian xi, 122
  brothers 6, 89
  brothers and sisters 6, 89
  duties 83, 90, 112, 122
  husband and wife xv
    afterlife 49, 106
    discontent 25, 35, 43, 44, 46, 81, 90
    good 51, 53, 114
    relationships change 3, 122
  parents 21, 23, 49, 53, 81, 83, 120
  patrilineal xi
  problems xi, 112, 113, 122, 124
  relations xii, xv, xiv, 6, 22, 30 , 53, 56, 80

  sisters 91, 100, 107
  sons xvii, 10, 33, 59, 90
fate(s) 40, 55–8, 61, 112, 119
  death and 80, 86
  free will 32, 57
  marriage as 35, 57
  as power 81
  predestination 80
Fatemeh 56, 97
Five Pillars 25, 27
folklore xi, 2, 8
  folktales 1, 38, 66
food xi, 59, 123, *see also* agriculture
  bread xi
  children 114
  for dead 88, 89
  game xi, xii
  God and 113
  in humoral schema 110, 112, 113
  hunger 2, 5, 36, 57, 111, 114, 123
  improvement 3, 81
  theft of 36

gender 9, 10, 44, 80
  differences 9, 117
  expectations xvi
Germany 101
gnostic 11, 14, 27
  agnostic 30, 62, 79
God 22, 96
  accessibility 55, 75, 85, 121
  all-knowing 99, 102
  angry 41
  authoritarian 2, 40
  averts eyes 37, 119, 121
  'Big' God 11, 13, 37
  creator 2, 10, 11, 13, 14, 18
    creates order 14, 30, 79
    next world 49, 119
    origin myth 47
  cruel 13, 40
  demands 22, 25, 42
    gratitude 21, 23, 34, 57, 124
    lack of gratitude 121
    obedience 61, 109, 119, 123
    disobedience 116
  and fear 33, 36, 46
  first cause 14, 29
  good 31, 124

inscrutable   14, 32
justice   6, 37, 104
   unjust   14, 40, 81, 109
   is light   13
   limited powers   32, 42, 54, 81, 117
   mercy   27, 32, 33, 37, 43, 50, 83
   monotheist deity   19
   moralistic   10, 13, 27
   name of   29, 85, 117
   Necessary Being   27, 42
   omnipresent   33
   proof for   31
   is reason   14, 61
   remote   10, 15, 37, 51, 63
   salvivic power   7, 36, 37, 81, 84, 112
   sins   105
      forgiven   36, 37
   success   110
   is truth   37
   uncaring   32, 55, 114
   Will of   21, 33–7, 55, 60, 79, 81, 95, 106, 110
      as final cause   80, 92, 112, 117, 119
      as safety hatch   75
   wishes   32, 45, 98
government   xvi, 51
   administration   xvii
   employee   xiv, xv
   Islamic   xv, 5, 91, 92
      pre-Islamic cult places   66
      shrines   66, 69
   judged   52, 114, 122
   police   40
   -religion   7, 96
      criticised   90, 92, 103, 114, 117
   soldiers   xvii, 86
graves, *see also* dead; saints
   children's   67
   dance at   89
   desecrate   89
   difficult   89, 98
   gravestone   86, 105
   graveyard   xix, 68, 98, 100
   house of the dead   73, 88, 89, 96
   light on   69, 88, 93
   and memory   67, 88, 89, 99
   visitation   10, 90, 91
   wailing   88, 93

hadith   38
hajj   17, 27, 115
health   xiv, 35, 108, 116
   allergy   112
   birth control   xv, 112
   cleanliness   117
   clinic   xviii, 82, 85, 111, 114, 125
   diseases   32, 40, 80, 111, 114, 117
   drug addiction   50, 83, 114
      opium   117
   epidemic   115, 117
   fertility   xiii, 41, 111
   healer   36, 111
   humoral balance   111
      Galen   110, 112
   malnutrition   111
   management   110, 113
   medicine   xv, 39, 82, 111, 112
   mental health
      depression   18, 111, 112, 115
      hope   121
      in Iran   121
      memories and   123
      obsession   61
      and religion   121
      stress   7, 115, 118, 119
   miscarriage   33
   pharmacopoeia   35, 111
   physician   xvi, xviii, 3, 15, 17, 24, 50, 52, 57, 66, 82, 101, 112
   problems   3, 27, 50–2, 54, 57, 59, 119
      modern   111, 114
      and wealth   113, 114
   wind   116
hell   5, 21, 33, 45, 49, 96, 100
   dark   52
   doubts about   102
   features   102
   fire   50, 102
herding (pastoralism)   xvi, 22, 27, 58, 65, 66, 69, 119
   animals   xi, xii, 59, 115
   migration   xi, xii
hezbollah   7, 8, 73, 103, 104, 119, 122, 123
   benefits   8
   and health   111
houri   48, 102
human

agency 86, 112, 120
  conflict 10
  dispositions 112
  and God 122, 124
  humanist values 53, 103
  nature 53, 54
  responsibility 21, 51–3, 56, 61, 96, 115, 118, 124
    for death 80, 82, 83, 91
    self-reliance 61
humor
  jokes xvi, 50, 56, 57, 95–7
    afterlife 98, 102, 105
    anticlerical 18, 23
    bitter 122
    saints 70, 72
  Mullah Nasreddin 89
  self-deprecatory xvi, xix, 113
hunting and gathering x, xi, xii, 86, 115, 123
Husein 73

Imam 7, 19, 25, 46, 63–5
  hidden 21, 39, 49, 50, 96, 97, 101
  Reza 75
Imamzadeh, *see* pilgrimage; shrine
Iran 99
  elite and politics 23
  -Iraq war 23, 37, 68, 83
  Pahlavi 125
    Reza Shah xiii
  saint veneration 7
  theocracy 7
Islam 20
  benefits of 18, 19
  critics of 91
  ethics 16, 17
  hegemonic power 9
  and human rights 122
  Islamization of 5
  kinds of 1, 2, 5, 7, 8, 13, 17, 90, 102
  mysticism (*erfan*) 21
  and politics 7, 8, 23, 24, 118
  pre-Islamic 64, 66, 75, 76
  is reasonable 30
  rituals in 19
  'true' Islam 16
  and saints 63
  sharia law 6

Shia 4–7, 27
  clergy 13
  Shia texts 8
  women and Shia 8
Islamic Republic xiii, xviii, 22, 68, 76, 123
  changes 3, 6, 68
  education 11, 96
  mourning 90
  political identity 30, 117
Israel 85

jinn 4, 18, 36, 54, 61, 84, 116, 117, 119
  in trees 86
  and children 116
justice 40, 50, 100
  after death 103
  law 5–7, 90

Kerbela 73
khan x, xii, xiii, 36
  feud xvii
  and tribal people 37
kin
  hostilities 6
  in other world 105
  patrilineal 64, 65
  support 2, 10, 39, 99, 103, 107, 112
knowledge
  vs. belief 15, 50, 92, 106, 108
  empirical 13, 34, 38, 56, 60, 110, 113, 117
Kohgiluye and Boir Ahmad, *see* Boir Ahmad
Kuweit 43

land reform xiii
  ownership xii, xvi
  White Revolution xv
language x, xiii
  Arabic 7, 42
  bilingual xvi
  Luri, Farsi 1
  vernacular 4, 13
lie 44, 45, 97
  'good' 39, 53
  Lur 38, 39
  well 24, 38
life

ageing   79, 80
  difficult   109
  from God   32
  limits of   47, 56, 79, 95, 119
  meaning of   81
  misery   110, 122
  mythology   98
lifestyle
  changes   3, 44, 49, 81, 86
  hedonism   11
  rising expect   xvi, 3, 11, 121
light   69, 88, 93
  God is   13
literature   8, 9
logic   30
  narrative   41, 81
  scientific   6, 13
  vernacular   6, 13
Lur   x, xii, 9, 86
  character   xvii, 33, 38, 39
  cooperation   xvi
  costume   xi
  dangerous   xvii, 2
  identity   xi, xvi

magic   14, 60, 61, 63
marriage   xvi
  age   xv, 33
  arranged   xv, 59, 72, 122
  celibacy   20
  choice   xv, 75
  co-wives   41, 60
  divorce   3, 35, 122
  expectations   xv
  polygyny   3, 23, 122
    as sin   42, 81
  time-limited   11
Mecca   17, 22, 25, 50, 56, 73
Medina   73
men   3, 80
  jobs   xiv, xviii, 57, 60, 123
  neglectful   23
  oppressors   xi, 22, 122
  responsibility   x, xi, xiv, 82, 122
merits   xv, 36, 41, 43, 44, 117
  for the dead   90, 98
  defined   103
  and wealth   43, 114
millenarian anxiety   49

money
  buys health   113
  debt   3, 112
  and women   xv, 122
morality   100
  citizens   7, 11
  dilemma   39, 115
  elastic   17
  and formalism   96
  Islamic   111
  obligations   57 (*see also* responsibility)
  weakness   36
mosque (prayer room)   xviii, 7, 25, 60
  criticised   43, 103
  rituals   17
mourning   90, 92
  rituals   10, 22, 23
  songs   105
Muharram   22, 60, 62, 89
Mullah   xii, 23, 37, 52, 74
  afterlife   91
  clerics   7, 17, 18
  humanism   16
  itinerant   10
  as job   3
  preacher   xvi, 33, 54, 75, 83, 86, 102, 117
  and science   110
  wealthy   17, 36
music   xi, 104, 120, 123
Muslim   5, 101
  good Muslim   19–25, 43, 51, 90, 110
  identity   27, 45
  obligation of   22, 51
  and war   119

nature   31
  dangerous   36
  health   123
  human   53
  laws of   14, 27
  natural order   32, 40, 79, 80, 91
  physical universe   13
neighbours   21, 22, 25, 39, 42, 45, 74, 80, 83, 97, 112
necessity   36, 40, 53, 54
  and morality   10, 110, 116
  of survival   115

New Year   56

opportunism   xvi, 18
Other World   46, 88, 103, *see also*
        afterlife; hell; paradise
    images of   100, 106, 123
    unknown   21, 39

paradise   5, 47, 49, 52, 54, 55, 73, 83, 86,
        114
    Adam and Eve   55, 97, 116
    boring   101
    features of   101, 102, 108, 109, 117
    as garden   98, 101, 106, 108, 123
    key to   98
    obligatory belief   101
    as projection   101
    unknowable   101
Party of God, *see* Hezbollah
peace   25, 42, 52
philosophy   xvi, 2, 22, 34
    balance   58, 59
    common sense   4, 5, 79, 98, 109, 112
    of death   79, 80, 119
    effort, reason, knowledge   110, 117
    empiricism   14, 27, 60, 80
    existential challenges   124
    homocentric   62, 79
    methodical doubt   14
    of nature   115, 116
    neo-platonic   13
    realism   98, 119
    reason   30, 61, 110
        lack of   80
    stoic   10, 21
    of well-being   111, 119
    of work   56
piety   7, 19, 60, 117, 122, 124
    addictive   22
    arguments against   20
    distrust of   8, 16, 23, 123
    kinds of   8, 13, 15, 17, 18, 22
    rituals   21
    uses of   18
pilgrimage   19, 22, 59, 72
    benefits of   73, 120
    as diversion   26, 72, 73, 76, 115
    increase   76
    meanings of   73

pilgrim   67–9, 73
    subsidized   73, 115
pir   64, 65, 69, *see also* shrine
power   61, 83
    apotropaic   84, 114, 117, 118
    dangerous   32, 42, 80, 116
    extra-human   13, 14, 18, 27, 85, 92,
        124
    and health   81–3, 117
    jewellery   85, 114
    minerals   82, 84, 85
    in people   84, 100
    personified   58
    plants   84
    smell   117
    time as   118
    in words   4, 10, 36, 60, 117 (*see also*
        amulet)
    spells   10, 60, 118
poverty   xiii, xiv, 14, 81
    ill health   113
    and merits   43
    as pain   113, 121, 124
    and politics   xvi
    poor   8, 17, 33, 39, 57, 59
progress   xiii, 4, 11, 17, 22, 27, 42, 44
    developmental idealism   xiii
    halted   119
    modernity   84, 86, 119
    as problem   122
    shrines and   69
    and well-being   111, 117
Prophet Muhammad   xii, 7, 25, 42, 63,
        65, 67, 75, 76
psychology   81, 39, 114
    cognition   4, 5
punishment   80, 81, 104

Quran   16, 18, 19, 22, 37, 38, 42, 48, 49,
        56, 85, 105, 110
    Fateha   74, 88
    jinn in   86, 116

reason   38, 53, 82, 83, 86
    lack of   80
religion   xvi, 2, 4, 7, 8
    authorities   15
    as code   22
    critics of   4, 15–17

education 8
formalist 96
helps people 110
'irreligion' 4, 9
local *vs.* urban 5, 9
moralist 23
and power 5, 118
public 30
rituals 7, 10, 15, 59, 60
and science 4, 15
'superstition' 9, 10, 16, 18, 44, 56, 60
   Islamic 91
symbols 11
taxes 10
is universal 4, 5
use of 17, 24, 26
responsibility x, xi, xiv, 82, 122
revolution xv, 5, 29, 30, 86, 119
   Revolutionary Guards 8, 40, 66, 69
   White Revolution xv
rituals 120, 121
   benefits 119, 120
   domestic 10, 36, 84, 104, 107, 114, 119–21 (*see also* pilgrimage; saints)
   mourning 121 (*see also* grave)
   mullahs disparage 121

sacrifice 58, 59
   for protection 10, 41, 120
saint 63–5, *see also* shrine
   bones of 74
   cult of 74, 76
   efficacy 71, 72
   hagiography 65
   help 64, 72, 73, 76, 111
   'house' 68, 73
   martyr 64, 65
   miracle 65, 75, 120
   and morality 71
   needs 74
   patron-client 70–2
   power of 71, 73, 115
   promises to 64, 70–2, 83
   temple sleep 120
   trees 66, 70
   visits to 64, 70, 72, 76
   women 64–7
science xvi, 4, 17, 112, 117

sexual relations 11, 35
   pederast 83
   prostitution 11, 35
Seyed xii, 5, 10, 19, 23
   marriage 59
   meaning 64
   opportunist 45, 69
   power 65
   shrines 67–70
Shiraz xvii, 8
shrine xii, 8, 22, 31, 50, 59, 65, 76, 77
   abandoned 72, 73
   creation 67–9
   destroyed 66, 76
   kinds of 64, 67, 69
   light on 69
   renovated 69, 76, 77
   Sisakht xviii, 8, 9, 67
   trade routes 69
   travel brochure 70
   water-tree 66, 67, 69, 70, 75
sin xvi, 2, 36, 40, 108, 116
   against God *vs.* people 44, 97, 103
   of ancestor 41, 81, 112, 113, 116
   defined 103
   and gender 44, 80
   innocent 34, 35, 40
   kinds of 44, 118, 122
   and merits 49, 51, 53, 60, 103
   punishment 40, 80, 81, 112, 116
   repent 36, 38
   retribution 81, 104
   unimportant 105
Sisakht x, xii, xiii, xvi, 1, 2, 3, 8, 68, 69, 122
   business xvi, xvii, xviii, 2, 18
   growth xix, 24
   images xix, 28, 46, 62, 93, 94, 107, 108, 124
   Qobad Nikeqbal xii
   shrine xviii, 8, 9, 67
   social features xii, 8, 11
soul(s) 32
   after death 95, 96
   doubts about 106
   leaves 74, 86
   life soul (*jun*) 47
   ruh 47, 49, 97
Sufi 36, 66

ethos 104
mysticism 61
suicide 30, 41, 52, 54, 109
   decreasing 44, 80
   and jinn 116

Tehran xvii, 63
theodicy 33, 34, 41, 52, 117
   options 113
theology 14
   death 9, 79, 86, 91, 96, 106, 119
   logos 31
   problematic 76, 80, 90, 98, 109
   theologians 99
thief 53, 66, 117
time 38
   as agent 118
   allotted (*ajal*) 47, 56, 95, 119
   and decay 91, 92, 119
   as God's order 118
   and health 118, 119
   wheel of 36, 118
travel 70
   benefits of 72, 111, 115, 123
   tourism xv, xvi, 50
tribes 69, *see also* Lur
   Bakhtiari x, 8, 67
   Basseri 9
   chief xii, xiii, xiv, 11, 36, 37, 40
   dominance x
   Doshmanziari 9
   dress xi, 24
   feuds xiii
   graveyards 9
   integration xv
   Komanchi 9
   law xiv, 6
   Lur 9 (*see also* Lur)
   Mamasani 9, 37
   power xii, xiii
   Qashqa'i 9
   structures xvi
   tribal life xi, xiii

votif 74
   cook-out 60, 74, 107
   sacrifice 10, 52, 59, 115, 120
   social aspects of 74, 75
vaqf 60

women 10, 123
   afterlife 99, 100, 102
   and children xvii
   depression xiv, 113
   education xv
   healer 16, 36, 111, 116
   inheritance 6
   laughter xvii
   misogyny 35
   social status xv
   suicide xiv, 22, 109
   as wife 21, 122
   work xi, xiv, xv, 3, 32, 54, 74, 100, 109, 114
   changes in 3, 37, 122
world
   characteristics of 14, 39, 61
   end of 119
   next 49, 119

Yasuj xvii, 65, 66
young people 17, 22, 68
   afterlife 102
   dating 11
   death of 30, 82, 83
   women 44, 111

Zagros x, xii, 69
Zar cult 61
Zoroastrian 13
   burial 66, 68, 97

www.ingramcontent.com/pod-product-compliance
Lightning Source LLC
Chambersburg PA
CBHW070639300426
44111CB00013B/2174